THE

GUIDE TO

USING ECONOMICS AND ECONOMIC INDICATORS

ROMESH VAITILINGAM

(subject

PITMAN PU

Pitman Publishing
128 Long Acre, London WC2E 9AN

A Division of Longman Group Limited

First published in Great Britain 1994

British Library Cataloguing in Publication Data
A CIP catalogue record for this book can be obtained from the British Library.

ISBN 0273 60969 6

All tables and figures are reproduced by kind permission
of the *Financial Times*. The author would also like to
thank Mark Allin, Annemarie Caracciolo, Helen Pilgrim
and Skanda Vaitilingam.

3 5 7 9 10 8 6 4 2

Typeset by PanTek Arts, Maidstone, Kent.
Printed and bound by Bell and Bain Ltd., Glasgow

*The Publishers' policy is to use paper manufactured
from sustainable forests.*

CONTENTS

Introduction   *iv*

PART I ESTABLISHING THE PRINCIPLES

1 **Microeconomics**   **3**
2 **Macroeconomics**   **21**
3 **International economics**   **39**
4 **Statistics and econometrics**   **61**

PART II UNDERSTANDING THE NUMBERS

5 **National output, income and expenditure**   **75**
6 **Production and employment**   **101**
7 **Prices and competitiveness**   **121**
8 **Money and finance**   **143**
9 **Trade and exchange rates**   **164**

PART III FORECASTING AND POLICY

10 **Governments and global organisations**   **189**
11 **Managers, investors and academics**   **204**

Index   *214*

INTRODUCTION

Economic news is pervasive. Almost every day sees publication of new facts and figures for one economic indicator or another: consumer credit, retail sales, industrial production, the public sector borrowing requirement, the exchange rate mechanism, the level of unemployment, the rate of inflation, the balance of payments, and so on. Newspapers like the *Financial Times* regularly report these latest developments in the economies of the United Kingdom, Europe and the world.

But what does all this information mean, and in what ways might it be useful to you in making your key business, investment and lifestyle decisions? These are the questions this book attempts to address. It aims to take you behind the scenes of all the main economic indicators (those for jobs, prices, manufacturing output, trade, the money supply and many more), explaining, in a straightforward way, the basic principles of economics that drive the statistics, their compilation, reliability and significance, and how they are used by individuals, companies and governments.

The state of the economy is important to everyone. Closest to hand, it affects whether you have a job, how much you get paid, and/or the profitability of your business or financial assets. Certain economic forces are particularly powerful: the rate of interest, for example, determines how much your savings can earn or how much you pay on your mortgage or on money borrowed for investment. Similarly, the rate of inflation determines the value of both your income and savings, as well as influencing your future pay claims or your pricing policy. The rate of taxation you are obliged by the government to pay also affects the value of your income, as well as your access to such publicly provided goods and services as health care and education.

A little further out, the exchange rate can affect whether you can afford to go on holiday abroad. More broadly, if you manage a business reliant on export sales, it might determine whether or not your products can be priced competitively for foreign markets. The level of oil prices influences the proportion of your income taken up by running expenses on a car or the proportion of your production costs taken up by energy; the level of unemployment influences the ease with which you can find work or the wages and salaries you have to pay to hire staff; and so on.

Economic and financial statistics can have an enormous influence on business expectations and financial markets. But reports in the media often fail to explain exactly why they are so important, what impact they might have on particular businesses and sectors of the economy, and how they relate to each other. A basic grasp of how the market economy works will give you the ability to make sense of the mountain of data published by the government and other economic forecasters. It will enable you to assess the intentions and efficacy of government interventions (what is going on when it cuts taxes or raises interest rates?), to compare the performances of national economies (why do Japan and Germany seem to outdo France and the United Kingdom?), and simply to understand the economic content of the news.

But a grasp of economics also offers more. The national and international economic environments shape business conditions, and are themselves shaped by business decisions. Appreciating how economists think about these interactions can reveal the ways in which managerial decisions are made, sometimes unconsciously, on the basis of economic principles. Economics can be a powerful tool for managers as they seek to match the supply of their goods and services to the market's demand in a way that is profitable. It can provide means of assessing the likely consumer response to your new product, the potential profitability of a new investment, the degree of competition in a new market, the appropriate timing of an acquisition, or the nature of your pricing policy. For equity investors too, it offers a method of measuring company shares and other financial assets in the pursuit of the best returns.

Being able to use economics to interpret economic information, and make decisions on the basis of it, is a valuable skill for any manager or investor: this book gives you the basic tools you need. It is arranged in the following pattern, with Part I explaining, in lay person's terms, the essentials of economics, breaking it down into four broad areas:

- **Microeconomics:** how individual consumers, firms, managers, employees and investors make decisions, and how markets work.

- **Macroeconomics:** how the whole economy fits together, and how the government deals with major issues like unemployment, inflation, taxation, economic growth and the business cycle.

- **International economics:** how a national economy fits into the bigger picture in terms of trade, international finance, exchange rates, and integration into regional and global economies. Here the primary focus is on the position of the United Kingdom in the European and world economies, but the lessons are universal.

- **Statistics and econometrics:** how the statistics work, where they come from, how to make sense of them, and how significant and reliable they are.

Part II explores the indicators of economic activity for which regular information is published, and interprets their significance for a manager in a small, medium-sized or multinational company, and for a private or institutional investor. It also examines the impact the data tend to have on the financial markets. There are five broad areas:

- **National output, income and expenditure:** the level, growth and fluctuations of a country's total output of goods and services (its gross domestic product or GDP), roughly equivalent to the total of how much everyone receives in income and how much they spend. This chapter also looks at government economic activity (spending, tax revenues and budget deficits), and at the breakdown of overall output by business sector.

- **Production and employment:** the output of the manufacturing and industrial sectors, sales through the wholesale and retail trades, and the number of people in and out of work. This chapter also considers cyclical indicators, ways of forecasting the future pattern of the business cycle.

- **Prices and competitiveness:** inflation in earnings, and in the prices of commodities, of other producer inputs, and of retail goods. This chapter also examines how inflation and exchange rates influence the abilities of a countries' producers to sell their output abroad.

- **Money and finance:** the money supply, consumer credit, interest rates, and the financial markets, primarily those for stocks and bonds.
- **Trade and exchange rates:** the balances of overseas trade in physical goods and invisible services, the cross-border financial flows of profits, rents, interest, and dividends, and the currency markets that allow it all to happen.

Lastly, Part III illustrates how managers, investors and governments use economic information to forecast the future direction of the economy and make better informed decisions. It explores the foundations of both public and private sector forecasts, and their implications for public policy and business and investment strategies. In addition, it covers the forecasts of the major global economic organisations: the World Bank, the International Monetary Fund (IMF) and the Organisation for Economic Cooperation and Development (OECD). Again, while the primary focus is on the UK economy, the principles and practice of forecasting and policy are universal.

This book is intended for anyone whose business and investment decisions are affected by economic indicators. It aims to provide a simple guide to understanding the statistics and the language of modern economics. Right from the first chapter, tables of figures and samples of FT reporting are introduced to accustom the reader to the ease with which the numbers, reports and comments can be interpreted and used with just a little background.

Before turning to economics, the economy and their statistical analysis, some basic and recurring mathematical concepts might be valuable:

- **Average:** a single number used to represent a set of numbers. It can be calculated variously as: a mode, the number that occurs most frequently in a set of numbers; a median, the number with 50 per cent of the rest lying below it and 50 per cent above, or if there is an even quantity of numbers, the average of the middle two; the arithmetic mean, the total sum of the numbers divided by the quantity of them; and the geometric mean, the figure that derives from multiplying the numbers together and taking their nth root, where n is the quantity of numbers.

- **Percentage:** the proportion that one number represents of another or the change in a number from one period to another. To calculate the proportion or percentage of y that x represents (whether x is another number or the difference between one number over two periods), x is divided by y. The result will be a fraction of 1, and to convert it into a percentage figure, it is simply multiplied by 100. Movements of a percentage figure might be mentioned in terms of points (one point is 1 per cent) or basis points (one basis point is one hundredth of 1 per cent). Percentage points or basis points are different from percentage changes.

- **Inverse and positive relationship**: the connection between two numbers. Numbers with an inverse relationship move in opposite directions; those with a positive relationship move together. This is the mathematical explanation of why, for example, bond prices and yields move in opposite ways; if x is equal to y divided by z, and y is constant, then as x rises, z falls or vice versa. But if x or z is constant, x and y or z and y will rise or fall together. The two pairs are in a positive relationship.

- **Index:** a number used to represent the changes in a set of values between a base year and the present. Index numbers distil many different ingredients into a single index, and measure changes in it by changes in its parts. This involves giving appropriate weighting to the components according to their importance in what is being measured. A weighted average is usually calculated as an arithmetic mean, either using the same weights throughout (a base weighted index) or adjusting the weights as the relative importance of different components changes (a current weighted index). Base weighted indices may have the base shifted periodically.

With these simple tools and applied economic developments of them explained in the text and in chapter 4, the reader should be well equipped to negotiate the economic indicators, analysed in what follows.

Part I

ESTABLISHING THE PRINCIPLES

1

MICROECONOMICS

Most of the economic indicators discussed in the media are macroeconomic, broad aggregates of trends and cycles in output, prices, jobs, trade, money, and so on. But economics really begins at the level of the individual decision-maker. This branch of economics, known as microeconomics, is concerned with the forces that influence the economic behaviour of individual consumers, firms, employees, and investors, and of the basic economic institutions of industries and markets. Though individuals frequently make economic decisions instinctively, and though markets might appear to move randomly, there are consistent principles underlying their behaviour.

Investors naturally find it valuable to understand the market in which they are operating. But for company managers, it is absolutely essential to be able to make sense of the market, to appreciate exactly what shapes the demand and supply of goods and/or services in which they deal. To be 'market-driven', to respond effectively to changing market conditions, implies an elementary grasp of the fundamental principles of consumer behaviour, of investment decision-making, of the firm, and of demand and supply. These principles must then be worked out in the three main types of market: product markets, where goods and services are bought and sold; labour markets, where jobs and wages are offered and accepted; and capital markets, where lenders and borrowers of money come together.

CONSUMERS

Microeconomics begins with the demand side, the consumer. Most people have a weekly or monthly income, remuneration for the work they put in at their job. The choices for what they do with it are essentially two. They can spend it on their basic needs of food, drink, clothing, and accommodation, as well as more 'luxurious' items, such as holidays, music and books. This is known as consumption. Alternatively, they can save it: for future spending by them or their heirs, as a precaution against unanticipated future needs, or to generate future income.

How consumers make the choice between consumption and saving is more typically an aggregate issue in macroeconomics (see chapter 2), while how individuals allocate their savings is more the subject of investment theory (see below). The theory of consumer decision-making is about how they allocate their consumption budgets to particular goods and services. It is a theory about choice, since the limited income (or budget constraint) any consumer faces means that tough decisions have to be made on which products will be purchased and in what quantities.

Because the tastes and preferences of individual consumers are all so different, it is impossible to make definitive statements about their behaviour. What can be suggested, though, is how their choices might respond to changes in the relative prices of different products. For example, if the price of one good falls relative to all others, it has two effects. Firstly, there is the substitution effect whereby the consumer buys more of it because of its relative cheapness: people always choose to substitute a cheaper good for a more expensive one, and so the substitution effect always causes an increase in consumption.

But there is also the income effect whereby the price fall increases the consumer's real income. Here the direction of the effect is less predictable: often more will be consumed, but there are certain goods for which the amount consumed might fall in response to higher incomes. These are usually 'inferior' goods (perhaps, margarine in contrast to butter) which consumers will buy when they are poorer but which they will replace with something preferable but more costly when they are better off. For some goods, the income effect might outweigh the substitution effect, leading to a drop in consumption in response to a price fall.

Managers should be aware of whether their products are normal, inferior or possessing some other property that causes their consumption to behave in unusual ways. For example, for some consumers, the fall in prices of package holidays might make their attraction diminish: the increase in popularity and reduced prices put these people off through the snob effect! Typically, however, managers can expect products to be normal, responding in the standard way that if the price goes up, consumption will go down. This is the basis of the demand for goods, the key feature of which from a company's point of view, is its elasticity, how much demand changes in response to given price changes. Understanding elasticity is essential to a company's pricing policy.

Elasticity of demand

In the first instance, consumer demand for a product is determined by its price, consumers' tastes and preferences, and their incomes. It is also affected by the availability and prices of substitutes (perhaps cake instead of bread, or bicycles instead of cars), the prices of complementary goods (butter for bread, petrol for cars), the number of other buyers (telephones are not much use if few other people have them), and a range of other less important factors.

For a firm selling the product, the key element is the price because it is the one over which they have the most control. Its managers will want to know if, when they increase the price, demand will fall to such an extent that total revenues (price multiplied by sales) will diminish, stay constant, or increase. Consumer responsiveness to price changes is at the core of firms' abilities to set and change prices.

This is the elasticity of demand for a product. If it is inelastic, demand does not respond very much: this might be the case with essential items like basic foods, for which demand is fairly constant. If demand is elastic, it responds much more to a price change: this is more the case with non-essentials or luxurious goods, perhaps computers, cars, or theatre tickets. In fact, the properties of luxury or necessity are important influences on product elasticity. Others include the number of substitutes available, the product's price relative to consumers' income, and the time period in which buyers can react. Usually, the more substitutes are available, the greater the proportion of income the price takes up and the longer the time to decide on the purchase, the more elastic a product's demand.

In addition to this price elasticity, there is income elasticity, the responsiveness of demand to changes in consumers' incomes. This is determined by the type of good (normal, inferior or something else peculiar), and is particularly useful for assessing how demand might increase in response to general rises in incomes resulting from economic growth or recovery after a recession (see chapters 2 and 5). Some goods will be affected more than others: for example, demand for supermarket food is unlikely to change a great deal, though demand for restaurant food may be dramatically affected.

There is also cross-price elasticity, the responsiveness of demand to changes in the prices of other products, whether substitutes or complements. Understanding this is fundamental to a firm's ability to compete effectively on prices, and the basis for huge amounts of money being spent on advertising, as firms attempt to establish brand loyalty. The intention is that once a brand is popular, the product will be less cross-price elastic: relative decreases in the prices of its rival products will tempt away fewer customers. Cross-price elasticity is also important to firms selling complementary goods such as video recorders and video cassettes or computers and software. Reducing the price of one may stimulate demand for the complementary product.

Investors

Investment decision-making is related to consumer decision-making, but deals with the narrower market for financial assets. In a sense, the theory underlying it is about how people allocate their savings budgets to the purchase of particular financial assets. Investors are suppliers to the capital markets (see below), people who have a surplus of money from their income that they want to save. They can do this by keeping it in cash, or by putting it in a bank account or building society, the traditional meaning of savings. Alternatively, they can buy something that they expect at least to maintain its value, that might provide a flow of income, and that can be resold when needed (that is liquid).

The companion volume to this book, *The Financial Times Guide to Using the Financial Pages* explains in detail the principles on which investors base their decisions (as well as providing much broader coverage of all financial markets). Essentially, their aim is to construct a portfolio that might include shares, bonds, unit trusts, cash, gold or a variety of other financial assets, and which offers them the prospect of the best possible return consistent with the maximum level of risk with which they feel comfortable.

Investors select their assets by a number of criteria. The first is their annual return, perhaps an interest rate or dividend yield; the second is their potential for capital appreciation (together with annual return, this forms total return); and the third is their degree of risk, the possibility of making a loss on them. The characteristics of risk and return that all assets possess are intimately related: generally, the riskier they are, the greater the prospective return.

Furthermore, the potential risks and returns of different assets in one portfolio serve to temper one another. This is the principle of not putting all your eggs in one basket: the typical investor will pursue a strategy of what is called portfolio diversification. With investment objectives that seek a certain degree of safety, but also some potential of higher rewards, it makes sense to own a balanced portfolio, a range of different assets with varying degrees of risk and potential returns.

The theory of investment operates on the premise that an individual investor is the dominant player on the supply (saving/lending/investing) side of the capital markets, making and implementing his or her own investment decisions. In reality, individual investors acting alone form only a small part of the investment community. Nowadays the bulk of investment is done by large investing institutions such as pension funds and insurance companies, operating on behalf of the millions of people who put money into them. Nevertheless, the principles by which they invest are the same.

FIRMS

Some of the main assets an investor might own are shares in companies, organisations established for some kind of commerce and with a legal identity separate from their owners. The owners are the shareholders who have rights to a part of the company's profits, and who usually have limited liability. This means that their liabilities for company debts are limited to the amount paid for their shares. They can only lose what they invested.

Companies are often run by people other than the owners, though in theory at least the ordinary shareholders control the company:

management is expected to act in the best interests of the owners. That, at least, is the typical assumption of microeconomics in this, its supply side, the theory of the firm (where lie the roots of management theory, the study of how businesses make decisions). Although many of its later developments tackle issues arising from the separation of ownership and control, it is instructive to think about the firm in the rudimentary economic way: operating with a sole management goal, to maximise its short-term profits (or, at least, minimise its losses).

Managers of a profit-maximising company must ask themselves a number of key questions: should the company be in a particular business? if so, how much of the product should it produce? and how much should it charge for it? Assuming managers believe a business is profitable enough to be in, the level of output they supply is a function of the price they are able to charge. Depending on the competitive structure of the market, they may be able to charge whatever they like or limited to a narrow range of choice. Supply is also affected by such factors as the costs of production, the level of available technology, the prices of other products (whether substitutes or complements), and the number of other companies selling in that market.

Once managers have decided on their output, firstly, whether to enter or exit a market, and secondly, once in, whether to expand or contract their output, they must decide on the allocation of their resources to producing that output. This is the fundamental issue of selecting and varying the combination of the two key inputs to the production process, the two factors of production, capital and labour. It is partly a question of how to use existing plant, equipment and staff; and it is partly about whether, when and at what cost to take on new staff or invest in new capital goods. Hiring and the capital expenditure process will both depend to some extent on the prices of labour and capital: wage and salary levels and interest rates, the costs of production.

Costs of production

The economic analysis of costs is quite similar to the process of management or cost accounting with which company managers will be familiar. Such managers will recognise the need to have a thorough understanding of their costs of production in order to determine the optimal level of production at any given point in time. They will also be aware of the distinction between different types of costs: for example, opportunity costs, the costs of any given outlay expressed in terms of the next best thing on which it could have been spent; replacement and historical costs, two ways of accounting for assets, either in terms of how much they would cost to replace or how much was originally paid for them; and sunk costs, expenditures that are already committed.

Sunk costs lead to another central distinction of cost analysis, that between short and long run costs. In trying to understand how firms allocate their resources to production, microeconomics assumes that there are short run costs of which certain parts are sunk or fixed. For example, it is typically assumed that in the short term, capital is fixed and that output can only be increased by adding more labour to the production process. The more labour is added, the smaller the amount of additional output generated, according to the law of diminishing returns. This relates to discussions of productivity in chapter 2.

With long run costs, all is variable: firms can vary the inputs of both capital and labour, they have time to adopt new technology, to develop better production techniques and to be more efficient. In the long-term, company managers can explore potential economies of scale whereby increasing the level of production decreases the average cost of producing each unit of output; technological innovation, where productivity is improved through enhancing the output potential of capital as well as labour (see chapter 2); and economies of scope in which the production of two or more products together costs less than the total of producing each of them separately.

Once the managers of a firm have understood the way in which their costs of production vary with the level of output, their interaction with one another, and the period of time under consideration, they need to be related to revenues and profits. Microeconomics provides numerous ways of analysing company incomes and expenditures in order to calculate the most profitable level of output and the optimal price at which that output can be sold. All of the decisions that arise from such calculations depend on the nature of the product markets in which the firm is operating. For example, if it is a dominant force in the industry, it has far more control over its prices, output and profitability than if it is one among many competing companies.

Investment

It is important to clarify one potential source of confusion early on and that is the use of the words 'investor' and 'investment'. Popularly, and especially in financial markets, an investment is an asset purchased by an investor with a view to making money, either through its yield or its appreciation in price. But this kind of investment involves only a transfer of ownership. No new spending has taken place: in the language of economics, the 'investor' is actually saving! It might better be called financial investment.

Economists, on the other hand, define investment as spending by companies or the government on capital goods: new factories or machinery or housing or roads. This is capital or business investment. Generally, it is funded by borrowing from savers, perhaps through the issue of stocks or bonds. Thus, investment in this sense is the other side of the market from saving; it is borrowing rather than lending, spending rather than saving.

The economics and financial pages of a newspaper may well use the words in both senses. Usually, though, the context will make it quite clear which is intended. In each case, the cost of the investment is determined in the markets for financial assets. The price of a stock or bond is on the one hand what an investor will have to pay to own it; on the other hand, it is what a company or government can expect to receive for the issue of a similar security.

But before making the financing decisions of how they should try to raise new funds (something again covered in detail in *The Financial Times Guide to Using the Financial Pages*, along with information on how firms present their figures, reward their shareholders, and contest corporate control) company managers have to make decisions on whether they should make new capital investments at all. The basis on which they assess this issue is the extent of expected returns, and, as this FT extract suggests, this is a highly controversial issue:

> As the Confederation of British Industry's investment appraisal survey comes out today, the main topic engaging the analysts is how far it might explain the elusive nature of UK business investment. For the evidence that many companies are setting high hurdles – minimum rates of return – for investment projects has given new statistical input to the debate about

the alleged 'short-termism' of UK businesses. By demanding high rates of return, the argument goes, businesses are fuelling inflationary expectations and stifling viable investment projects. (*Financial Times*, 25 July 1994)

Investment appraisal (the capital expenditure process) is one of the most difficult management tasks. The hurdle rates technique mentioned in this extract is one popular way of doing it. By discounting the value of expected future cash flows from a potential investment back to the present, managers calculate the expected return on the project, and then compare it to a set required return or hurdle rate. This hurdle rate usually bears some relation to the current level of interest rates; such calculations also need to take account of prospective inflation during the life of the project (a reason why inflation indicators are so important; see chapter 7). If the expected return exceeds the hurdle rate, the investment typically gets the go-ahead. An alternative way of evaluating an investment is the payback technique, which assesses a project in terms of how soon the company will recoup its investment.

DEMAND AND SUPPLY

The economic behaviour of consumers and firms is driven by a number of different factors, but the pre-eminent one is the price of the product they are seeking to buy or sell. It is essentially the patterns of response of consumers and firms to price movements that determine demand and supply. Clearly, both of these fundamental forces are shifting repeatedly over both the short and long-term: but economics is all about how they can be brought into some kind of dynamic balance, matched together in 'equilibrium'. It typically happens in the context of the marketplace, and it is the workings of this central institution of the free market economy that managers and investors need to appreciate.

Markets

A market is essentially an institution that allows buyers and sellers to come together to trade goods, services, labour or financial assets with one another through the discovery of prices with which all parties are satisfied. It could be something like the traditional idea of a market with numerous stalls selling fruit and vegetables; it could be the jobs section of a newspaper or magazine; or it could be a network of telephones and computer screens conveying information on foreign exchange rates.

In each case, what is taking place is a form of auction. In fact, an early economic theorist imagined an auctioneer offering for sale a certain quantity of a product. If there are too many or too few buyers at the suggested price, the auctioneer lowers or raises the price until the number of buyers exactly matches the number of products available for sale. In effect, consumers wishing to buy a product are looking for firms offering it at a price they find acceptable; firms are doing the reverse. If neither side finds a counterparty willing to trade at that price, the buyers will increase the price they are prepared to pay, while the sellers will reduce their preferred price. Eventually, a compromise price is reached, and that becomes the current market price.

This process is the balancing of demand and supply: the price of an item moves to the level where demand and supply are equal. And since demand and supply continually shift with the changing patterns of individuals' objectives and expectations, the price is continually moving to keep them in balance. In this environment of constant flux, it should, in principle, be possible for a seller to extract an excessive price from an unwary buyer if that buyer is kept unaware of the market price. Hence, another angle on the nature of a market is that it is a means for providing information. The more widely available the information, the better that market will operate.

Aggregating from the market for an individual product leads to a market in the recognised sense, an institution providing and generating prices for a range of products with similar properties. These may be different types of dead fish, they may be students looking for jobs in the creative and media industries, or they may be shares in UK companies.

In financial markets particularly, the market is often personified as having an opinion or sentiment. What this means is that the bulk of the traders in a market consider it to be moving in a particular direction: if buyers overwhelm sellers, it will be up (a seller's market), while if more traders are trying to leave the market than to come in, it will be down (a buyer's market). 'Conditions' are something that afflicts all types of market: for example, they might be 'favourable', in which case it needs to be asked for whom, buyers or sellers? Or they might be 'slow', in which case neither buyers or sellers are much interested in doing any business.

Markets are also defined by what trades on them. There are three broad types: the main markets are the ones in which everyone participates virtually every day, those for goods and services, the product markets. But there are also the vital markets for the inputs that are used to produce those goods and services. The most important are the markets for the two key factors of production, labour and capital.

PRODUCT MARKETS

Product markets can be markets for consumer goods (bread, cars, computers), for capital goods (machine tools, photocopiers, paper clips) or for services (airlines, insurance, online information). They are each part of what are often described as industrial sectors: the food retailing industry, the office equipment industry, the media industry, and so on. Within both markets and industries, there are a variety of forces that determine the demand for and supply of their products, and the prices that firms charge and consumers pay. Many of them arise from the structure of the market or industry, in terms of the number of companies operating in it, the costs of production they face, the power they have to control prices, and the revenues and profits they can expect to generate.

Market structure and the industrial structure overarching it can be different. For example, the word-processing software market might be highly competitive, but the software industry dominated by a handful of major suppliers, an oligopoly. From the point of view of a firm operating in a range of markets with different degrees of competition, this will be very important, but it does not make a great deal of difference to the microeconomic analysis which typically focuses on markets.

In either case, the classic example of a structure is that of perfect competition where numerous firms compete for small slices of the action. Because of the competition, each firm has to accept the standard level of prices, and can only expect to make barely acceptable profits. If profits are rising, new competitors will be attracted to enter the market; if they are going down, there will be an industry shakeout. Firms can succeed only by being low cost producers, by being permanently wary of existing or potential competition, and by always trying to be one step ahead of the pack.

At the opposite end of the market structure spectrum is the case of monopoly where one firm dominates an industry, and is able to set the price and output that earn it the maximum profits. In many such industries, the huge costs of entry mean that there is only room for one producer: these are natural monopolies, such as the provision of electricity or rail services. They are often under the control of governments, either through ownership or regulation, in order to protect consumers, whose demand is likely to be highly inelastic, from excessive exploitation.

Firms with a monopoly of a particular market (perhaps achieved through a patent or specialist knowledge) are in a powerful position, but this may only last a short time, and they should always watch out for potential competition. They might be particularly vulnerable to competition from a new substitute product, as in the way personal computers replaced typewriters. They might also be threatened by monopsonies, buyers with considerable market power, such as nationalised health services in relation to pharmaceutical companies.

The third type of market structure covers all kinds of imperfect competition, ranging from monopolistic competition, where a large number of firms can achieve temporary monopolies through product differentiation and branding; to oligopoly where a handful of suppliers dominate the market, and are obliged constantly to assess the likely response of their competitors to pricing and production decisions they make. These are the very recognisable types of market seen in the real world, such as the European car market where a limited number of firms are mutually interdependent (see Figure 1.1). Companies in such markets might use variations on some of the ideas of game theory and competitive strategic analysis to formulate the decisions and actions that will bring them industrial success.

Prices

Awareness of both the current market structure in which a company is operating and its possible future evolution is essential for managers. But whatever the structure, the key, over both the short and

WEST EUROPEAN NEW CAR REGISTRATIONS
January-May 1994

	Volume (Units)	Volume Change(%)	Share (%) Jan-May 94	Share (%) Jan-May 93
TOTAL MARKET	5,425,000	+5.5	100.0	100.0
MANUFACTURERS:				
Volkswagen group	889,000	+1.5	16.4	17.0
– Volkswagen	581,000	–1.6	10.7	11.5
– Seat	142,000	+20.8	2.6	2.3
– Audi	140,000	–4.2	2.6	2.8
– Skoda*	25,000	+20.6	0.5	0.4
General Motors#	695,000	+6.3	12.8	12.7
– Opel/Vauxhall	666,000	+5.6	12.3	12.3
– Saab**	23,000	+32.3	0.4	0.3
PSA Peugeot Citroen	685,000	+13.5	12.6	11.7
– Peugeot	411,000	+11.0	7.6	7.2
– Citroen	274,000	+17.3	5.1	4.5
Ford#	643,000	+7.5	11.8	11.6
– Ford Europe	637,000	+7.4	11.7	11.5
– Jaguar	5,000	+5.3	0.1	0.1
Fiat group##	623,000	+2.6	11.5	11.8
– Fiat	483,000	+6.2	8.9	8.8
– Lancia	82,000	–6.4	1.5	1.7
– Alfa Romeo	53,000	–11.9	1.0	1.2
Renault	575,000	+7.1	10.6	10.4
BMW group†	332,000	+5.9	6.1	6.1
– BMW†	167,000	–0.8	3.1	3.3
– Rover†	165,000	+13.6	3.1	2.8
Mercedes-Benz	189,000	+38.8	3.5	2.7
Nissan	177,000	–1.4	3.3	3.5
Toyota	140,000	–4.0	2.6	2.8
Volvo	91,000	+23.9	1.7	1.4
Mazda	85,000	–11.0	1.6	1.9
Honda†	71,000	+5.2	1.3	1.3
Mitsubishi	54,000	–17.9	1.0	1.3
Suzuki	38,000	–19.4	0.7	0.9
Total Japanese	596,000	–6.5	11.0	12.4
MARKETS:				
Germany	1,455,000	–0.6	26.8	28.4
Italy	887,000	–4.3	16.3	18.0
United Kingdom	822,000	+13.3	15.1	14.1
France	803,000	+16.0	14.8	13.5
Spain	359,000	+17.5	6.6	5.9

Figure. 1.1: West European car market

long-term, is to try to enter a growing market ahead of the competition; to be always prepared for competition, whether it comes bearing cheaper products, better products or substitute products that make the existing ones redundant or at least less in demand; and when there can be no effective product differentiation or when brand loyalties are waning, to be the lowest cost producer.

Each market structure has different effects on corporate pricing behaviour. Firms in competitive industries are essentially stuck with the going price: they are said to be price takers. Monopolists in contrast have a considerable degree of market power over price, and are said to be price makers. In both cases, though, and in all in between, firms need to be aware of the elasticity of demand in response to their price making or taking. They also need to be aware of the elasticity of supply, to what extent new firms are tempted by the attractive profit opportunities in their markets, and able to enter them. Managers need to be able to anticipate shifts in demand and supply to prepare for more or less competitive environments.

Advertising and promotion will also play a part in the structure of a market, and the dominance a company can achieve in terms of pricing, production and profitability. Such activities aim to influence consumer tastes and preferences, and are often based on detailed market research. What the research is really all about is estimation of the elasticity of demand for the company's products. If it is found that different groups of consumers have different demand elasticities for the same product, it may be possible for the firm to employ price discrimination, that is charging different prices for the same product in different markets. A common example is firms offering discounts for volume purchases.

LABOUR MARKETS

Product markets vary considerably in their degree of flexibility in response to changes in demand and supply. For example, if demand increases in the market for dead fish, suppliers can relatively easily raise their prices or increase the supply by doing a little more fishing. On the other hand, demand increases in the housing market will often affect prices rather more slowly, and it is naturally difficult to increase the supply of properties overnight. This issue of flexibility is a useful way to think about the two markets that are logically prior to the product markets, those for the labour and capital resources that generate products.

According to microeconomic theory, the labour market is where workers offer their services in return for pay (to compensate for the loss of leisure time which it is assumed they would prefer), and companies seek their services in order to make products (the demand is said to be derived demand because it derives from consumer demand for products). These two groups represent the demand for and supply of labour, and, in the way of all markets, they interact to determine the levels of wages and employment.

Wages

Wages are the equivalent of prices in the product markets, but it seems to be very much more difficult to explain their determination. In theory, for example, demand and supply will respond to wage levels in the same way that they do to prices. Firms will supposedly hire staff only up to the wage level where it is profitable to do so, relating workers' productivity and costs (unit labour costs; see chapter 7) to anticipated revenues; ideally, they will pay as little as they can get away with. At the same time, workers will supply more labour the higher the level of wages; if they are unemployed, they will seek employment by undercutting the wages of workers in jobs.

But all sorts of impediments stand in the way of the labour market attaining a balance through such mechanisms. Free market economists claim that such forces as unions, unemployment benefits, minimum wages and tax disincentives prevent wages falling to the 'market-clearing' level, but it is not clear that removing such blocks by union legislation and market deregulation are effective or appropriate. For example, recent research indicates that employers do not necessarily find it rational to seek the workers who will accept the lowest pay; nor for reasons of corporate morale do they slash wages or lay off vast numbers of people just to ensure short-term profitability. Similarly, it is often not rational or even possible for unemployed workers to 'price themselves into work' by undercutting the current wage level.

Alternative theories of wage determination are legion, and this is understandably an area of great controversy among both economists and politicians. However, it seems to be increasingly clear that the labour markets are social institutions as much as economic ones, and, as Will Hutton writes in *The Guardian*, 'interaction between human beings cannot be interpreted in the same way as the supply and demand for dead fish. Ideas of fairness and morale imbue the labour market and turn on their head the way its operations should be modelled.'

Returning to the issue of the flexibility of markets in response to changes in demand and supply, it is clear that labour markets are for all sorts of social and cultural reasons not very flexible (even in the UK and US cases of extreme deregulation). Indeed, labour cannot be regarded as a commodity in the same way as products. In contrast, the capital markets discussed below consist solely of commodities in the form of easily tradeable financial assets. They are highly flexible markets, with prices often responding instantaneously to changes in demand and supply, and buy and sell orders shifting constantly in response to fractional movements in prices.

CAPITAL MARKETS

In this way and in others, capital markets (and financial markets more generally) are rather different from product and labour markets. They might be physical places where traders meet to bargain, but in an age of technology, they do not need to be: often, nowadays, they operate through computer screens and telephones. Open outcry is the term for an actual gathering of traders offering prices at which they are prepared to buy and sell. But a very similar process is happening when they list their desired prices over the telephone or on a screen.

There are essentially four kinds of market in the financial system, trading different groups of assets. The first is the securities market where new capital is raised (the primary market) and where trading in existing shares and bonds takes place (the secondary market). Such markets include stock exchanges around the world, as well as the international capital markets for bonds and Eurobonds. The other three are: the money markets where highly liquid financial instruments are traded; the foreign exchange markets where currencies are bought and sold; and the futures and options markets where these derivatives can be used to hedge or speculate in future interest rate, exchange rate, commodity price and security price movements.

All of these markets are organised in the sense that they operate on well-established custom and practice, and direct access to them is limited to professional participants. Investors and borrowers usually gain access to the markets through intermediaries. Beyond the organised markets are the over-the-counter (OTC) markets, places or, more often, computer screen-based or telephone networks where securities are traded outside the recognised exchange. The biggest of them all is the foreign exchange market, though the OTC derivatives market is also growing dramatically.

There are three basic functions that have to be performed in a financial market: distribution of assets into the portfolios of investors who want to own them, creation of new ones in order to provide funds for borrowers, and 'making' the markets, providing the means by which all of these assets can be easily traded. The first function relates more to investors, the second to companies, and the third is the central facilitating role to which all financial institutions contribute in one way or another.

Interest rates

Linking all the financial markets together are interest rates. These are prices for the use of money, comparable to prices in the product markets and wages and salaries in the labour markets. An individual holding cash rather than depositing it in an interest-bearing bank account is paying a price, the foregone interest. Once the money is deposited, it is the bank that pays the price for the funds it can now use, again the interest payable on that account. Lastly, when the bank lends the money to a company, the company is paying a price for being able to borrow: the interest the bank charges for loans, normally higher than the rate it pays the original depositor so it can make a profit.

At any one time, there are different rates of interest payable on different forms of money. For example, money deposited long-term receives more interest than a short-term deposit. Similarly, money loaned to a risky enterprise earns more than that in a risk-free loan. Thus, an alternative view of the rate of interest is as the price of risk: the greater the risk, the higher the price.

All of these rates are intimately related: if one changes, they all do. This works by the same process as the changing prices of products or assets, that is, the rebalancing of demand and supply. If, for example, the rate of interest payable on short-term deposits were to rise, money in long-term deposits would flow into short-term deposits. The sellers or suppliers of long-term deposits would decline, and to attract them back, the price, the interest rate would need to rise in line with the short-term rate.

A rise in interest rates has a beneficial effect on investors with cash deposits in interest-bearing accounts. On the other side of the market though, the buyers of money or the borrowers face increased costs since the price has gone up. This would be the experience of companies borrowing to finance new investment, or of homeowners with monthly mortgage payments to make. But a change in interest rates also has effects on the prices of other assets, as well as on many other key variables in the wider economy. These are examined in more detail in chapter 8.

The effects of changed interest rates could conceivably come before the change is actually implemented. This is because of the expectations of investors: for example, if a rate rise is anticipated, bond owners (whose asset prices have an inverse relationship with interest rates; see chapter 8) will probably sell in the expectation of being able to buy the bonds back at the new lower price. This will cause prices to fall automatically because of surplus supply. Financial markets often discount the future in this way, building into the prices of the assets traded on them all past, present and prospective information on their future values. For example, expectations of company profits can influence the current price of a share just as much as actual announced profits, and sometimes more so.

2

MACROECONOMICS

Vast numbers of economic decisions and actions of consumers, investors, firms, and workers add up to the whole economy, the macroeconomy. The aggregation and interaction of all this individual economic behaviour form the subject of the second of the two main branches of economics, macroeconomics. Focusing on aggregate economic conditions, macroeconomics is all about the broader environment in which companies and investors operate, the influence of overall economic effects on business, plus the feedback effects from firms and financial markets to the overall economy. A full understanding of that environment is invaluable in the making of sound business and investment decisions.

The core issues of macroeconomics are the size, constituents and determinants of total economic activity. This activity can be measured in a number of different ways: as the total output of goods and services produced and sold by firms, as the total incomes to the factors that generate that output (land, labour and capital), or as the total expenditure on that output. It can also be thought of as the number of jobs a given level of output generates (or fails to generate, when focusing on unemployment). Lastly, it can be considered dynamically: in terms of changes in the nominal value of the output over time (that is, taking account of inflation); or as dynamic changes in its real value, either as long-term economic growth, or in the shorter term fluctuations of the business cycle.

THE CIRCULAR FLOW OF INCOME

The microeconomic decisions of consumers and companies are the basis for the overall economy. Bringing them all together shows how the economy works as a total system, in what is known as the circular flow of income. Essentially what happens is that firms produce goods and services to be sold to households (aggregate supply). To generate that output, they employ members of households who in return receive incomes. Those incomes provide households with the means to purchase the output (aggregate demand).

The circular flow sounds a little strange at an individual level: a company hires workers to make a product that they can buy with the income received for producing it! At the aggregate level, though, it makes perfect sense, with the myriads of consumer-worker-households producing and purchasing countless different goods and services through the medium of the firms that employ them. Grossing up from microeconomic decisions, output is equivalent to income on the supply side of the economy; and both are equivalent to expenditure on the demand side.

The most comprehensive measure of economic activity, as reflected in the circular flow of income, is known as gross domestic product (GDP). Its calculation, composition and significance are discussed in more detail in chapter 5; here it is simply necessary to know that it can be measured as output, income or expenditure. GDP expenditure represents overall market demand or aggregate demand. It consists of the four broad decision-making sectors of the economy: households, firms, governments and foreigners. Consumption by households, investment by firms, spending by governments (on both consumption and investment), and the net outcome of buying exports and selling imports by foreigners make up the total.

Increases in consumption, investment, government spending or exports are known as injections to the circular flow of income. Their effect is to increase aggregate demand and boost GDP. Normally, GDP rises not only by the amount of the increase in demand: a rise in consumer spending creates income for firms and their workers, who in turn might raise their spending, creating income and spending power for others, and so on. This is known as the multiplier. On the other side are withdrawals from the circular flow, essentially savings, taxation and imports. These too can have multiplier effects, but ones that, in contrast, reduce GDP: an increase in savings means consumers are spending less, which in turn reduces firms' incomes, cutting their spending, and so it continues.

On the aggregate supply side of the economy are the factors of production, land, labour and capital, the combination of which determines the level of production. This in turn generates the levels of output and employment. GDP output measures the value of the output, while GDP income measures the receipts of the factors of production: rents to land, profits to capital and wages and salaries to labour. It is generally assumed that the total supply of labour and capital determine the maximum level of output possible at any point in time. This is the economy's productive potential or full capacity, and it is expected to grow over time, through growth of the labour force and growth of productivity (see below).

Consumption, investment and savings

In most countries, consumption accounts for a half to two-thirds of GDP. Its level is determined by a number of factors, principal of which is the level of income. For example, if incomes are boosted through wage rises or tax cuts, households will save some and spend some. The amount that is used on consumption varies, but it is generally assumed that as income increases, the proportion that is spent, rather than saved, diminishes. Macroeconomic theories of consumption attempt to construct foundations in microeconomics, based, for example, on individuals' projections of income, consumption and saving patterns over their lifetimes.

Other influences on consumption include price expectations (rising prices might encourage spending now, rather than saving income that will lose its value to inflation), interest rates and the ease of consumer credit (low borrowing costs and/or low potential returns for savings might also encourage consumption), and a range of social factors. For example, Japan saves a far higher proportion of its national income than the United States, a fact that arises largely from cultural differences. Whatever the cause, the part of income that is spent becomes someone else's income, with potential multiplier effects. The fact that some income is saved means that the multiplier eventually peters out: the amount that is spent and becomes someone else's income gets smaller each time the income flow goes around.

The multiplier will also only continue as long as there is supply to meet the increased demand. Increased output will only occur as long as growth in demand goes into production rather than higher prices. However, if an economy is close to full capacity, increased consumption and stronger growth can cause inflation through mechanisms discussed below and in chapter 7. Exactly where the point is at which growth in demand causes higher prices rather than higher output is an issue of great debate among economists and politicians.

Taxes and benefits also play a role in consumption; the latter depends, in fact, not on total income, but on the amount of income available to households after payment of income taxes and national insurance contributions, and receipt of any benefits. This income is called personal disposable income: the difference between personal disposable income and consumer spending is called personal savings. This can be actual savings held in a deposit account, it can be repayments of debt, or, at an individual level, it can be negative ('dissaving') if consumption exceeds income through borrowing. The savings ratio is the proportion of income that is saved, expressed as a percentage of personal disposable income.

An increase in savings typically acts as a withdrawal from the circular flow, reducing GDP initially. But savings also provide the finance for industry to invest, something that is essential for future production, income and consumption. Investment is thus the twin of savings. By definition, investment equals savings: leaving exports/imports out of the picture, if consumption plus savings equals total income, income equals expenditure, and consumption (household and government) plus investment (private and public) equals expenditure, then investment and savings are equivalent. What happens is that income saved rather than consumed is available for investment: savings and investment are both about deferring current consumption for future prospects of consumption.

Like consumption and savings, investment is determined by a variety of factors, including actual and anticipated profitability, interest rates and inflation (see chapter 1 for the microeconomic explanation). This investment might be done by local firms or come from overseas through what is known as foreign direct investment (FDI) or inward investment (see Figure 2.1). This chart illustrates the number of projects of inward investment into the United Kingdom over two years, including the national sources of those projects, and the main benefits they generate in terms of created jobs. The impact of FDI and of

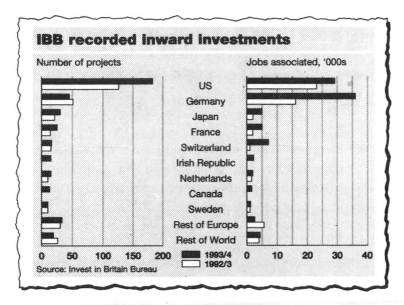

Figure 2.1: Inward investment to the United Kingdom

other important overseas interactions with the domestic economy are discussed in more detail in chapters 3 and 9.

GROWTH AND THE BUSINESS CYCLE

The circular flow of income is a static view of the macroeconomy, representing its position at a given point in time or over one year. Looking at its changes over time gives a dynamic view of the development of a national economy. Long-term, an economy is typically on a growth path, with national output, adjusted for inflation, increasing in a secular trend. However, year to year, this growth might be very irregular with pauses, retreats and spurts in economic activity, output and the general level of employment. This is known as the business cycle.

The business cycle is characterised by four phases: expansion or recovery when output and employment are rising; boom when both are at high levels; recession when both are falling; and slump or depression when both are at low levels. Within these four phases are two turning-points: peaks when booms turn into recessions; and troughs when a recovery finally begins after a period of slump or recession. There is no law that says a cycle will follow this smooth pattern with each phase lasting a certain period of time. For example, a weak recovery may turn back into slump: this has been called a double dip recession.

Recession does not necessarily imply falling output or negative growth, though it might lead to that. It can simply be a growth recession, meaning growth at a lower rate than previous years or than the long-term trend dictated by the rate of increase of the economy's productive potential. This productive potential is the fundamental reason that continuing above average growth is unsustainable over more than a few years. What happens is that recovery may be fuelled by increased consumption, investment, government spending or exports; alternatively, it may arise from reduced savings, taxes or imports. Any of these means greater demand throughout the economy. Eventually this puts pressure on supply, which in turn can lead to inflation, higher interest rates, increased savings, reduced investment and so on into recession.

This pattern comes up time and time again in discussion of economic indicators, as the following report from the *Financial Times* illustrates. Growth and the business cycle are fundamental to the reported figures, and many of these figures can best be understood in terms of their relationship with trends (long-term patterns) and cycles (short-term fluctuations around a trend). The many determinants of why growth fluctuates around a trend (such as investment and stock cycles, external shocks and government policies) and their interactions are some of the most important questions facing managers and investors making short-term decisions.

> The present business cycle has much in common with that of the 1980s. Each downturn has engendered a desperate belief that the world has entered a long-term depression phase; then there have been mutterings that recovery will not create new jobs; and finally concerns about inflationary overheating have re-emerged. It is, of course, nonsense to disconnect output and jobs. Unless newly employed workers produce nothing or negative amounts the two must go together. Unemployment has fallen in the US and the UK, where output has been rising briskly; and the OECD expects it to level off in Europe as growth returns to trend. (*Financial Times*, 25 July 1994)

Samuel Brittan, the author of this extract, has also observed that 'Businessmen have a tendency to think that any point on the cycle is unique.' Managers should be very wary of making this error, no matter how much governments protest that the booms over which they are presiding might go on forever. Although the actual shape of a cycle is not predetermined, managers who appreciate its existence, look for the signs of its turning-points and plan accordingly, will undoubtedly have an advantage over their competitors.

Productivity, technology and innovation

The extract also alludes to some of the key determinants of longer term changes in output, namely employment and productivity. Although these variables naturally change over the cycle, they have a more important impact on the longer term trends of economic growth. For example, productive potential is largely a result of the number of people employed, the hours available per worker (core hours plus overtime), and their education and training. It is also influenced by the size of the population and its age structure. For example, a substantial number of people of working age may be good for productive potential, but, if it is not realised through education, it could end in widespread unemployment.

Economic growth is determined by growth of the labour force plus growth of productivity. Productivity is a measure of the quantity of output produced with given quantities of factor inputs. It usually refers to labour productivity (typically defined as output per worker or output per hour), which is influenced by such factors as social attitudes, work ethics, unionisation and training. More importantly, it is affected by capital investment, depending to a large extent on the quality of plant and equipment. For example, it is difficult to increase productivity on obsolete machines close to being scrapped.

Substantial increases in productivity depend on new investment: labour can only increase its output up to a certain point with a given stock of capital. Beyond that, the supply of labour if not capital reaches a limit; productivity gains from there rely on product and process innovations, which allow increases in the potential output from a given stock of capital and labour. Innovation is the principal engine of economic growth, and it is driven by scientific and technological progress, invention and improvement.

Many economists understandably consider this area, the long-term determinants of economic growth and development, to be the core of economics. Understanding the factors that will improve future economic competitiveness, productivity and employment, they claim, should be at the heart of governments' economic ambitions. These ambitions to improve, to innovate and to 'beat the competition', are also at the heart of corporate concerns. While short-term fluctuations in output, employment and prices are of great immediate importance, both to governments and firms, longer term innovation and productivity growth should not be neglected.

Productivity is clearly a driving force for long-term growth, but it is also highly cyclical. This is because employment and capital are less flexible than demand and output: when demand rises in the early stages of a recovery, the first reaction is for spare capacity left over from the recession to be used. Employment typically rises slowly, while output might increase quite rapidly: firms tend to respond to increased demand initially by asking for greater productivity from its current workforce. Only if demand is sustained will a firm increase employment: if employment remains static, but productivity increases, it is possible to have 'jobless growth'. However, if output is growing, in all likelihood, so eventually will employment. This, as the extract suggests, will itself create further output.

THE ROLE OF GOVERNMENT

The government acts in many different ways: as a consumer, investor, lender, borrower and market regulator. Overarching all of these roles is the government's position as primary economic agent, attempting to monitor and influence the state of the economy. The principal means by which it does this are: fiscal policy, the budgetary balance between public spending and taxation; and monetary policy, essentially control of the money supply and manipulation of interest rates.

These policies aim for a number of different goals, the balance of which depends on government beliefs about the way an economy works. They generally centre on management of the level of employment at a high and stable rate, management of the general level of prices at a low and stable rate, and achievement of short- and long-term economic growth at a reasonably satisfactory rate. A healthy balance of payments (the state of national transactions with abroad) is also frequently a goal, targeted with trade and exchange rate policies, as well as fiscal and monetary ones. At the microeconomic level, a government may also be concerned with efficiency in the broad allocation and use of national resources, and equity in the distribution of income.

Balancing the budget

Governments spend money on a range of different goods, services, salaries, subsidies, and other payments. These include defence, education, health, public transport, public infrastructure, public housing, the pay of public sector employees, social security, and interest on government borrowing. To help pay for the services this spending provides and, to some extent, to redistribute incomes from the wealthier to the poorer, the government raises money, primarily through taxation. Some taxes are direct, levied on personal and corporate income; some are indirect, levied on sales, value added, imports, and certain products such as petrol, cigarettes and alcohol.

The difference between public spending and taxation is known as the budget balance, the budget being the collective term for the government's annual decisions on how its tax and spending plans will be designed and implemented. It might be a balanced budget where revenues equal expenditure, a budget surplus where revenues exceed expenditure, or, most typically for the UK government, a budget deficit, where expenditure exceeds revenues. Net income is known as the public sector debt repayment (PSDR) since the surplus allows repayment of debts from previous years. This was the UK government's position for a brief period in the late 1980s. More commonly, there is a net outflow, the public sector borrowing requirement or PSBR. The cumulative total of all PSBRs and PSDRs is known as the national debt.

Throughout the 1980s, the UK government had one other source of revenue, namely the receipts from the sale to the public of nationalised industries, the process of privatisation. The influx of cash from 'selling the family silver' had a very positive effect on government finances, essentially being responsible for those PSDRs.

Fiscal policy

Fiscal policy is used by the government in a variety of ways: to provide services, such as education, health, defence, and infrastructure, that might not be so well provided by the free market; to meet social goals of alleviating poverty and assisting the disadvantaged; to influence the behaviour of individuals and companies, encouraging desirable activities like investment and discouraging undesirable ones like smoking; and to manage the overall level of demand for goods and services in the economy, and hence the degree of economic activity and the rate of inflation.

Achievement of the government ambition of demand management is generally attempted through countercyclical policy: the government aims to smooth out the more extreme patterns of the business cycle, damping demand in a boom and boosting it in a recession. This can be done in a boom either through raising taxes or cutting spending; in a recession, it may try lowering taxes or increasing spending. To some extent, there are built-in stabilisers, and this is what is meant by the cyclical effects of the business cycle.

For example, in a recession, people are earning and spending less which means that the government's tax revenues fall. Of course, if the budget is already in deficit at that point, the deficit will expand even further. The government's problem then is to decide between raising taxes and cutting spending to ease the deficit or the reverse to help pull the economy out of recession. At such a point, it may turn to monetary policy.

Controlling the money supply

In order to finance their frequent budget deficits, and in common with any other individual or organisation that wants to live beyond their means, the government has to borrow in the financial markets. This it does by issuing securities with a range of different maturities, from long-term gilt-edged stocks traded on the Stock Exchange to three-month Treasury bills issued weekly in the money markets (see chapter 8). For a period in the late 1980s, the government's budget surplus meant that there were no new issues of gilts. However, as the budget returned to deficit, the government resumed issuing new ones early in 1991.

The government's agent for the sale of its debt instruments is the Bank of England, often known simply as the Bank. The stocks are first created by the Treasury and then the Bank arranges their sales, purchases and redemptions. New issues replace the ones that have matured in order to meet the government's continuing financing needs and the market's demand for a balance of differently dated stocks. Most are redeemable at some specified date, though a few are irredeemable; most pay a fixed interest amount or coupon, though for some, interest payments are index-linked to the rate of inflation.

In addition to financing its own spending, the government seeks to control the expansion of the money supply that is driven by the major financial institutions. Banks, for example, 'create' money through what is known as the money multiplier. What happens is that a bank receives a deposit, some of which is kept in liquid form as a safeguard in case the depositor needs it back, with the rest being lent on. The borrower will then spend the money on an item, the seller of which will deposit it in a bank. Again, part of the deposit will be kept liquid with the rest lent on, and so the cycle continues.

If it were not for the fact that the banks do not lend all that they receive in deposits, the process would continue indefinitely with the amount of money in the economy, the money supply, ballooning. In fact, the proportion of their deposits not lent determines how much a given deposit eventually becomes within the whole banking system. If, for example, all banks keep back 10 per cent of their deposits, an initial deposit can expand tenfold: of a £100 deposit, £90 is lent and deposited, of which £81 is lent and deposited, and so on. The eventual total of bank deposits is £1,000.

Open market operations, interest rates and monetary control

Expansion of the money supply is arguably one of the most important determinants of inflation and the overall level of economic activity. The funding of government spending also forms a critical part of the macroeconomy. These two economic variables come together in monetary policy, conducted through the Bank of England and its interactions with the institutions of the financial markets, notably the discount houses. Monetary policy can also be targeted at the exchange rate, as discussed in chapters 3 and 9.

The discount houses have a special relationship with the Bank that is central to the implementation of the government's monetary policy. First of all, they act as marketmakers in the money markets and, as such, they are obliged to cover the amount of bills on offer in the weekly Treasury bill tender, as well as having a bid price for other bills of exchange and certificates of deposit. These then are their assets; their liabilities are deposits by banks of what is known as call money. This is money borrowed at interest rates lower than the discount houses earn on bills (again, as marketmakers, they are obliged to take the deposits), but which can be withdrawn at very short notice.

Discount houses can take on these obligations because the Bank stands behind them as the 'lender of last resort'. If they run short of funds, either because banks have withdrawn money or because they have been obliged to purchase other money market instruments, they can go to the Bank. Every day the Bank estimates the market's fund shortage and usually meets it by buying bills from the discount houses. In doing this they are injecting funds into the whole financial system; if instead they sell bills, they are withdrawing funds, effectively mopping up surplus money. This is known as open market operations and is one of the means by which the government controls the money supply.

The extension of this control is how the Bank of England manipulates the level of interest rates. Since it deals actively in the bill markets through open market operations, it is in a position to create a shortage of cash when it wishes to. In that case, the discount houses are obliged to borrow, and as the lender of last resort, the level at which the Bank provides funds is an indication of the level of short-term rates of which it approves. These rates can then be used to influence rates across the whole economy.

The rate of interest, that is, the price of money, is one of the most powerful forces in the financial markets. Under the relatively free market approach of recent UK governments, interest rates have been allowed, for the most part, to be determined by market forces with the Bank's guidance. But, with this system, the Bank has to be careful to give only very subtle indications of where it wants rates to go: if it alerts the market to its intentions, the force of expectations will have immediate ramifications throughout the economy as traders discount the future.

An alternative method of controlling the money supply is using direct controls on bank lending, aiming to limit money multiplier effects. This might be achieved by changing banks' reserve asset ratios, that is, the proportions they keep liquid from any given deposit; by imposing limits on total bank lending or consumer credit; or simply by persuading bankers to restrict their lending. These policies might also serve to fulfil the Bank's other obligation to maintain financial stability: it is critical that banks lend soundly since a large credit failure by one of their borrowers could have devastating consequences.

A further technique of monetary control, which has been popular in the United Kingdom since the late 1970s, is setting targets for monetary growth. An important target in the United Kingdom is the monetary base: this consists of cash in circulation plus banks' deposits at the Bank of England. To date, this appears to have been reasonably effective in restraining inflation, the primary goal of monetary policy. It is discussed in more detail in chapter 8.

CONTROVERSIES AND DEBATES

While microeconomics is a fairly uncontentious subject, macroeconomics is one of huge controversies and continuing debates. Why economic activity does not proceed at a smooth pace, what causes inflation and unemployment, how money affects the real economy, and the desirable extent of government involvement in the economy, are all issues about which economists argue extensively. And the debate is not limited to economists: indeed, many of these questions are at the heart of the ideological and policy disputes of rival politicians. Economic schools of thought that define positions on the issues (Keynesians, monetarists, supply-siders and so on) are frequently appropriated by politicians in pursuit of a new idea or a justification for their policies.

At the same time, much of the work of less theoretically or mathematically minded economists arises in response to developments in the economy and the effects of government economic policies. The Keynesian revolution, for example, which was essentially about how the government could manage demand, and hence the business cycle, through its budget, came about as a result of the failures of economic policy in the depression of the interwar years. The monetarist counter-revolution in turn arose from problems thrown up by Keynesian policies, notably their inability to restrain inflation.

Three issues, among many, recur in various forms in debates between competing politicians and policy-oriented economists. One is the causes of and relationship between inflation and unemployment, and, in particular, whether there is a trade-off between them. Another is the set of questions about the appropriate role of government, notably its use of taxation and budget deficits to influence aggregate demand and incentives to work. The third relates to the money supply, and the considerations surrounding the independence of central banks in their management of monetary policy.

Unemployment and inflation

The inflation–unemployment trade-off begins with the questions of which is worse, economically, socially and politically; and which therefore should be the primary goal of economic policy. Over the past decade, western governments have tended to argue that it is the control of inflation that should come first, traditionally the viewpoint of the political centre-right. Inflation makes it hard to distinguish between changes in relative price rises and general price rises, distorting the behaviour of individuals and firms and reducing efficiency; since it is unpredictable, it causes uncertainty and discourages investment; and it redistributes wealth unjustly, from creditors to borrowers, from those on fixed incomes to those on wages, and from everyone to the government.

Certainly, inflation is damaging to the performance of the real economy, but so is high unemployment. It is an incredible waste of productive resources, it is expensive in terms of government benefits, and it is miserable for all the individuals who experience it. Along with substantial earnings differentials, and tax policies that favour the better off, it can cause drastic disparities in the distribution of income, and potentially disastrous social disruption. Concerns about the consequences of high global unemployment in the early 1990s have seen a resurgence of interest in the pursuit of full employment, traditionally a key policy goal of the political centre-left. This raises the central issue of how unemployment and inflation are connected, and what full employment might mean.

It used to be believed that there was a simple trade-off between the two variables: what is called the Phillips curve, after its progenitor, suggested that to reduce inflation, society had to tolerate higher unemployment, and vice versa. This inverse relationship did in fact exist in the US economy and others through the 1960s; it subsequently broke down irretrievably, as later years witnessed both high inflation and high unemployment, what became known as stagflation. Such times led to the coining of a new economic indicator, the misery index, the combination of the rates of consumer price inflation and unemployment (an alternative misery index adds together inflation and interest rates).

Nowadays, the consensus of economic opinion seems to be that there is some level of output and employment beyond which inflation rises. For example, there is always a gap between the actual level of output and the potential level, a measure of the amount of slack in the economy called the output gap. If this gap is closed too far, supply cannot rise to meet any increased demand, thus forcing up prices; there exist what economic reports often call bottlenecks or supply constraints. This might be called a situation of excess demand: spending power, perhaps arising from tax cuts, increased consumer borrowing or a bigger money supply, exceeds the availability of goods and services, bidding up their prices.

Similarly, it is argued, below a certain unemployment rate, what has been called the natural or non-accelerating inflation rate of unemployment, higher demand becomes inflationary. At such a point, the supply and demand for labour are in balance; below it, higher demand for labour supposedly drives up wage costs, which feeds through to retail price inflation, which encourages demands for higher wages, and so on in an inflationary spiral.

Estimates vary of what that rate of unemployment really is, and arguments continue about whether it should be regarded as the 'full employment' unemployment rate. It is assumed to depend on such factors as the level of minimum wages, benefits, employment taxes, unionisation, the age structure of the labour force and other demographic factors, and these are now the issues of much economic and political debate. For many managers, though, it still appears that there is a simple trade-off, which can influence their business decisions (see chapters 6 and 7).

Taxation and the budget deficit

The issue of demand management is central to the pursuit of higher output and lower unemployment, without overheating the economy and causing inflation. This is Keynesian economic policy whereby growth is pursued through increasing government spending or cutting taxes, creating or raising the budget deficit, and increasing the PSBR. Tax cuts, for example, increase demand through their beneficial effects on personal disposable income.

The question is, though, how far can the government manage demand in this way before running into inflationary bottlenecks. Furthermore, it is not clear that governments can make accurate enough assessments to judge exactly how much 'pump-priming' or 'deficit financing' is needed to 'fine-tune' the economy to a non-inflationary growth path. Indeed, when demand should be restrained to avoid overheating, there are political reasons why governments might avoid raising taxes.

Lower taxes as a means of demand management in times of recession are typically a politically centre-left policy. But tax cuts may also be advocated by centre-right politicians who view them as having a different economic effect. These politicians and the economists who advise them (supply-siders) focus on the incentive and disincentive effects of taxation, arguing that lower taxes have a strong incentive effect, encouraging people to work harder, and thereby raising national output.

Certainly, taxation does affect incentives to some extent, but extreme believers in this position, who gained political power in the United States in the 1980s, took it a little too far. These supply side economists claimed that cutting the tax rate significantly would have such powerful incentive effects that the level of tax revenues would actually rise. In reality, the result was a series of massive budget deficits.

Debates about taxation also focus on the appropriate form it should take. For example, progressive income tax is a way of redistributing income from richer to poorer sections of the population, creating a more equitable society. Supply-siders prefer the use of indirect taxes, such as value added tax. These, they argue, are easier to enforce, and reduce the incentive to work by less than equivalent levels of income tax. The claim is that taxpayers experience 'money illusion': if they pay taxes concealed in product prices, they notice it less than taxes taken out of their pay, and are thus prepared to pay more tax on goods than on income. This might have a number of political and economic benefits: if people feel less heavily taxed, they will behave accordingly.

Central bank independence

Demand management through fiscal policy still has supporters, as does management of the economy through monetary policy. The latter used to be the preserve of monetarists, who focused on the importance of controlling the money supply as a way of keeping inflation in check. But monetary policy also affects growth: it is said to be neutral if the level of interest rates neither stimulates nor slows growth. If the interest rate rises, monetary policy might restrain consumer spending and encourage savings, hence reining in growth. Nowadays, the key roles of monetary policy in economic management of demand and inflation are almost universally acknowledged: the question is more one of who should control it, the government or independent monetary authorities.

The argument for central bank independence is that governments have done a bad job of managing their economies, providing monetary accommodation not only for their own deficits, but also for wage claims, oil shocks and so on. This has caused inflation: since government control of the money supply is open to manipulation in response to political expediency, there is a built-in inflationary bias. The bias can only be removed by handing control over to the central bank, which will be free of political pressures. The central bank can then pursue its twin goals of monetary and financial stability, a sound money supply and a safe financial system.

Naive monetarist versions of this view suggest that central banks can control inflation with interest rates without an intermediate effect on economic activity. This visualises a clear connection between interest rates, the money supply and inflation, that is separate from output and employment. This seems a rather unlikely scenario: given the powers over the whole economy an independent central bank would have, it is clearly important to make it democratically accountable.

The issue of central bank independence has become particularly important in the United Kingdom as a direct result of the failure of the UK government's monetary policy in 1992. This policy, discredited by circumstances, was to control inflation and pursue economic convergence with fellow members of the European Union (EU), by keeping the pound in the exchange rate mechanism (ERM) of the European Monetary System (see chapter 3). After the collapse of this policy on Black Wednesday in 1992, the government aimed to restore its credibility in 'the fight against inflation' by greater openness and an enhanced role for the Bank of England.

The UK government's post-ERM policy is something of a compromise response to this argument, going part of the way to bank independence, but still retaining substantial control. It is based on a specific inflation target of 1 to 4 per cent for retail price inflation excluding mortgage interest payments, and a promise to push inflation into the lower half of its target band by the end of the 1992–97 parliament.

The goal is to be achieved by the traditional means of using the interest rate to manage demand and the money supply. But in order to discourage a lax monetary policy (lowering or holding interest rates down too long to court political popularity), the goal is supplemented by the Treasury publishing a monthly monetary report, the Bank publishing a quarterly inflation report, and most importantly, the minutes of monthly policy meetings between the Bank governor and the Chancellor being published six weeks later (see chapter 7). Making interest rate policy more transparent in this way, it becomes harder for politicians to abandon the fight against inflation. It also strengthens the Bank's power, either to dictate policy or to discredit the government's economic policy if its policy recommendations are ignored.

3

INTERNATIONAL ECONOMICS

Business and investment decisions are increasingly made in an international context. Global flows of goods, services and capital are making national economies more and more interdependent, and this trend appears unlikely to be reversed. Firstly, there seems to be a strong consensus on the positive effects of liberal trade policies whereby barriers to trade between nations are reduced and removed. Secondly, national product markets are increasingly dominated by powerful multinational corporations, companies that cut across national boundaries, and are eager to produce and sell their output wherever they can do so profitably. And thirdly, there are the international financial markets (for debt and equity capital, for cash and currencies, and for commodities and derivative products), in which borrowers seek the cheapest funds available, and investors and speculators chase the highest possible returns.

Economic globalisation is having increasingly important effects on national economies, on local financial markets and on individual companies. In making business and investment decisions, it is no longer advisable simply to take account of the domestic economy, either with regard to particular markets or at the aggregate level. Even if you tend to rely on domestic suppliers, sell primarily to the home market, or restrict your portfolio to the local exchanges, it is still useful to consider international trade and financial flows, and economic developments elsewhere in the world. These can affect any business, adding an international dimension to micro- and macroeconomic considerations.

Alongside the process of globalisation are the processes of market integration and regionalisation, pursued by national governments.

The countries of western Europe are well advanced on the path to integrating their trade and currencies, as well as coordinating their economic policies, and many other regions of the world are following their example. These processes too interact with the business of exporting and importing, with running your business more generally, and with national and international asset markets. It is valuable to understand them and their coverage in the *Financial Times* in order to make more informed business and investment decisions.

THE WORLD ECONOMY

The collapse of communism at the end of the 1980s was expected to usher in a new era of prosperity for the 1990s, but so far this decade, global growth has proved disappointing. According to the IMF, total world output stagnated in 1991, did little better in 1992, and grew by 2.3 per cent in 1993. While the IMF anticipates world output growing by 3 per cent in 1994 and 3.7 per cent in 1995, the situation in the labour market is not so encouraging. Unemployment in the twenty-five industrialised nations of the OECD has jumped from less than twenty-five million four years ago to nearly thirty-five million today.

Better news on the global scene is that Latin America appears to be resolving its economic problems after a decade of low growth and falling living standards, triggered by the Mexican debt crisis of 1982. The dynamic economies of south-east Asia should also notch up more growth this decade although at a slower pace than in the boom years of the 1980s. The IMF forecasts that developing countries as a whole will grow by an average of 5.5 per cent in 1994 and 5.8 per cent in 1995, more than twice as fast as the industrialised world.

Meanwhile, the countries of eastern Europe are finding that the struggle to make the transition from a command economy to a market economy is far more difficult than expected. Worse still is the position of the former Soviet Union: Russia's economic reform efforts have run into ever greater problems, while the disintegration of the Comecon trading bloc has greatly increased the adjustment problems of all the former communist states. Africa continues to lag economically behind the rest of the globe.

The world economy breaks down into a number of key regional or other economic groupings based on standards of living, levels of output and trade, and historical or geographical connection. The three most powerful blocs are North America (the United States and its partners in the North American Free Trade Agreement or NAFTA, Canada and Mexico), the twelve member states of the European Union and east Asia centred on Japan. While the United States remains the world's dominant economy, representing a quarter of global output and a third of the industrialised countries' output, the other two blocs are certainly threatening its position. This post-communist balance is sometimes described as the tripolar world.

Japan and the NAFTA and EU countries, plus nine other industrialised countries, primarily located in western Europe, form the Organisation for Economic Cooperation and Development (OECD), the 'rich countries' club'. The leading countries of the OECD (the United States, Japan, Germany, France, Italy, the United Kingdom and Canada) make up the Group of Seven (G7), which as a whole accounts for two-thirds of world output. Then there are the 'newly industrialised countries' (NICs) of south-east Asia, the mainly Middle Eastern nations of the Organisation of Petroleum Exporting Countries (OPEC), the ex-communist countries of eastern Europe and the former Soviet Union, and the developing countries of Latin America, Africa and the rest of the world.

INTERNATIONAL TRADE

International trade is a central driving force of global economic growth and development, and the general trend since the war has been for both world trade and output to increase dramatically. Trade expansion has led the growth of output, though since 1973, the rates of growth of both have slowed (see Figure 3.1). Almost all countries have participated to some extent in the explosion of world trade and output, but some have done very much better than others. Today, the United States is the biggest exporter of goods and services at 12.6 per cent of total world exports, while Germany and Japan are neck and neck for second place.

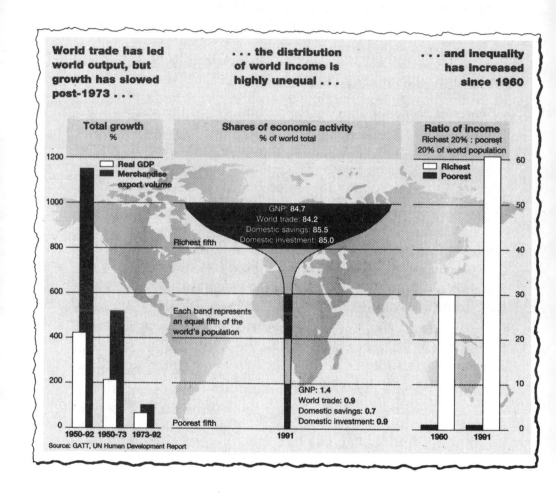

Figure 3.1: World output, trade and income distribution

- **Total growth of world output and trade**: total percentage growth rates for real (that is, inflation adjusted) world GDP and merchandise export volume (physical goods, as opposed to 'invisible' services) over a forty-plus year period and two sub-periods.

1973 is often seen as the turning point of the post-war period, marking the end of the high growth, low inflation, full employment, and fixed exchange rate years, and the beginning of the more uncertain times since. The problems of the latter period were launched by the floating of the dollar and the consequent chaos in the international financial markets; and by the oil crises, when the price of oil quadrupled within the space of three months.

- **Shares of economic activity**: the percentages of the world's total output, trade, savings and investment taken up by each fifth of the world's population, broken down by wealth. This indicates that the 20 per cent of the people in the world who are the richest, account for around 85 per cent of the key economic indicators; the poorest 20 per cent of the population make up around 1 per cent. The distribution of global income is highly unequal.

- **Ratio of income**: the 1960 and 1991 ratios between the total incomes of the richest 20 per cent of people of the world, and the poorest 20 per cent. These figures indicate that inequality has increased dramatically over the last thirty years.

The interaction of national economies through international trade increases world output by allowing countries to specialise in the production of those goods and services which they can produce most efficiently. Countries could cut themselves off from the rest of the world, and seek to provide for all their needs domestically. However, if, for example, their industries are particularly good at making high quality, low cost computers, and not so efficient at growing rice, it makes sense to focus their energies on the manufacture of computers, and, in effect, trade them for rice with other countries. Even if those other countries are not more efficient at rice-growing, but agriculture is still their most effective industry, specialisation in production followed by free trade should still be beneficial to all parties.

It is generally accepted that specialisation (to some degree) and free trade allow all countries to develop more rapidly, and expand global output and incomes. However, there are many obstacles to their working out in practice. These arise from the interests of particular groups within countries (including managers, investors and employees), and play out in governments' trade and commercial policies, in recurrent trade disputes between countries and trading blocs, and in the great debate between free trade and protectionism.

A number of arguments for protection are advanced. For example, companies in declining or internationally uncompetitive industries sometimes demand protection in order to avoid going out of business. Their managers might argue for the 'national interest', the importance of producing their goods domestically, the unemployment their failure would cause (here, they would be backed by their workforce), and the 'cheating' strategies their foreign competitors adopt.

Similarly, firms in 'infant industries' (often new, high technology sectors) might claim they need protection because they are as yet too young, small and weak to compete effectively at the international level. Governments themselves might pursue strategic protection of industries they believe it would be dangerous for foreigners to control.

The trade policies of the EU, for example, are the outcome of three conflicting compulsions: the liberal commitment to the idea of free trade, as reflected in multiple global trading initiatives; the protectionist desire to shield some domestic producers from foreign suppliers; and what is known as a 'pyramid of preferences', which ranks various trading partners, often on the basis of historical connection. The protectionist element of these policies has predominantly been directed at manufactured imports from other industrialised countries, but, increasingly, they also affect goods produced by competitive suppliers in less developed countries.

Trade liberalisation and the Uruguay Round

The growth of international trade is frequently hampered by the barriers erected to keep out imports and protect domestic industries. These might take the form of tariffs, quotas, duties, limits, 'voluntary export restraints' and a host of other schemes. Since the end of the war, big advances have been made in reducing these barriers to the free flow of goods and services, but there is still a long way to go. The recent world recession has threatened a renewed bout of protectionism as countries have looked inwards to deal with their own problems. For example, US car manufacturers and their workforces have combined to demand protection of the US car market from cheaper and frequently better quality Japanese imports.

The main forum for addressing trade issues is the General Agreement on Tariffs and Trade (GATT). This is a multinational institution set up in 1947 to promote the expansion of international trade through a coordinated programme of trade liberalisation. The GATT's primary two-pronged approach has been to eliminate quotas and reduce tariffs. It has supervised several conferences (or 'rounds') on tariff reductions and the removal of other barriers to trade, and, in late 1993, brought to completion the Uruguay Round of trade discussions.

Begun in 1986, the Uruguay Round was an attempt by the international community to negotiate a fundamental change in the world trading system. With the participation of over one hundred countries, it aimed both to repair the old GATT and to extend it to many new areas: it was the first negotiating round in which developing countries pledged themselves to substantive obligations; it was the first application of liberal trading principles to the services sector, foreign direct investment (FDI), and intellectual property rights; and it reintegrated into the GATT system two important sectors, textiles and agriculture.

The success of the Uruguay Round centres on, among other things, an enormous cut in tariffs. This, coupled with more transparent and orderly trading rules, should give a powerful boost to the world economy, stimulating competition and offering developing countries new opportunities for integration into international markets. The accords of the Final Act, agreed on 15 December 1993, should come into force in 1995 following ratification by all member countries.

The Uruguay Round has introduced a series of institutional innovations to back up the new rules: a semi-judicial dispute settlement system, a trade policy review mechanism and a new World Trade Organization to be based in Geneva like its predecessor, the GATT. The principal change is that the old GATT will lapse: the new system as it results from the Final Act of the Uruguay Round will be a very different and legally distinct institution. It should create a considerably more stable and more open framework for international trade relations.

EXCHANGE RATES AND INTERNATIONAL FINANCE

The cross-border exchange of goods and services is made possible by the fact that it is possible to convert one national currency into another. Thus, a UK company wishing to buy a US product (priced naturally in the local currency, dollars) can make the transaction by buying dollars with its pounds. The price it pays for those dollars in sterling is known as the exchange rate, and the markets on which it buys them are the international currency markets.

When these markets are allowed to work freely, with the price of currencies in terms of other currencies fluctuating according to demand and supply, it is known as a floating exchange rate system. That, for example, is the kind of system currently in place between the dollar and the yen. The opposite is to have rates set by governments with occasional devaluations and revaluations, a fixed rate system, such as the one that operated in the post-war world up to 1973. In practice, systems are typically somewhere in between, with rates allowed to fluctuate to some extent, but managed by national monetary authorities.

As well as providing the means for companies and countries to conduct trade across borders, exchange rates also allow various forms of international investment and speculation. Broadly characterised, there are three types: firstly, there is speculation by owners of large quantities of 'hot money', constantly moving their funds around the world in pursuit of the best return, and going in and out of money market accounts in response to minuscule shifts in relative interest rates. Secondly, there is financial investment in international asset markets by investors, who may be pursuing immediate profit or longer term financial goals. And thirdly, there is international capital investment or FDI by companies seeking low cost production facilities and/or access to new markets. Given the difficulties of planning such investment, FDI typically has longer term ambitions in mind.

Currency markets

The primary function of foreign exchange markets is to facilitate international trade. Companies involved in such trade might participate in them in the following ways: buying foreign currencies in order to purchase foreign goods, perhaps as inputs to their production processes; selling the currencies they receive for the sale of their products to overseas buyers; or hedging either of these kinds of transactions through the forward purchase or sale of the relevant currencies at a fixed rate. Floating exchange rates can make life difficult and unpredictable for exporting and importing companies, and hedging activities are designed to counteract any potential losses through future changes in a currency's value against other currencies.

But the currency markets also allow foreign investment and speculation. This is primarily in the form of speculation in the currencies themselves, but they are also important to investors in international stocks, or stocks that are particularly sensitive to currency or interest rate movements. In practice, the bulk of turnover in these markets is attributable to speculation, and while speculation provides the markets with necessary liquidity, it can also destabilise them. Greater volatility makes prediction of future market movements more difficult, hence creating a further need for hedging by longer term investors and companies.

As in all markets, the value of currencies in the international market is determined by supply and demand. The main players are the foreign exchange dealers of commercial banks and foreign exchange brokers. However, the market is often significantly affected by the intervention of central banks on behalf of governments. In this marketplace, there is considerable interaction between the authorities and market professionals. But despite this intervention, swings in currency values can be vast, and often not very attached to 'fundamentals', the state of the real economy. Such swings can be particularly damaging for companies that rely heavily on exports or imported raw materials.

The core determining factor of a currency's value is still the health of the real national economy, especially the balance of payments current account. The process is best demonstrated with an example: if there is a surplus on the current account, that is, a country sells more goods than it buys, then buyers have to acquire its currency to purchase goods. This adds to the selling country's reserves of foreign currencies, and bids up the price of the currency. As the price rises, exports rise in price: if there is a fall in the quantity sold, the currency too will fall.

The currency's value is also affected by the level of domestic inflation and the domestic rate of interest. High rates of interest and low rates of inflation make a currency attractive for those holding assets denominated in it or lending it to borrowers. As a result, a central bank may use interest rates to try to raise or lower the value of its currency. This may be done through short-term interest rates: usually, raising them attracts investors into buying the local currency, while lowering encourages selling. In general, one country raising interest rates while others remain the same, will raise the value of that currency as money flows into the country. This will have a limited effect if the fundamentals are wrong, that is, if there is a persistent deficit on the current account.

A central bank might also work on the currency by using its official reserves of foreign currencies to buy its own currency and, through the weight of its intervention, push up its value or at least hold it steady. But, nowadays, with the vast speculative volume of transactions in the foreign exchange markets, a successful intervention may need international cooperation. A government acting alone is increasingly unable to manage effectively the financial markets or indeed its own national economy.

One further significant factor determining short-term currency values is market sentiment. There is often a self-fuelling process in which enthusiasm for a currency, or the lack of it, drives the rate. Speculators might decide, as they did with the pound sterling on Black Wednesday (see below), that a currency is overvalued or simply that there are speculative gains to be made. Short selling (selling assets not owned with the expectation of buying them back after their price has fallen) will then cause it to fall, often in spite of government intervention.

Capital flows

'Hot money' flows in and out of countries in response to the pursuit of short-term gain and without any considerations of longer term issues of economic development of product markets or national economies. It moves simply on the basis of movements or expected movements of exchange rates and relative interest rates. However, there are two other important forms of international financial flows. One that is growing substantially is the flow of cross-border financial investment, as investors place larger portions of their portfolios in international equities and bonds. As with all financial investment, this might be short- or long-term investment, depending on the goals of the investors. It is reflected particularly in the increasing enthusiasm for the 'emerging markets' (see below).

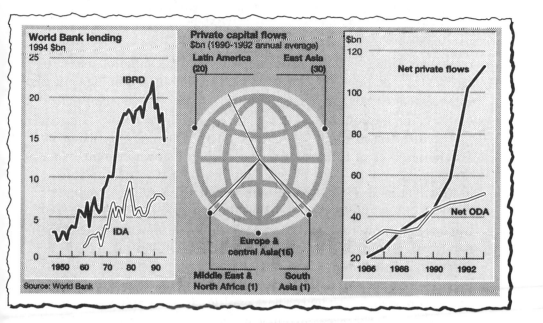

Figure 3.2: Global capital flows

More connected to the longer term growth of the world economy and its constituents is the third kind of international financial flow, capital investment by companies, governments and financial institutions in foreign countries. In the case of the private sector, this is called foreign direct investment (FDI); from governments, it might be in the form of loans, or conditional or unconditional aid. Such investment might also come from major global organisations such as the World Bank (see Figure 3.2).

- **World Bank lending**: supplies of development capital from the World Bank to developing countries in billions of dollars. The flows are from two arms of the Bank, the International Bank for Reconstruction and Development (its market-based lending arm) and the International Development Association (for countries that cannot borrow on commercial terms). The Bank also has an investment banking affiliate, the International Finance Corporation.

- **Private capital flows**: investment by the private sector in five key developing regions.

- **Net private flows and net overseas development assistance (ODA):** flows of private capital to developing countries, and of ODA or aid from governments. In the years from 1988, flows of the former have quadrupled.

MARKET INTEGRATION AND REGIONALISATION

Alongside the process of trade liberalisation across the globe are those of market integration and regionalisation. These processes typically begin with a free trade agreement, an arrangement between countries (usually in the same geographical region of the world) to eliminate all trade barriers between themselves on goods and services, but in which each continues to operate its own particular barriers to trade with the rest of the world. It may develop into a customs union or common market where arrangements for trade with the rest of the world are harmonised; subsequently into a single market like the EU; and perhaps on to full economic and monetary union (EMU).

A number of regional free trade agreements exist, most notably the North America Free Trade Agreement (NAFTA) and the Association of South East Asian Nations (ASEAN). NAFTA is due to be finalised in 1994; ASEAN was set up in 1967 by Indonesia, Malaysia, the Philippines, Singapore, Thailand and Brunei. Such initial efforts at market integration are spreading rapidly, including, for example, the Mercosur (Mercado Comun del Sur or 'southern common market') in Latin America, incorporating Brazil, Argentina, Uruguay and Paraguay; and Ecowas, the Economic Community of West African States, built around Nigeria.

There is some debate as to whether the integration of regional markets is a threat or an encouragement to the further development of free trade on a global scale, as the following FT extract illustrates:

> The trend towards regional economic blocs was likely to accelerate during the 1990s, but there was no evidence that it had damaged the growth of world trade, Mr Peter Sutherland, the director general of the General Agreement on Tariffs and Trade, said yesterday. 'The conclusion that the

world is witnessing the creation of three inwardly-oriented trading blocs, based in North America, western Europe and the Asia-Pacific region, is not supported by an analysis of trends in the pattern of world trade'. Mr Sutherland said he was confident that regional integration would complement multilateral trade, provided GATT members swiftly ratified the Uruguay Round trade agreement. (*Financial Times*, 8 July 1994)

The European Union

The regional economy that is most advanced in the integration and coordination of its economic policy, trade policy and currencies is the European Union. The EU is on its way to representing one third of world output, compared with one quarter for the United States and one sixth for Japan. As a market comprising twelve countries, the Union accommodates around a quarter of all world commerce within its frontiers. Furthermore, it is the world's most substantial source of foreign direct investment, its most important provider and consumer of services and the largest global supplier of aid.

The European Union has been through a number of transformations in its history, the most economically significant of which, to date, is the '1992' project, the creation of a single market. On 1 January 1993, that single market came into effect: in principle and to a large extent in practice, the remaining obstacles to the free flow of goods, services, capital and labour between the twelve member states of the EU were removed, and the Union moved significantly closer to its goal of becoming a genuine 'common market'.

In spite of serious upheavals in European currency markets, notably in the latter halves of 1992 and 1993, the EU's long-term goal is to establish a full economic union, involving a close harmonisation of member countries' general economic policies, the centralisation of fiscal and monetary control procedures, and a single currency. The single market has already produced a number of benefits for European consumers and businesses, and it is anticipated that there are many more to be reaped from the process of 'ever closer union'.

One of the most important steps towards that full economic and monetary union in Europe was taken in 1979, when the then European Community set about creating a 'zone of currency stability' known as the European Monetary System (EMS). Since then, the Treaty on European Union, agreed at an EU summit in Maastricht in 1991 and signed the following year, has established a timetable for further advancement of the EMU goal.

The European Monetary System

The idea behind the European Monetary System was to achieve currency stability through coordinated exchange rate management. This would facilitate intra-Union trade and set the stage for a single currency towards the end of the 1990s. The exchange rate mechanism (ERM), a system of fixed but flexible exchange rates, was the central plank of the EMS. Countries participating in the ERM would keep the value of their currencies within margins of 2.25 per cent either side of agreed central rates against the other currencies in the mechanism. Sterling, the peseta and the escudo, all of which joined the ERM several years after its inception, were allowed to move within margins of 6 per cent.

The ERM worked by requiring members to intervene in the foreign exchange markets in unlimited amounts to prevent currencies breaching their ceilings or floors against the other currencies. For example, if the peseta fell to its floor against the D-Mark, the Bank of Spain was required to buy pesetas and sell D-Marks. Other members could help by intervening on behalf of the weak currency. This, in theory, would prop up the peseta before it fell through its floor. Alternatively, the country whose currency was under fire could raise its short-term interest rates to make its currency more attractive to investors.

If intervention on the foreign exchanges and adjustment of short-term rates failed to stop a currency from sliding too low or rising too high, an absolutely last resort was a realignment of the central rates to relieve the tensions in the system. In the early years of the ERM there were several realignments but from 1987 until 1993, when the ERM was effectively suspended, there were none. Many economists argue that it was the failure of the mechanism to realign in response to the strength of the D-Mark that led to the tensions of the autumn of 1992 and the summer of 1993.

Currency market volatility in 1992 and 1993

After five years of relative calm, the currency markets of Europe erupted in a sequence of dramatic market events from the summer of 1992. The explanation for these events lies in German reunification at the end of the 1980s. In order to pay for unification without excessive taxation, the German government had to borrow substantial amounts of money, which forced up the cost of borrowing in Germany. High German interest rates coincided with low US interest rates and the result was strong international demand for D-Marks, forcing German rates even higher.

This happened just as the rest of Europe, heading into recession, needed lower interest rates to stimulate economic activity. However, since all the other countries were committed to maintaining their currencies' central rates against the D-Mark, they were forced to keep their interest rates at levels that were damaging to their economies. So long as Germany's rates were high, countries like the United Kingdom and France were unable to lower their lending rates without causing a run on the pound and the franc.

In the case of the United Kingdom, the tensions became too much for the system in September 1992. The country was suffering its longest recession since the 1950s yet had interest rates of 10 per cent. With inflation low, the real cost of borrowing was exceptionally high. The markets took the view that such high lending rates at a time of recession were unsustainable. Pressure on the pound mounted over August, but the UK government, mindful of the hardship being caused by the high cost of borrowing, was unwilling to raise rates further in order to protect the pound. Its only weapons were intervention on the foreign exchanges and repeated assurances by ministers that there would be no devaluation.

Events came to a head on 16 September 1992, Black Wednesday (or White Wednesday to 'Eurosceptics', delighting at its negative implications for future European union), when sterling and the Italian lira were forced out of the mechanism. Speculative investors, losing confidence in the currencies and seeing the opportunity for significant profits, shifted vast funds out of sterling and the lira into the D-Mark. Many, for example, sold the pound short, expecting to be able to buy it back at a much reduced rate.

The effect of all this selling was to drive the pound down. On the day, the UK government tried to save it by buying large quantities of pounds, and by announcing an increase in interest rates to 15 per cent. But this was not enough to stem the flow against sterling: effectively, the Bank was transferring its reserves to the short selling speculators. After a steady drain on reserves, the government pulled out. Both sterling and the lira sank well below their ERM floors as soon as the authorities gave up the struggle to keep them within their old bands.

For the next eleven months, relative calm returned to what was left of the mechanism. However, in August 1993, tensions arose once more, this time centred on the French franc. The problems were familiar: France was in a recession with high unemployment yet was unable to cut its very high interest rates. One solution would have been for Germany to ease its lending rates, but the Bundesbank, the German central bank, would not contemplate such a move for fear of encouraging inflation at home. According to the German constitution, the prime duty of the Bundesbank is to monitor domestic monetary policy. Thus it was required by law to put the need for low German inflation before the travails of the ERM.

As pressure mounted, EU finance ministers met to find a solution. The answer was to widen the currency bands for all except the D-Mark and the Dutch guilder to 15 per cent. The bands were so wide that although the ERM survived in name, the currencies were effectively floating. With the new bands a currency could theoretically devalue by 30 per cent (from its ceiling to its floor) against another member without falling out of the system. That has been the system of the ERM since then (see chapter 9 for further details on its operations).

Prospects for economic and monetary union

Following the upheavals of the ERM, plans to introduce a single currency in Europe by 1999 at the latest, as agreed at Maastricht, look somewhat optimistic. It was after all agreed that EMU would only be possible after participating countries had achieved a broadly similar economic performance. It was anticipated that the discipline of the former version of the ERM would help European economies to converge but, without it, countries are freer to pursue their own monetary and fiscal policies.

For EMU to take place, convergence is required in a number of key areas, including interest rates, which should be at broadly similar levels across countries; and inflation, which should be at comparably low and sustainable levels. With a system of irrevocably fixed exchange rates, or a single currency, persistent differences in inflation could lead to certain countries experiencing significant competitiveness problems and, as a result, serious employment losses.

Government deficits and national debts are also an important feature of convergence: high fiscal deficits and/or high public debt as a proportion of gross domestic product (GDP) would have to be avoided by all member states, both to counter inflation and to guard against the emergence of excessive real interest rates for the EU as a whole. During the 1980s while the ERM was in place, EU inflation rates converged to a large extent. Big divergences remain, however, in the spheres of fiscal balances and unemployment. There is considerable scepticism about the EU's abilities to bring the different economies into line by the end of the decade.

Alongside the process of 'deepening' the Union (not only through EMU, but also through plans for political union as well as the social dimension of Europe) is one of 'widening', extending the membership to other countries in Europe. The EU currently has twelve members, but negotiations for the accession of Norway, Austria, Finland and Sweden have all been completed and merely require ratification by national referendums in those countries. Poland, Hungary, Slovakia and the Czech Republic are all keen to join in the not too distant future. Some EU governments, notably that of the United Kingdom, believe enlargement of the EU should be given priority over rapid moves towards economic and monetary union.

ECONOMIC DEVELOPMENT

All countries pursue economic growth, an increase in their output of goods and services, and their incomes to purchase those goods and services as well as those produced abroad. For countries outside the industrialised world, this is generally termed development. Numerous different policies have been tried since the war to achieve this goal, but nowadays, it is typically pursued through a combination of encouraging production of goods for export, attracting foreign direct investment as well as overseas aid and loans, macroeconomic stabilisation policy (reducing balance of payments and fiscal deficits, and controlling inflation), and market liberalisation. Much debate centres on the appropriate 'sequencing' of internal economic policies for development, meaning which ones should come first.

The economies of south-east Asia have been the most successful at development, becoming the newly industrialised countries (NICs). Much of that achievement has been a result of high export orientation as measured by exports as a proportion of GDP, what is known as export-led growth. Many of the countries of eastern Europe, Latin America, Africa, and elsewhere in Asia (notably India and China), are eager to follow the progress of the NICs, and, as a consequence, it is important for the markets of the developed world to be open to their products. But developing countries' share of world merchandise trade, that is, manufactured goods, food, fuel, and raw materials, was actually higher in 1950 (at around 40 per cent) than in 1992 (at just under 30 per cent).

Annually, the World Bank publishes its *World Development Report*, charting the progress of the developing world and examining certain fundamental issues in detail. For example, the 1994 edition, entitled *Infrastructure for Development*, focuses on services essential for development, such as transport, telecommunications, water and sanitation, power and gas and major water works (see Figure 3.3). It explores the ways in which developing countries can improve the quantity and quality of their infrastructure services.

● **Infrastructure expansion in recent decades**: the average decade rate of growth of five key infrastructural services in both middle and low income countries, according to appropriate measures.

Part of such development can be funded by foreign aid: in 1992, for example, the rich industrial countries gave $60 billion in aid to poor countries, 0.33 per cent of their total GDP. Two-thirds was in the form of bilateral grants and loans, as opposed to contributions to multilateral institutions. An average of 28 per cent was tied to the purchase of goods and services from donor countries. This kind of aid is less beneficial to poor countries since it forces recipients to pay higher prices for imports, encourages them to invest in vast capital

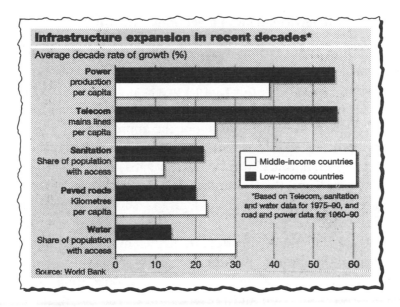

Figure 3.3: Infrastructure in developing countries

projects, and does little for the relief of poverty, one of the most pressing problems of the developing world.

Another notable problem for developing countries has been the debt crisis when numerous governments defaulted on their loans from western banks. This has eased considerably since the late 1980s when Latin American countries particularly had very high debt service ratios, the proportion of export revenues taken up by debt repayment. The IMF prediction for 1994 is that interest and capital repayments will take up around 30 per cent of Latin American export revenues, down from 45 per cent in 1986. At the same time, the Asian countries' debt service ratio is 6.7 per cent; for African countries, it was 33.2 per cent in 1993, but is expected to fall.

The World Bank discerns five major development challenges for the future. These are the promotion of economic reforms likely to help the poor, perhaps in contrast to the inequitable 'structural adjustment' (somewhat extreme free market) programmes of the past; increased investment in people, particularly through education, health care and family planning; protection of the environment; stimulation of private sector development; and public sector reform that provides the conditions in which private enterprise might flourish.

Migration, the environment and economic transition

Alongside the longstanding issues of economic development in the 'third world' are the more recent development problems of the formerly planned economies of eastern Europe and the ex-Soviet Union. The transition of these countries to democratic market economies has thrown up many new questions about the appropriate sequencing of economic policies and the extent to which market reforms (including price liberalisation, trade liberalisation, privatisation, establishment of capital markets, and the institution of a legal and regulatory framework) should be implemented suddenly, as 'shock therapy'. There is also concern in the traditional developing world about the diversion of industrialised nations' attention, trade preferences and capital.

A major issue in both developing and ex-communist countries is the environment, and whether the goals of expanded trade and development, and protection and preservation of the environment, are compatible. For example, should developing countries adopt less strict regulations on pollution by 'dirty' industries than the developed world in order to attract investment by firms in those industries? At the heart of this debate is the concept of 'sustainable development', whether there are policies that promote both economic growth and an improved environment. This is a highly contentious issue: many developing countries ask why environmental concerns should hinder their progress when the industrialised countries had ignored such concerns in their own development.

Another issue high on the international agenda is also very contentious, that of migration. Flows of goods, services and capital are well covered by the institutions of global capitalism, but there is little policy on the treatment of international flows of people. Indeed, there is much hypocrisy among believers in the free market system, demanding 'free markets, free trade and free enterprise', but at the same time, strict immigration controls. If trade and finance can flow freely, why not labour, some ask. Such considerations have stressed the importance of free trade and foreign investment to discourage mass migration: by investing directly in the poorer parts of the world and providing open markets to their products, the industrialised countries will not experience so much migratory pressure from those places.

Emerging markets

Both for multinational businesses and for private and institutional investors, the markets of the developing world are becoming more and more appealing. This is partly a response to such political developments as the collapse of communism and the increasingly global embrace of liberal democratic values, which may have reduced the sovereign or country risk of overseas investments. But naturally enough, economic forces also play a critical role: relatively lower labour costs are an attraction to multinationals to shift production to the developing world, as are the vast markets those workers represent for global brands like Coca-Cola, Marlboro and McDonald's.

EMERGING MARKETS: IFC WEEKLY INVESTABLE PRICE INDICES

Market	No. of stocks	Dollar terms July 1 1994	% Change over week	% Change on Dec '93	Local currency terms July 1 1994	% Change over week	% Change on Dec '93
Latin America	(209)	586.47	+2.7	-9.9			
Argentina	(25)	836.08	-1.6	-15.9	513,040.53	-1.6	-15.9
Brazil	(57)	250.52	+6.9	+7.6	937,410,992.9	+15.4	+822.4
Chile	(25)	655.73	-0.4	+18.8	1,099.45	-0.9	+15.3
Colombia[1]	(11)	937.83	+0.4	+45.6	1,359.92	-0.6	+46.7
Mexico	(68)	814.44	+2.8	-19.1	1,192.16	+2.9	-11.7
Peru[2]	(11)	138.18	-1.0	+14.3	185.05	-1.0	+16.4
Venezuela[3]	(12)	437.25	-8.2	-26.1	1,980.38	-8.2	+39.3
Asia	(557)	238.89	-2.2	-17.9			
China[4]	(18)	85.65	-4.0	-42.6	93.64	-4.0	-42.9
South Korea[5]	(156)	127.72	+0.2	+8.1	135.15	+0.1	+7.7
Philippines	(18)	275.39	-3.0	-19.1	352.68	-3.0	-20.6
Taiwan, China[6]	(90)	132.45	+0.5	-2.0	133.81	-0.0	+0.0
India[7]	(76)	133.02	-1.3	+14.2	147.10	-1.3	+14.2
Indonesia[8]	(37)	98.47	-2.5	-21.0	115.89	-2.5	-18.6
Malaysia	(105)	260.05	-3.2	-23.3	249.93	-2.7	-25.8
Pakistan[9]	(15)	396.50	+0.4	+2.2	551.18	+0.4	+4.4
Sri Lanka[10]	(5)	181.49	+2.7	+2.4	194.29	+2.5	+1.7
Thailand	(55)	359.90	-0.8	-24.6	357.69	-1.1	-26.0
Euro/Mid East	(125)	104.74	-1.8	-38.1			
Greece	(25)	212.29	-1.8	-6.8	346.20	-1.3	-10.0
Hungary[11]	(5)	180.79	-1.0	+8.5	222.60	-0.3	+10.3
Jordan	(13)	164.17	+1.7	-0.8	232.69	+1.1	-2.8
Poland[12]	(12)	506.58	+9.6	-38.1	720.38	+9.5	-34.8
Portugal	(25)	107.78	-2.8	-5.3	121.78	-2.5	-11.8
Turkey[13]	(40)	98.54	-2.8	-53.7	1,438.16	-4.8	-1.1
Zimbabwe[14]	(5)	248.46	-10.1	+22.9	298.97	-8.2	+39.9
Composite	(891)	299.52	+0.1	-15.8			

Figure 3.4: Emerging markets indices

Local businesses as well as financial institutions also seem to be developing rapidly. On Monday and Thursday, the FT carries data on the emerging stock markets of Latin America, east and south Asia, Europe and the Middle East, which are attracting increasing investor attention. Thursday's tables are prepared by the International Finance Corporation (see Figure 3.4).

- **Market and number of stocks**: countries' stock exchanges and the number of stocks on each one that are included in the local index.
- **Dollar terms**: the latest value of the local market index, the percentage change over the previous week, and from the end of the previous year.
- **Local currency terms**: the same figures in the local currency.

Monday's FT has an entire Emerging Markets: This Week page with a column on 'The Emerging Investor', a news round-up, a table of the ten best performing emerging market stocks by percentage price rise of the previous week, and a further table of emerging market indices prepared by Baring Securities. This table covers markets in four Latin American countries, three European and seven Asian plus composite indices for Latin America, Europe, Asia and the world.

4

STATISTICS AND ECONOMETRICS

Economics is a numbers-based subject, but that should not make it daunting. Admittedly, the highly technical nature of much of modern economics has put a great deal of its written output beyond the reach of the lay reader. But aside from high theory, where there is occasionally an overemphasis on technique rather than the underlying ideas and their policy relevance, the mathematics does serve a purpose. In constructing models of how the economy or a part of it works, in testing them against the empirical data, and in measuring the performance of key economic variables, economists are trying to calculate what the policy implications are, whether for governments, companies or financial institutions.

PRINCIPLES OF MEASUREMENT
AND MODELLING

Statistics, at least in its relation to economics, is all about measurement and estimation. In the first instance, this means the ways in which numbers on jobs, wages, output, and so on, are collected and measured. It is concerned with the gathering of data, usually either time series (changes in one variable over time, perhaps the national rate of unemployment); or cross-sectional (one variable measured in different but comparable places, perhaps the rate of unemployment in different regions of the country). In such data compilation, some sources are recognised as being more reliable than others; and there is awareness that revisions may be necessary over time as better information becomes available.

Economics meanwhile will set out the major issue to be resolved, bringing together various methods and tools to analyse it. This typically involves building theoretical models that isolate critical problems, and then testing them against the statistical data. For example, a very simple and testable model might involve the relationship between the money supply and the rate of inflation. Isolating this relationship from related variables such as the rate of interest or the level of output, the model might start from the theory that growth in the former directly causes increases in the latter. This can then be tested using a collection of time series data on money supply growth and inflation.

Econometrics (the 'metrics' or measurement of economics) is all about using statistical techniques to estimate the relationship between economic variables like this. For example, if it is theorised that there is an inverse relationship between unemployment and inflation (that when one goes up, the other goes down), econometrics takes a series of simultaneous values of the two variables and then calculates how closely they are related. If closely, there is said to be a high correlation between their movements.

A basic technique of econometrics is known as regression analysis. This takes the behaviour of a variable and tries to explain it by estimating how important an influence each of a list of potential determinants has on it. For example, this might be done at a macro-economic level, hypothesising that unemployment is determined by output, inflation, the interest rate, the level of benefits, the degree of unionisation, the quality of education, and any of a number of other factors. Running a regression should be able to tell you which explanation has the most power, which factors have the most impact.

At the level of the firm, this technique can be enormously valuable, and it is why large corporations often hire teams of econometricians. Managers understandably want to estimate the demand for their products, and, as chapter 1 showed, this can depend on a variety of factors. In order to work out how much control they have over influencing that demand, and to put a little more precision into their production planning, they might run some regressions. The demand for a company's airline tickets from London to Paris, for example, might be theorised to depend on their price, the price of rivals' tickets, the price of the train or coach, the franc-sterling exchange rate, the level of trade between France and the United Kingdom, and any number of other things.

TECHNIQUES OF ANALYSIS

The introduction to this book included a handful of even more fundamental mathematical concepts that are invaluable in the appreciation of economic data. Others include understanding the principle of aggregates (where the results of individual decisions are added together to calculate broad patterns, typically moving from micro- to macroeconomic concerns) and the distinction between nominal and real figures, between value and volume. This is about distinguishing the effects of inflation and changes in the real level of economic activity. Value figures are calculated as volume multiplied by price, and thus include inflation; volume figures are calculated as value divided by price, and thus exclude inflation. Values are in nominal terms at current prices; volumes are in real terms at constant prices.

It is also important to distinguish trends and cycles, to understand economic indicators in terms of long-term movements and short-term fluctuations around those movements. A trend is generally long-term, though the word may be used loosely to refer to a short-term change that may reverse over the course of the business cycle. Nevertheless, it is very important to be aware of which changes are likely to be relatively permanent, and which more temporary. This is the basis for interpreting turning points (peaks and troughs of the business cycle) and cyclical indicators: leading indicators which signal future developments; and lagging indicators which reflect the past (see chapter 6).

Seasonality

Another important factor in the calculation and evaluation of economic indicators is the pattern of seasonality, as the following FT extract makes clear:

> A statistical health warning accompanies the UK consumer credit figures released yesterday. The data, the Central Statistical office noted, may

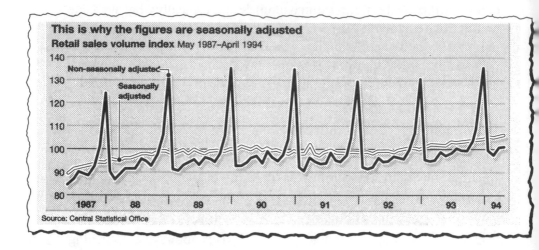

Figure 4.1: Seasonal adjustment

have been distorted because of Easter and its effect on seasonal adjustment. Such warnings are not entirely new. Spending and borrowing both surge before public holidays and statisticians have always floundered over the fact that Easter is a moveable feast and Christmas can occur on any day of the week. But the timing of Easter this year has created particular problems. Because the holiday straddled both March and April, statisticians have been uncertain which month they should adjust to account for the anticipated surge in high street activity. (*Financial Times*, 7 June 1994)

Most figures show a seasonal pattern that is repeated year to year. The classic case is the substantial increase in retail sales volume in the period before Christmas (see Figure 4.1). This pattern also shows up in such figures as average earnings, reflecting the extra hours worked in retailing and postal services. In such cases, the data are frequently 'seasonally adjusted' to smooth their pattern over the course of the year and to aid their interpretation. A figure for a given month is seasonally adjusted by calculating what percentage of the year's monthly average it represents, and dividing it by the percentage.

Managers are frequently well aware of seasonal patterns. For example, those in seasonal industries such as tourism will anticipate the summer boom in their business, as well as the increased availability of temporary staff. However, it is important for managers to note that while economic data are usually seasonally adjusted, their own company data (sales figures and accounts) are typically only available in unadjusted form. When calculations of relationships between national economic performance and firm performance are made, this needs to be borne in mind. It is also important to be able to distinguish seasonal patterns from the business cycle or longer term trends.

Index numbers

The introduction to this book referred to index numbers but it is worth emphasising their importance. Many of the economic indicators published in the FT are presented as indices, assuming constant prices from a given date, usually 1990=100. The reference date is arbitrary and merely provides a convenient landmark for comparison. What matters is not the index numbers themselves but the change from one period to the next.

Indices are also used to represent a collection of data in one figure, attempts to create order and direction out of diversity. This is notably the case with financial market indices. For example, stock market indices are designed to pull together the disparate movements of different share prices, each responding to a myriad of individual pressures, to find out whether the market, or a subsection of it, is moving up or down, in a bullish or bearish direction.

There are numerous ways of composing equity indices, each with advantages and disadvantages, and the one selected will depend on just what it is that is being tracked. Indices are important benchmarks for measuring the performance of the fund managers who put money into the stock market on behalf of investors. Most will try to outperform the various benchmarks, though some will passively aim merely to 'track' the rise and fall of the indices. In its simplest form, this could be attempted by buying the stocks that constitute the index.

For managers too, such benchmark information is highly valuable for understanding both the performance of their individual companies and investors' evaluation of their prospects. For example, it is important to ensure that the company's share price is not underperforming the overall market, perhaps making the management vulnerable to a hostile bid. Indeed, increasing numbers of companies are making the share price a key management target through programmes of corporate value creation and value-based management.

Statistics to be released this week

Day Released	Country	Economic Statistic	Median Forecast	Previous Actual
Mon	Japan	May current a/c, IMF	$9bn	$14bn
July 4	Japan	May trade balance, IMF	-	$13.3bn
	Japan	May foreign bond investment	-	$12.5bn
	UK	June official reserves	£50m	£25m
	UK	May credit business	£350m	£413m
	UK	June M0*	-0.1%	0.2%
	UK	June M0**	6.6%	7.1%
Tues	US	Johnson Redbook, w/e July 2	-	3.6%
July 5	Japan	June trade balance, 1st 10 days	-	$872m
	France	Apr indust production*†	0.4%	0.2%
	France	Apr manufacturing production*†	0.4%	0.9%
	UK	May housing starts	-	16,500
	Aus'lia	May retail trade†	1.2%	-3.7%
Wed	US	May home completions	-	1.36m
July 6	US	June domestic auto sales	7m	7m
	US	June domestic light truck sales	5.4m	5.5m
	Germany	June unemployment rate, West††	10,000	9,000
	Germany	May employment rate, West††	-12,000	-16,000
	Germany	June vacanies, West	-	-7,000
	Germany	June short-time, West	-	-42,000
	Germany	June unemployment rate, East	-20,000	-57,000
	UK	May manufacturing output*	0.2%	1.1%
	UK	May manufacturing output**	1.6%	3%
	UK	May industrial production*	0.2%	1.6%
	Canada	June foreign reserves – change	-C$475m	C$324m

Figure 4.2: Diary of economic indicators

SOURCES OF ECONOMIC INFORMATION

On Saturday and Monday, the *Financial Times* publishes an Economic Diary, detailing all important statistics to be released in the coming week (see Figure 4.2). This covers indicators not only for the United Kingdom, but for all of the major economies of the OECD, notably the other leading countries of the EU, Japan and the United States. There are often accompanying notes on the results that observers are expecting, and what impact they might have on future movements of the financial markets, and on government policy. Similarly, there are details of upcoming political events (elections, summit meetings, White Papers, legislation, and so on) that have implications for business and the markets.

Government statistics

For the UK economy, FT coverage is particularly intense. Each month a wealth of figures is produced by the Central Statistical Office (CSO), the government department responsible for compiling economic statistics. These official figures, many with track records that go back decades, together throw light on the state of the economy, indicating to businesses, consumers and the government whether the economy is in recession, growing or at a turning point. The FT tracks much of this monthly and quarterly data. Figures for such key economic indicators as unemployment, inflation, output and GDP are especially likely to make the headlines, particularly when the monthly or quarterly changes are sharp.

The data compiled by the CSO usually refer to the previous month's economic activity. They are collected through nationwide surveys with the results analysed by teams of statisticians at the CSO's centre in Newport, Gwent. By the time the figures are announced to the public, they have generally been smoothed to take account of seasonal patterns and to give a clearer picture of the underlying trend. Annually, the CSO publishes the United Kingdom's full national accounts, known as the *Blue Book*.

Economic Trends is the CSO publication that brings together all the main economic indicators discussed in chapters 5 to 9, while *Financial Statistics* provides data on a wide range of financial topics. These include financial accounts for various sectors of the economy, government income and expenditure, public sector borrowing, banking statistics, monetary aggregates, institutional investment, company finance and liquidity, security prices and exchange and interest rates.

Economic news reports appear in the first section of the *Financial Times* the day after they are released by the CSO. For easy reference, a table of UK economic figures appears on Thursday. The UK economic indicators table gathers together a range of key economic statistics to give an instant overview of activity in the UK economy. The figures are broken down into five principal sets of values, indices and rates of change: Output, Economic Activity, Inflation, Financial and External Trade. Chapters 5 to 9 are organised to correspond roughly to each of these broad areas.

CSO data are published by Her Majesty's Stationery Office, the government's publishing department; they are based on information supplied by an estimated 28,000 UK companies. Recent new financing has allowed extensions of this research, notably to surveys covering the service sector and company finances. Other official CSO publications include the *Monthly Digest of Statistics*, and the *Pink Book*. The latter gives detailed balance of payments data for the country, including the City of London's contributions to UK overseas earnings, total transactions with the rest of the EU, and details of overseas assets and liabilities. The previously massive 'balancing item' in the data, covering data shortages and discrepancies, has now been shrunk by newly financed research.

The CSO is the main collector of UK economic statistics, employing a quarter of total government statistical staff. The rest are spread among more than thirty other departments, notably the Department of Trade and Industry, the Department of Employment (which publishes, among other things, the *Employment Gazette*) and the Treasury (the key publication of which is the annual *Financial Statement and Budget Report*, the *Red Book*). One further source of official economic information is the *Bank of England Quarterly Bulletin* incorporating the Bank's inflation report.

Economic data collection has traditionally been conducted by government departments, but in the United Kingdom, it is increasingly being put out to private sector competition. The first project offered for tender was the collection of retail price index data; this has been followed by compulsory business data. Bids are taken from both government departments and private sector market research groups. The CSO is also entering into private sector partnerships to publish and market its business and trade statistics, mainly annual reports and quarterly data on a detailed sectoral basis.

Surveys and forecasts

A number of surveys, produced by bodies such as the Confederation of British Industry (CBI), supplement the FT's regular reporting of UK economic statistics. Some of the most important are the CBI's quarterly and monthly industrial trends surveys of manufacturers. These give strong indications of future trends in manufacturing output by asking industrialists about their price expectations, their investment plans and investment appraisal techniques, the state of their order books, and whether they are driven by export or domestic demand. The surveys typically question over 1,000 firms, representing about half of British manufacturing. The CBI also conducts surveys of the distributive trades sector (see chapter 6).

Other unofficial but longstanding and widely regarded economic surveys include the British Chamber of Commerce's quarterly economic survey of its members which, unlike the CBI industrial trends survey, includes the service sector. There is also an annual survey by the Invest in Britain Bureau which examines the number and origin of inward investment projects into the United Kingdom, and the quantity of jobs they create (see chapter 2).

In addition to surveys of companies' expected and actual economic experiences, there are also numerous forecasts for the UK economy, published in both the public and private sectors. The Treasury's forecast, produced at the time of the Budget, is the most prominent and probably the most influential, but hundreds of other bodies produce their own forecasts, including researchers in large financial institutions, corporate planning departments, specialist forecasting companies, and independent academic institutes. These are discussed in more detail in chapter 11.

World Statistics

Although economic statistics from outside the United Kingdom are reported by the *Financial Times* on a less systematic basis than the UK figures, a broad range of figures is published throughout the year. For the world, the most regular and reliable statistics are collated by the International Monetary Fund (IMF) in its monthly publication *International Financial Statistics* and its twice yearly

World Economic Outlook. Another useful source of statistical information is the OECD, in particular its annual country reports and the twice yearly *Economic Outlook* (see chapter 10).

On Tuesday, the FT includes a table of international economic indicators comparing key variables for the six main economies of the OECD: the United Kingdom, the United States, Japan, Germany, France and Italy. These include a quarterly presentation of figures for National Accounts plus, in rotation, monthly figures for Production and Employment, Prices and Competitiveness, Money and Finance, and Balance of Payments. Chapters 5 to 9 are organised to correspond directly to these categories.

For countries outside the OECD, especially in Latin America, Africa and Asia, the most detailed economic coverage, in addition to IMF statistics, is often the FT's special survey of the country, published once a year.

RELIABILITY AND SIGNIFICANCE
OF THE NUMBERS

In assessing the reliability of economic indicators, it is wise to ask a number of questions. These should include who produced the statistics, whether they will be revised, to what period they relate, whether they are seasonally adjusted, and do they take account of inflation. There is often a rush to publish the information, and the initial figures may only be estimates. This is notably the case with GDP figures which go through several revisions. For example, with the US GDP figures for 1992, early projections may have cost George Bush his job: while he probably lost the election of that year on poor economic news, revised figures for 1992 indicated that the recovery was much more robust than it seemed at the time!

Economic indicators may be inaccurate for a number of reasons. For example, GDP figures may have grown less reliable because they have ignored the shift of production from manufacturing to service industries. They may also be inaccurate as a result of government manipulation. Accusations of massaging official figures come easily: one classic example is the UK Department of Employment's thirty changes to the definition of unemployment in the 1980s, all but one of which reduced the jobless total. When a statistic like this becomes a political objective, there is naturally a temptation to make it easier to achieve by changing its definition. This suggests the value of denying government the absolute power to control official statistics.

The Economist newspaper has periodically published rankings of countries on the basis of the accuracy and integrity of their economic statistics. These they measure by the size of revisions (small revisions do not necessarily mean better figures since some countries do not bother with them), the timeliness of publication (clearly, there is a trade-off with accuracy), the statisticians per head of population, the government statistics budget per head, the freedom from political interference, the methodology, and the relevance. *The Economist* reports that although US and UK figures seem to be both accurate and timely, there are lingering suspicions that they are not immune to political meddling.

Economic indicators are also frequently manipulated by whoever is discussing them. As is well-known there are three kinds of lies (lies, damned lies and statistics), and it is often the case that economic figures can be manipulated to prove anything you want. For example, in the United Kingdom, the Conservatives might claim that health spending is higher than ever; Labour would reply it is the smallest it has ever been in living memory as a percentage of GDP. Similarly, Conservatives might point to a fall in unemployment; Labour might show that there has been no corresponding rise in employment. There are often two or more ways of analysing related data like this.

In terms of the significance of the data, to some extent, this too is in the eye of the beholder. Bond markets, for example, are extremely wary of any signs of economic recovery turning into overheating and inflation (see chapter 8): they might see a fall in unemployment as a potentially dangerous indicator. Other parties might be less threatened by relatively minor changes in economic news, but will need to be aware of what such news can do to the financial markets. Business managers will pay particularly close interest to indicators of growing demand for their products, to inflationary prospects, and to interest rates: these might, for example, affect their production planning, their pricing policies, and their intentions for new investment.

Furthermore, managers should always ask whether they need extra information to aid their interpretation of various indicators.

Certainly, data on broad trends in output need to be supplemented with detailed industry-specific figures before firm decisions can be taken. But it is also essential to note the interconnections of the indicators. For example, a devaluation of the currency might suggest improved national competitiveness and the value of exploring export markets more thoroughly. But if domestic inflation rates exceed those in export markets, the boost to competitiveness may be illusory.

The economic information discussed in the next five chapters focuses primarily on the six leading economies of the OECD, including more detailed material on the UK economy. In each case, examples of regularly published tables and reports are presented with a commentary on what the figures cover, how they are calculated, and what their significance might be to investors and managers across a broad range of industries. Brief suggestions are given as to how businesses may use the data, as well as how financial markets might be expected to react.

Part II

UNDERSTANDING THE NUMBERS

5

NATIONAL OUTPUT, INCOME AND EXPENDITURE

The state and composition of a country's overall economy are typically summarised in measures of gross domestic product (GDP), broad indicators of the total value of goods and services produced and purchased in the economy. This total economic activity can be assessed in three different but equivalent ways: firstly, as national output, the value of all goods and services produced; secondly, as national income, flows of money to the factors producing that output, most importantly (since land is fixed) labour and capital; and thirdly, as national expenditure, total spending by individuals, businesses and the government on the output. Output is produced; expenditure occurs when that output is sold; and all spending becomes income.

GROSS DOMESTIC PRODUCT

Calculations of national output, income and expenditure become a country's national accounts. Each quarter, the *Financial Times* presents figures on these National Accounts in its international economic indicators table. They cover the six leading economies of the Organisation for Economic Cooperation and Development (OECD), the 'club' that comprises the twenty-five industrialised countries of the world (see Figure 5.1). The economies covered are those of the United States, the United Kingdom, Germany, France, and, as in this example, Japan and Italy. The figures are for GDP measured by expenditure, the aggregate demand side of the economy; but they could equally be presented as GDP by income or output, the aggregate supply side.

■ **JAPAN**

Gross National Product	Private Cons.	Total Invest.	Govt. Cons.	Net Exports
		as a % of GNP		
1,780.2	58.7	28.0	9.5	3.7
2,033.3	58.4	27.7	9.6	4.3
2,102.2	58.4	28.4	9.4	3.8
2,466.0	57.5	30.4	9.1	2.9
2,625.2	57.3	31.5	9.1	2.1
2,322.0	57.0	32.5	9.0	1.4
2,726.2	56.1	32.3	9.1	2.5
2,852.8	56.6	30.9	9.2	3.3
3,629.0	57.2	30.1	9.5	3.2
3,277.5	57.0	30.1	9.4	3.6
3,550.6	57.0	30.5	9.5	3.0
3,924.5	57.2	30.2	9.5	3.2
3,835.2	57.6	29.7	9.6	3.2

% growth in				
GNP	Cons.	Invest.	Govt.	Exports
5.1	3.3	6.5	1.7	6.5
2.7	3.4	4.3	4.5	-5.3
4.3	4.2	8.2	0.4	4.6
6.3	5.2	14.2	2.2	10.7
4.8	4.3	9.6	2.0	15.0
4.8	4.0	7.9	1.9	10.6
4.3	2.2	4.5	1.6	5.0
1.4	1.7	-2.3	2.2	2.7
0.1	1.1	-1.6	3.0	-1.4
0.3	1.0	-3.5	1.8	2.5
0.0	0.8	-1.7	3.7	-1.1
0.1	0.7	-0.6	3.8	-2.7
-0.2	1.8	-0.6	2.8	-4.1

■ **ITALY**

Gross Domestic Product	Private Cons.	Total Invest.	Govt. Cons.	Net Exports
		as a % of GDP		
615.7	62.2	20.9	16.5	0.4
658.4	62.4	21.0	16.9	-0.3
710.5	61.9	21.5	17.1	-0.5
790.8	62.4	21.3	16.9	-0.6
861.1	61.8	21.0	17.7	-0.4
931.6	62.1	20.5	17.8	-0.3
947.0	63.1	19.4	17.7	-0.2
830.8	63.0	16.8	17.7	2.5
857.0	62.5	17.3	17.5	2.7
860.1	63.1	16.4	17.6	2.9

% growth in				
GDP	Cons.	Invest.	Govt.	Exports
2.6	3.0	1.7	3.4	3.2
2.9	3.7	1.4	2.6	2.5
3.1	4.2	4.6	3.4	4.7
4.1	4.2	6.3	2.8	5.4
2.9	3.5	2.3	0.8	8.8
2.1	2.5	3.7	1.2	7.0
1.3	2.3	1.1	1.5	0.3
0.7	1.8	-1.9	1.0	5.3
-0.7	-2.1	-17.5	0.8	10.0
-1.3	-2.5	-20.4	1.0	9.6
-1.0	-3.1	-18.8	0.9	11.8
-0.7	-2.2	-17.9	0.7	9.5
0.3	-0.7	-12.4	0.5	9.4

Figure 5.1: International economic indicators: national accounts (Japan and Italy)

Reading the figures

- **Gross domestic/national product**: measures of overall economic activity in these countries, calculated by adding together the total value of the annual outputs of goods and services (with quarterly figures annualised), and expressed in billions of European currency units (ecus). In this case, the value of GDP is calculated by the expenditure method. The first breakdown is in current prices, the actual prices of all that output in the marketplace. The second breakdown shows growth rates in constant prices, adjusting for the effects of inflation and thus measuring changes in volume: the growth rate is the percentage change over the corresponding point in the previous year. The figure is gross because it does not incorporate a deduction for the depreciation of capital goods.

- **Private consumption**: the percentages of GDP expenditure made up of consumer spending on goods and services. These figures typically include imputed rents on owner occupied housing, but not interest payments, purchases of building or land, transfers abroad, business expenditure, buying of second-hand goods or government consumption.

- **Total investment**: the percentages of GDP expenditure made up of capital investment (as opposed to financial investment) by both the private and public sectors. This is spending on new factories, machinery, equipment, buildings, roads, accommodation, raw materials, and so on. 'Gross domestic fixed capital formation', as investment is sometimes termed, is a key component of current growth of GDP, as well as a critical foundation for future expansion. Obviously, investment in machines has greater potential for future output than that of houses, though the contribution of infrastructure such as roads may be harder to assess.

- **Government consumption**: the percentages of GDP made up of consumer spending by the public sector. Government spending on such items as infrastructure is accounted in these figures under total investment, though in some presentations of GDP, government spending encompasses both consumption and investment.

- **Net exports**: in the current prices series, the percentages of GDP made up of the difference between the value of national exports of goods and services and that of imports. This balance of trade in goods and services in the United Kingdom is typically negative with the value of imports exceeding that of exports. Adding in net income from abroad in the form of profits, rents, dividends, interest and transfers, this becomes the current account of the balance of payments. In the constant prices series, the export figures show the growth rates of exports alone, rather than of net exports.

There are various alternative concepts of total economic activity to GDP, including gross national product (GNP) and net national product (NNP). The difference between GDP and GNP is that the latter includes net property income or net earnings from abroad. That means the return on UK investments overseas less the return on foreign investments in the United Kingdom. NNP is GDP minus capital depreciation, an item that is very difficult to account for. For such reasons, most countries now use the GDP measure, except Japan and Germany.

In the United Kingdom, new data for the national accounts are produced as follows. A month after the end of each quarter the Central Statistical Office (CSO) produces a provisional estimate of GDP based on output data (GDP-O), such as industrial production and retail sales (see chapter 6). A month later the CSO provides a further estimate taking account of income and expenditure data (GDP-I and GDP-E). Finally, one month after that, the full national accounts are produced based on complete information. Although GDP-O, GDP-I and GDP-E should be the same, for a variety of reasons there is often a discrepancy between their results. Usually, an average is taken (GDP-A).

As well as revisions to the provisional GDP figures, the national accounts show a full breakdown of economic activity during the previous quarter by sector, and identify trends in such key GDP components as personal disposable income, personal consumption and savings, and fixed investment and stock building. The CSO publication that contains the annual UK national accounts is known as the *Blue Book*.

GDP data is collected by survey which naturally can miss a certain amount of economic activity. Deliberately omitted from GDP calculations are such transactions as transfer payments (pensions, social security, unemployment benefit, and the like), gifts, unpaid and domestic activities, barter, second-hand and intermediate exchange of goods, leisure, resource depletion and environmental costs. But there are plenty of concealed transactions that should be added in, but are missed. These typically arise from tax avoidance or evasion, and transactions in what is variously called the black, shadow or hidden economy.

Interpreting the information

A typical FT report on new GDP figures looks like this:

> The strength of Britain's economic recovery increased in the second quarter of the year, in spite of April's tax rises, as total output rose above levels seen before the recent recession. With the manufacturing sector playing a key role in the growth, the data suggested that the UK recovery is becoming increasingly broad based.
>
> Gross domestic product grew by a seasonally adjusted 0.9 per cent in the three months to June, compared with the previous three months. Compared with the same period a year ago, second quarter output was 3.3 per cent higher. This was the fastest level of growth for more than five years and suggests that the Treasury's forecast for 2.75 per cent GDP growth this year will be comfortably reached. (*Financial Times*, 23/24 July 1994)

When the level of GDP falls compared with the previous quarter, the economy is said to be contracting. Two consecutive quarterly falls, and it is said to be in recession. When GDP rises quarter to quarter, the economy is expanding. The movements of GDP from slump to recovery to boom to recession to slump again are what was described in chapter 2 as the business cycle. This extract indicates how the data can be used to assess the economy's position on the business cycle, and its likely future trends.

As chapter 2 described, government macroeconomic policy is often aimed at smoothing this cycle, easing the pain of recession and applying restraint when the economy is in danger of overheating. This is known as countercyclical policy, and would typically be done through fiscal policy (boosting public expenditure and cutting taxes, or the reverse) or monetary policy (loosening or tightening the money supply, perhaps through lowering or raising interest rates). In this extract, tax rises designed to reduce the government's budget

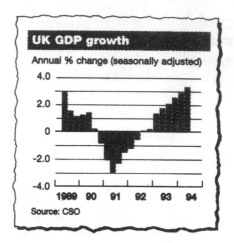

Figure 5.2: UK GDP growth

deficit, rather than restrain the economy, seem not to have had the undesirable side-effect of choking off the recovery.

The extract also indicates that the UK GDP growth rate has attained a five year high. The FT frequently demonstrates changes in the growth rate graphically (see Figure 5.2). These figures are calculated by comparing the average level of output in the quarter with the average level in the previous quarter. The annual rate of growth is the figure that is most widely discussed in forecasts, as well as being the target of government policy, and often an input into business planning. This is calculated as the amount by which the latest quarter's output surpasses the equivalent quarter's a year ago as a percentage of the equivalent quarter's.

Rates of growth should not be confused with the actual level of output. In the extract, the rate of growth has hit a five year high, while the level of output has surpassed the peak of the last boom. But these are different events: the output peak will have come a little later than the growth rate peak, since it will not have been reached until growth rates actually went negative and the level of output began to contract. Levels of output are reflected in other FT charts (see Figure 5.3), in this case revealing patterns of real UK GDP, but which could equally show nominal GDP.

Nominal GDP describes the total level of production, measuring total demand in cash terms or at current prices. Real GDP tracks

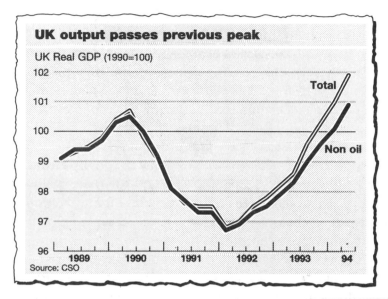

Figure 5.3: UK real GDP

activity in constant prices, showing changes in output after adjusting for inflation. This is the pattern of the business cycle. In this case, it is shown both as a total, and with the oil sector's output excluded: North Sea oil is such an erratic part of the economy that output trends are often best measured without it.

Real GDP can also be presented on a per head basis as output per person. This is calculated as GDP divided by the number of people in the population, and is a good indicator of cyclical changes in overall economic welfare, as well as a guide to trends in living standards. If real GDP per head increases, so does overall economic well-being. This means that real GDP must grow at least as fast as the population in order to maintain living standards. At the same time, it is important to consider the distribution of income. Migration either in or out of a country will also have an effect, as will the age structure of the population, particularly on the economy's productive potential and the prospects for future trends in GDP.

The publication of GDP figures will have a variety of effects on investors and managers. It is often the first estimate, based on output, that is the one that most affects financial markets, given their demand for rapid and accessible information. Output data is, in fact, usually the most reliable in the short-term, though longer term, expenditure is more accurate. Either set of figures will give an indication of where the economy is heading, and, if it is in a recovery, for example, whether this is being driven by industry or consumers. Faster and fairly broad based growth, as in the above extract, will usually be taken as a good sign, though if the economy is perceived to be near its productive potential, it may lead to fears of capacity constraints fueling inflationary pressures.

For company managers, economic growth usually means greater demand, suggesting an expanding market for their products. The extent of the market expansion will depend on how responsive the products are to changes in demand, and managers might attempt to work out what the relationship is between the rate of growth of GDP and of their products' sales. For example, a buyer for, say, a retail clothing chain will expect demand to rise in a recovery. But to plan for that demand by purchasing appropriate levels of stock requires some idea of exactly how much it will rise.

Obviously, the buyer will need more than just broad GDP data (notably, information on the clothing industry and the retail sector, the kind of more detailed data discussed below and in chapter 6), but it is often worthwhile to relate a firm's operations to those of the overall economy. Thinking about the links between demand for a particular product and aggregate demand, between individual companies and aggregate supply, and between micro- and macroeconomics, is a valuable approach to making key management decisions.

INCOME AND EXPENDITURE

GDP-I or national income is the economy's total of wages and salaries, income from self employment, trading profits and surpluses, and income from rents. These are the factor incomes, returns to land, labour and capital, the factors of production in the circular flow of income. They may be presented either in nominal or real terms.

Incomes are determined by a number of factors: for example, income from employment depends on the numbers of people in employment and the hours they work. This is the main constituent of total income, the next most significant being income from self-employment.

Gross domestic product and its components (£bn at 1990 prices, seasonally adjusted)

	Consumers' expenditure	General government consumption	Total fixed investments	Stock-building	Domestic demand	Exports of goods & services	Total final expenditure	Less imports of goods & services	Less adjustment to factor cost	Plus statistical discrepancy#	GDP at factor cost
1993	348.5	116.4	95.3	0.3	560.5	140.3	700.8	153.3	71.8	-0.8	474.9
1994	359.3	118.1	99.2	0.6	577.2	148.9	726.1	162.2	74.5	-1.0	488.4
1995	370.1	118.6	103.2	1.6	593.6	157.2	750.8	170.9	76.9	-1.0	501.9
1993 1st half	172.5	57.9	47.4	0.4	278.1	69.3	347.4	75.7	35.7	-0.4	235.6
2nd half	176.00	58.5	47.9	0.0	282.4	71.0	353.4	77.6	36.1	-0.5	239.3
1994 1st half	178.5	58.9	49.4	-0.3	286.5	73.5	360.0	79.9	36.9	-0.5	242.7
2nd half	180.8	59.2	49.8	0.9	290.7	75.4	366.1	82.3	36.7	-0.5	245.7
1995 1st half	183.6	59.3	51.0	0.7	294.6	77.6	372.2	84.3	38.3	-0.5	249.2
2nd half	186.5	59.3	52.2	0.9	298.9	79.7	378.6	86.6	38.8	-0.5	252.7
Percentage changes on a year earlier*											
1993	2½	¼	¼	½	2	3	2¼	2¾	2¼	0	2
1994	3	1½	4	0	3	6	3½	5¾	3¾	0	2¾
1995	3	½	4	¼	2¾	5½	3½	5¼	3¼	0	2¾

#Expenditure adjustment *For stockbuilding and the statistical discrepancy, changes are expressed as a percentage of GDP

Figure 5.4: UK GDP components

Interest and dividend income depend on company profits, the level of interest rates, and the overall state of the economy. Indeed, the business cycle has important effects on income of all kinds.

For governments, sustainable growth in real incomes is the long-term target. Companies will be more concerned with shorter term developments. For example, if they are in the consumer goods sector, they will be interested in personal income (current income received by the personal sector), and personal disposable income, the amount of income available to households after payment of income taxes and national insurance contributions, and receipt of any benefits. In the United Kingdom, this has been called 'the pound in your pocket'! Emerging trends in personal disposable incomes, disaggregated as far as possible into income groups, will be of particular interest to marketing companies, to retailers, to advertising agencies, and many other companies dependent on consumer demand.

GDP-E or national expenditure represents the national accounts from the demand side. As the FT's National Accounts table indicates, (see Figure 5.1 above) expenditure can be broken down by the four categories of spending that correspond to the circular flow of income (explained in chapter 2): consumption, investment, government spending, and net exports. The National Accounts present these components as a proportion of the total, so that percentage changes of each can be compared with changes in the total. Thus, consumer spending might grow at a faster rate than overall GDP, suggesting a consumer-led recovery. The accounts are also frequently presented in actual nominal values, as in this example of UK GDP (see Figure 5.4).

Consumption

- **Consumer's expenditure**: another term for private consumption, consumption by the household, consumer, or personal sector, or personal expenditure. Consumption accounts for around 60 per cent of total GDP in most industrialised countries.

- **General government consumption**: spending by the government on consumer goods and services. Sometimes, as in the United States, government expenditure includes its spending on investment rather than, as here, counting that under total fixed investments. It generally makes sense to consider the determinants and impact of government spending as a whole, as below. However, in presented UK figures, total consumption includes consumption by the government.

In examining consumption trends, it is important to focus on the real percentage growth rates, and on changes in spending on particular types of consumer goods. For example, increased spending on durable goods (motor vehicles, televisions, washing machines, and so on) can be an early signal of recovery. The cyclical pattern of consumer spending is especially evident with durables, although, strictly, these should be considered investments since the use of them will extend over a number of years. Figures for consumption might be supplemented by surveys of consumer confidence. These are often a valuable early indicator of future demand: the more optimistic consumers are, the more likely they are to spend money.

In terms of the state of the overall economy, growth in personal consumption often leads a general recovery from recession, encouraging manufacturers to invest. For example, in the first two years of recovery beginning in the second quarter of 1992, virtually all of the increase in GDP was accounted for by consumer spending. Given its proportion of the total, consumption is clearly a critical target of government macroeconomic policy.

The problem with consumer spending booms is that the trade deficit often begins to grow and inflation takes off. If consumption grows faster than productive capacity, imports are sucked into the national economy. This can have adverse implications for both the balance of payments and for domestic inflation where prices of imported goods drive up the general price level. A sustained recovery of this kind requires the balance of spending to shift from consumption to investment. This might require the government to act countercyclically, perhaps raising personal taxes and reducing personal disposable incomes. Combined with rising profits for industry, this may sustain recovery.

For managers, it is critical to assess the pace of demand as it develops in a recovery and is potentially managed by the government. In particular, they need to calculate whether there are productive capacity constraints in their own company. For example, a manager responsible for planning production in a factory producing consumer durables might ask: how is the pace of demand moving relative to my available factors of production, labour and capital? Can I increase production to meet increased demand using the present equipment, perhaps by having my workforce work longer hours? Do I need to hire additional workers or, further down the road, if this demand is likely to continue to rise, should I invest in new plant?

The retail sector is particularly affected by consumer spending patterns, benefitting considerably from a recovery. A shop selling durables or other high price items is likely to see a lot of new business at such a time, as consumers finally make those purchases they put off during recession. As with GDP figures, shop purchasing managers may do well to calculate a relationship between their sales and overall consumer spending levels, in order to know exactly how much new business they can expect. They might also want to consider regional patterns of consumption and the extent of recovery in their local areas. For example, a region dominated by one industry that is in decline might not see the benefits of enhanced incomes and increased consumer spending.

Cyclical industries, businesses that are strongly affected by the business cycle as it plays out in consumer spending include the holiday industry: at the first sign of 'green shoots', companies selling holidays push their service very hard, sometimes seeking to sell months in advance. Countercyclical industries are those that produce the goods consumers buy more of in a recession. The publishing business might be one: with the small amount of discretionary spending they have in harder times, consumers cannot afford to go on holiday, but stay at home and read! Business books might do especially well, giving the advice and tools a reader needs to take advantage of the recovery when it eventually arrives!

Investment

- **Total fixed investments**: total spending on physical assets by firms from which a stream of goods or services can be produced over future years. This is the main indicator of industrial and commercial expenditure, though it is usually available only after a lag. There are numerous anomalies in the classification of investment as opposed to consumption. For example, motor vehicles bought by a business are investment; by an individual, they are consumption.

- **Stock building**: stocks or inventories are finished products, work in progress and raw materials held by companies; stock building is a change in the level of stock. It is expressed as a percentage of GDP since what is important is not its total level, but the rate of change. Increased stocks reflect output that has not been consumed.

- **Domestic demand**: total demand for goods (consumer and capital) and services produced domestically. Adding in net exports and various adjustments gives nominal GDP.

Like consumption, investment is cyclical: firms will invest if there is a high and sustainable level of demand for their output, and if they are already close to full capacity. Investment is also affected by interest rates as chapter 1 showed, but some sectors are more sensitive to interest rates than others.

Changes in stocks are more erratic, and do not necessarily move with the business cycle. For example, there might be a decline when demand outstrips production; alternatively, firms may already have anticipated increased demand, and raised production and stock levels accordingly. Inventories will probably rise when demand slows; on the other hand, they may fall if firms have already cut production, or are keen to reduce their stock holding costs. Essentially, inventories provide the buffer between production and consumption.

The pace of investment demand will be of particular interest to companies supplying capital goods. For example, the purchasing manager for a chain of shops selling computers or other office equipment, will look to increase stock levels if investment demand is picking up in a recovery. This might be indicated locally by increased demand for office space. Similarly, the equipment manufacturers themselves will plan for increased output. Either company might calculate links between overall investment demand and their own sales in order to predict the likely growth of demand accurately.

At a time when the economy is close to full capacity, sectoral stock levels might be of particular interest to the wholesalers and retailers who provide the link between manufacturers and end users. Low stock levels might encourage a shop purchasing manager to increase orders in order to avoid a future shortage and inability to meet local demand. Sectoral indicators for manufacturing, wholesale or retail inventories make useful guides to changes in total stocks.

International trade

- **Exports of goods and services**: total overseas demand for goods and services produced domestically.

- **Total final expenditure**: total demand for goods, services and capital goods produced domestically. A related figure, sometimes given, is total domestic expenditure, total demand at home for products from both home and abroad.

- **Imports of goods and services**: total domestic demand for goods and services from overseas. This figure can be added to domestic demand to calculate total domestic expenditure.

The fourth element of total GDP (after consumption, investment and government spending) arises from the fact that the economy is open to international trade and financial flows. Exports contribute to growth; in contrast, imports can stifle it, reducing increases in national output relative to growth in demand. For example, increasing imports might suggest that demand is outstripping what can be provided by domestic output. This is discussed in more detail in chapter 9.

Longer term increases in imports might imply declining competitiveness on the part of national industries. If the level of imports is consistently and substantially higher than that of exports, and the deficit is not balanced by net inflows of interest, profits, dividends, rents and transfer payments, the current account balance stays in deficit. This can be financed in the capital account temporarily, but longer term leads to exchange rate problems, as discussed in chapters 3 and 9.

- **Adjustment to factor cost**: many transactions are subject to taxes and subsidies, and GDP-E includes them by recording market prices of the products bought by consumers, firms, foreigners and the government. In contrast, factor costs (excluding taxes and subsidies) are used in calculating GDP-I and GDP-O. This adjustment allows the measures to be compared and converted between factor costs and market prices. It also indicates the extent of government involvement.

- **Statistical discrepancy**: an adjustment to GDP-E calculations that brings it to GDP-A, or an average with GDP-I and GDP-O. This adjustment arises from differences in the way GDP is calculated by the three methods, and the statistical discrepancies that result.

- **GDP at factor cost**: GDP-E converted so as to exclude taxes and subsidies. The reports of GDP-E typically refer to it at market prices.

Alternative measures of economic activity

Problems of data collection, hidden transactions and deliberate omissions all mean that GDP measurements are not representations of total economic activity. For example, it is very difficult to measure output and productivity in service industries. Similarly, the black economy, by definition, does not want to be measured and subject to the mainstream economic demands of taxation. A particularly notable omission is activity that bypasses markets, such as services produced and consumed in the home, housework. The difficulty is that it is easier to evaluate goods and services that are bought and sold than those that are not.

A further issue of measurement relates to the multinational nature of many firms. For example, a foreign subsidiary of a UK firm contributes its output to the national output of the host country, that is, the GDP calculation is based on location rather than ownership. If it were the other way around, adding in net sales of foreign subsidiaries to exports, a deficit might turn into a surplus. Trade could be measured entirely on the basis of ownership: cross-border sales to foreigners, net sales to foreigners by subsidiaries abroad, and sales by domestic firms to local subsidiaries of foreign firms would all become exports.

Such considerations have been borne in mind by the new System of National Accounts, published early in 1994, and arising from a joint effort of the United Nations (UN), the IMF, the World Bank, the OECD, and Eurostat, the European Union's statistical equivalent of the UK CSO. The new system takes into account changes in both the world economy, and in accounting practices over the past twenty-five years. For example, inflation accounting, measurement of trade flows and foreign direct investment, and valuation of non-market activities have all been incorporated into the new system.

Another new measure is that launched by the UN Development Programme in 1990, the human development index. This was developed as an alternative measure of economic and social progress, in response to a further problem of GDP: because of inconsistencies in its use, it is a poor measure for international comparisons, particularly

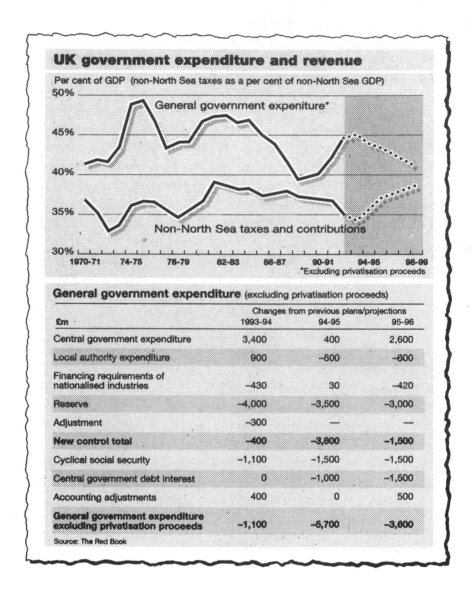

UK government expenditure and revenue

Per cent of GDP (non-North Sea taxes as a per cent of non-North Sea GDP)

General government expeniture*

Non-North Sea taxes and contributions

*Excluding privatisation proceeds

General government expenditure (excluding privatisation proceeds)

£m	1993-94	Changes from previous plans/projections 94-95	95-96
Central government expenditure	3,400	400	2,600
Local authority expenditure	900	−500	−600
Financing requirements of nationalised industries	−430	30	−420
Reserve	−4,000	−3,500	−3,000
Adjustment	−300	—	—
New control total	−400	−3,600	−1,500
Cyclical social security	−1,100	−1,500	−1,500
Central government debt interest	0	−1,000	−1,500
Accounting adjustments	400	0	500
General government expenditure excluding privatisation proceeds	−1,100	−5,700	−3,600

Source: The Red Book

Figure 5.5: UK government expenditure and revenue

of relative living standards. The new index is made up of life expectancy, adult literacy, average years of schooling and GDP per head measured at purchasing power parity; it is calculated regularly for over 150 countries.

GOVERNMENT SPENDING AND REVENUE

Clearly, a vital component of GDP is government spending on both consumption and investment. This is financed by government revenue, primarily from taxation of individuals and corporations, either directly or indirectly. The difference between government revenues and spending is known as the public sector borrowing requirement (PSBR). In the United Kingdom, forecast and historical figures for these fiscal indicators are published by the Treasury at the time of the annual government budget in what is known as the *Financial Statement and Budget Report* or the *Red Book* (see Figure 5.5).

- **General government expenditure**: spending by central and local government on consumption and investment, plus net lending to publicly owned corporations (in the chart, represented as percentages of GDP, and in the table, as changes from previous plans, rather than actual levels). In the United Kingdom, government expenditure generally excludes the income from sales of public companies to the private sector, because it can be so substantial, and each privatisation is a one-off. More detailed figures are available on public spending by government department (health, education, and defence are frequently discussed spending departments), and by current or capital account spending (for example, government employees' pay or investment in roads).

- **Non-North Sea taxes and contributions**: government revenues from all direct and indirect taxes (except those due on the North Sea oil sector) plus national insurance contributions, as a percentage of non-oil GDP. The oil sector is excluded because of its highly erratic nature.

- **Reserve**: an amount set aside for unforeseen contingencies, a kind of precautionary fund. In the table, figures are changes rather than actual levels for this and the remaining items. The fund is reduced more for the immediate future and is kept higher for more distant years on the basis of the time available for unforeseen contingencies to arise. Reducing the contingency reserve is an easy way to reduce the PSBR at a stroke, and is accepted as normal practice.

- **Control total**: the amount of government spending over which it has a large degree of direct control, and which is not determined mainly by the business cycle or the level of interest rates. For example, spending on education can be directly reduced, while taxes can be manipulated in the budget. The control total is actually calculated backwards as spending minus debt interest and cyclical social security.

- **Cyclical social security**: such items as state pensions and unemployment benefits, arising from longstanding government obligations, and many of which change cyclically. For example, in a recession, when unemployment rises, the amount of benefits payable naturally increases.

- **Central government debt interest**: the amount payable on all outstanding government debt, that is the gilt-edged stock discussed in chapter 2 and any loans. Debt interest is determined by the level of interest rates, and the size of the national debt, the cumulative total of government spending less revenues.

In the 1993 UK budget, the Treasury separated current and capital spending. It plans to change the way government departments account for public money, adopting the accounting practices of private firms, particularly with regard to accounting for depreciation of assets and the cost of capital. The ambition is to achieve better management of public finances and resources, and focus thinking on the long-term consequences of current policies. There is also talk of 'hypothecation', making a clear connection between where taxes come from and where they are used; for example, taxes on alcohol and cigarettes might be used in the National Health Service.

The most important consideration for a manager in relation to changes in government spending is how they are likely to affect aggregate demand. In addition, the annual budget often has particular measures aimed at the small business sector. These may involve various subsidies or other incentives to invest or take on more staff; they should be carefully scrutinised by any manager owning or running a firm that qualifies.

More broadly, government spending policy, perhaps in public procurement, might mean greater demand, increased turnover and incentives to invest for companies in the relevant industries. Being a government supplier can be a very lucrative business. From the point of view of the investor, the potential rises in companies' profitability from securing big government contracts might have a positive effect on their share prices.

Taxation

Taxes come in two basic forms: direct and indirect. The former fall on income: taxes on individuals and corporations, such as income tax, corporation tax, capital gains tax and inheritance tax. The latter fall on expenditure on goods and services, such as value added tax, duties on imports and excise taxes on products such as cigarettes and alcohol. Direct taxes are often progressive, falling more on individuals on higher incomes; indirect taxes are generally regressive, the same tax representing a bigger slice of a poorer person's income.

In the United Kingdom, changes in taxes are announced in the annual budget, and generally come into force the following spring at the start of the new tax year. The tax goals of a budget are frequently varied: at a macroeconomic level, they might be raised to finance government spending or reduce borrowing, or to stimulate or depress consumer demand. Another common goal is to raise tax thresholds so that inflation does not drag people into higher tax brackets. Still another might be to influence behaviour, or alternatively, to achieve fiscal neutrality, aiming to reduce the distortions that taxes cause in people's decisions to work, spend and save.

The government goal that may affect financial markets most significantly is that of influencing behaviour. For example, different tax treatment of different categories of assets will influence investment decision-making. Similarly, the tax treatment of corporate earnings will affect a company's dividend policy and its choice between raising capital through debt or equity.

Company managers will also want to consider the effect on their business of changes in income tax: for example, will they have a positive or negative impact on consumer spending, and hence demand for their products? Similarly, managers in certain industries will want to consider the effect on their own costs and on prospective consumer demand of tax changes on specific products. Increased fuel taxes, for example, will certainly raise production costs significantly for companies involved in manufacturing. The reduction of mortgage interest tax relief might have damaging effects on the business of companies involved in the housing market: estate agents, architects, interior designers, building societies, and the construction industry.

A range of other tax changes can have an impact on business, in these examples all negative, though they could go the other way.

PSBR by sector (£bn)

	Budget forecast	1993-94 Provisional outturn	1994-95 Forecast
Central government on cash basis			
Receipts:			
Inland Revenue#	76.9	77.0	88.5
Customs and Excise#	66.9	66.9	73.8
Soc sec contributions (GB)	37.1	36.9	41.7
Interest and dividends	9.1	9.3	8.7
Other	18.4	18.8	19.5
Total receipts	208.4	209.0	232.2
Outlays:			
Interest payments	18.8	18.8	21.7
Privatisation proceeds	-5.4	-5.4	-5.5
Net departmental outlays	245.2	243.4	254.2
Total outlays	258.6	256.9	270.4
Central government borrowing requirement*	50.2	47.9	38.1
Local authority borrowing requirement	-0.8	-2.8	-1.0
Public corporations' borrowing requirement	0.4	0.9	-1.0
Public sector borrowing requirement	49.8	46.0	36.1

#Payments to the Consolidated Fund
*Own account borrowing; excludes net lending to local authorities and public corporations

Figure 5.6: UK government PSBR

Increases in value added tax, for example, might be harmful to firms dependent on household expenditure, such as retailers; its extension to products such as books might be a problem for booksellers and publishers; and rises in the duties payable on alcohol might mean less business or reduced profits for breweries or public houses.

In all of these cases, the companies themselves are responsible for paying the taxes, and could bear the extra cost themselves, cutting their margins. Alternatively, and more typically, they will raise prices to the consumer, with the possibility of this depressing demand and hence their sales. All of these considerations must be borne in mind by a manager assessing the impact of the latest government budget.

The public sector borrowing requirement

Annual figures for the PSBR show how much the government has borrowed or paid back in the year, how it has performed against its targets, plus forecasts for future years (see Figure 5.6). When tax revenues are weak and government spending high, for example in a recession, the PSBR is likely to grow. It will narrow once the economy picks up and tax revenues rise again as more people find jobs, the built-in stabiliser.

Thus, the state of public sector finances is, in part, dependent on the state of economic activity: this part of the deficit is referred to as the 'cyclical' deficit. However, governments also incur persistent debts by systematically spending more than they collect in tax revenues: this part of the deficit, which exists regardless of economic activity, is referred to as the 'structural' deficit.

- **PSBR by sector**: central government cash receipts in billions of pounds and consisting of taxes paid to the Inland Revenue, the recipient of income taxes; taxes paid to Customs and Excise, the recipient of many indirect taxes and duties on imports; social security contributions; and interest and dividends on government loans and investments.

- **Outlays**: expenditure on interest on the national debt, on the nationalised industries (in this case, negative as a result of privatisation income from, for example, the sales of electricity company debt and equity), and on general government department consumption and investment, all in billions of pounds.

- **PSBR**: the total amount the government has to borrow to finance its spending for the year in billions of pounds, and broken down by central government, local government and nationalised industry borrowing. When the government collects more revenues that it spends, the PSBR becomes the public sector debt repayment.

Government policy on the PSBR has two basic effects on the economy. The first is through fiscal policy: if the PSBR is increased in times of stagnant or falling output and high unemployment, the directly higher spending of the government and/or the indirectly higher spending of consumers resulting from their lower taxes and greater disposable incomes stimulate demand. Through various

UK ECONOMIC INDICATORS

OUTPUT- By market sector; consumer goods, investment goods, intermediate goods (materials and fuels), engineering output, metal manufacture, textiles, clothing and footwear (1990=100); housing starts (000s, monthly average).

	Cnsmer. goods	Invest. goods	Intmd. goods	Eng. output	Metal mnfg.	Textiles etc.	Housg. starts*
1st qtr '92	95.6	90.4	96.9	90.1	87.1	88.2	14.0
2nd qtr.	96.3	90.4	96.3	90.0	87.4	88.6	14.5
3rd qtr.	96.3	91.7	98.0	90.8	86.9	90.1	13.1
4th qtr.	96.5	93.1	98.6	91.5	84.0	90.8	10.6
1st qtr '93	97.0	93.6	97.7	91.6	86.8	89.5	15.6
2nd qtr.	97.3	93.7	98.8	92.4	86.7	90.0	16.7
3rd qtr.	97.8	92.6	101.6	91.8	85.2	90.3	15.3
4th qtr.	98.7	91.5	104.0	91.3	85.6	90.1	13.8
April	96.8	94.0	97.1	92.2	86.9	89.1	16.5
May	98.2	95.4	99.5	94.1	88.3	91.7	16.4
June	96.9	91.8	99.7	90.8	84.9	89.1	17.3
July	97.7	93.5	101.1	92.7	85.9	90.2	15.1
August	97.4	92.7	101.7	91.4	84.7	90.5	14.7
September	98.2	91.7	101.9	91.5	84.9	90.2	16.0
October	98.0	92.3	103.9	91.7	86.0	89.9	15.3
November	98.9	91.5	104.6	91.3	86.1	89.7	15.7
December	99.1	90.6	103.7	90.7	84.7	90.7	10.3
1st qtr '94	100.0	94.5	103.5	94.5	84.2	90.6	16.7
January	99.7	94.4	103.3	94.1	84.8	91.2	15.3
February	100.0	95.2	104.0	95.0	84.1	90.0	16.2
March	100.4	94.0	103.2	94.3	83.6	90.5	18.6
April	100.7	95.3	105.9	95.7	84.1	90.5	18.4
May	100.7	95.0	106.2	95.0	85.2	91.0	18.6

Figure 5.7: UK economic indicators: output

multiplier effects, this can lead to recovery, increased output, reduced unemployment and growth.

However, the second effect may temper this: high, persistent and/or growing annual PSBRs may drive up the cost of borrowing, discouraging both consumption and investment. In this way, excessive borrowing might result in disincentives to invest, and a crowding out of private capital investment. Governments are frequently torn between the conflicting effects of the macroeconomic policies at their disposal. Companies and investors must always be wary of these effects, and factor them into their decisions and plans.

OUTPUT

In addition to the breakdown of GDP by consumption, investment, government activity and international trade, the CSO produces a breakdown by output of various market sectors in the UK economy. The FT presents the essentials of this data in the Output section of the weekly UK economic indicators table (see Figure 5.7). All of these except housing starts are indices based on 1990=100.

- **Consumer goods**: an index of output of finished goods bought directly for use by individuals and households, for example, televisions. This index is indicative of trends in the consumer sector and its important role in the economy as a whole. Key components of it are often reported separately, such as output of motor vehicles (car registrations) and consumer durables: up or downturns in either of these are a good leading indicator of the stage of the business cycle. That means that their up or downturns come before those of the business cycle, indicating what is to come.

- **Investment goods**: an index of output of capital goods bought by industry and the government for the production of other goods, for example, printing presses. Again, this index is a leading indicator of the state of the economy.

- **Intermediate goods**: an index of the output of goods that require further stages of processing (raw materials or fuels), or which will become parts of other finished consumer or investment goods, for example, computer microchips.

- **Engineering output, metal manufacture, textiles, clothing and footwear**: indices of output in these sectors, all important in the UK economy.

The key sectors can be analysed by comparing their percentage change over a period with the percentage change in overall GDP: relatively faster growing sectors, for example, are making a more substantial contribution to overall growth. A given percentage change in a dominant sector naturally has a larger effect on total activity than that of a less important sector.

It should be noted that these monthly output figures do not cover all sectors, service sector output being a notable omission. That is why the quarterly GDP output figures discussed above are so valuable, providing a high level of detail across manufacturing industry, services, construction and agriculture. For example, they provide data on the erratic oil and gas sector; on utilities and manufacturing industries, on transport, storage and telecommunications; and on the retail trade, hotels and catering.

All industry-specific data will be of value to investors in their shares, and to companies which are a part of them, which supply them, and which buy from them. For example, it is always valuable for a manager to benchmark his or her company's prices and output against those of the industry in which it competes. Similarly, if a company is supplying an industry in which output is growing (again, say, microchip manufacturers selling to computer hardware firms), it needs to plan for increased demand.

Expanded output in industries from which a firm buys might be read in all sorts of ways. For a chain of department stores, it might imply a need to put more emphasis on those products because of evidently expanding consumer demand: this might have been the case with video recorders, with compact discs, and with a host of other high-technology electronic products. For managers in a large conglomerate, it might suggest taking a stake in that industry themselves. Microeconomic analysis of industry data like this might make an important contribution to the consideration of entering new markets, perhaps by developing their own products or by acquisition.

Large firms may also want to examine the potential to produce or sell in overseas markets. The relative importance of certain sectors varies in different countries, as do the changes in those sectors' importance. This applies at the level of individual industries where some countries have natural advantages in the production of particular goods and services (see chapter 3); it also applies at the broader level of large industry categories such as manufacturing, agriculture and services (see Figure 5.8). For example, a shifting balance from the manufacturing sector to the services sector is often noted in mature industrialised economies. Developing countries in contrast are more likely to be starting with agriculture and shifting to manufacturing.

Housing and construction

- **Housing starts**: a monthly average of the thousands of new houses on which construction has begun in the period, figures provided by the UK Department of the Environment.

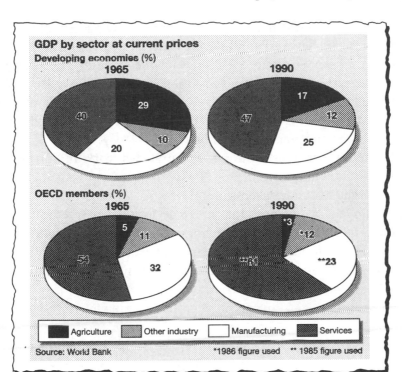

Figure 5.8: GDP by sector

Housing starts are another key leading indicator of economic activity, responding quickly to increases in earnings, employment and interest rates. For example, cuts in interest rates often prompt an upturn in construction, perhaps signalling that recovery is on the way. House sales are also very seasonal in nature: for example, they traditionally start to decline in the summer before picking up in the autumn.

As well as housing starts figures, there are regular published figures for total new construction orders. Particularly encouraging for the construction industry and the economy as a whole is a rise in private sector orders for offices, shops, factories and warehouses. This indicates increased investment by manufacturers and service industries.

Figures in the housing industry should be watched very carefully by all investors and by managers in a wide range of industries.

Construction work is fixed investment, and is very seasonal and sensitive to future demand and interest rates. However, it also has very significant knock-on effects throughout the economy. For example, when a construction recovery gets going, it first creates a demand for construction materials and labour, putting significant incomes into the pockets of workers and raw material suppliers, which will in turn be spent, boosting aggregate demand.

Secondarily, increased construction creates work and income for all sorts of ancillary businesses: directly related ones, such as architects, surveyors, estate agents, and home furnishings manufacturers; and indirectly related ones that make up local infrastructure, such as shops, restaurants, and leisure activities. In such a way might a boom get started, either national or regional, eventually to reach its peak with all these businesses' demand subsequently moving rapidly in the opposite direction.

6

PRODUCTION
AND EMPLOYMENT

In addition to the published information on national output, income and expenditure, there is a wide variety of important economic indicators relating to industry, commerce, and employment. All of these are valuable guides to the past, present and future movements of GDP and the overall state of the economy, as well as being of great interest in their own right to investors and managers across a broad range of industries.

The chief economic indicators in this area are published monthly in the *Financial Times*' international economic indicators table under the heading 'Production and Employment' (see Figure 6.1). This presents comparative, seasonally adjusted figures for retail sales volume, industrial production, unemployment and vacancy rates, and a composite leading indicator for the six main economies of the OECD. This example features Germany and the United Kingdom.

- **Retail sales volume**: the annual indices show the volume of retail sales calculated on the basis of 1985=100 (the same base is used for the industrial production and vacancy rate indicators); quarterly and monthly figures show the percentage change in retail sales volume over the corresponding period in the previous year. The data refer to total retail sales, except in the cases of France and Italy which cover only major outlets, and Japan where only department store sales are included.

- **Industrial production**: indices of the level of production in the industrial sector. These exclude the contribution of the service and agriculture sectors. In this case, the data come from national government sources, and include mining, manufacturing, gas,

INTERNATIONAL ECONOMIC INDICATORS: **PRODUCTION AND EMPLOYMENT**

■ GERMANY

	Retail sales volume	Industrial production	Unemp- loyment rate	Vacancy rate indicator	Composite leading indicator
1985	100.0	100.0	7.1	100.0	105.2
1986	103.4	102.2	6.4	136.4	105.0
1987	107.4	102.6	6.2	149.4	106.1
1988	110.5	106.3	6.2	164.8	112.3
1989	114.1	111.4	5.6	218.7	115.1
1990	123.5	117.2	4.8	261.1	115.7
1991	130.5	120.8	4.2	270.7	112.8
1992	127.7	119.1	4.6	260.2	106.3
1993	122.8	110.8	5.8	198.5	113.2
2nd qtr.1993	−3.6	−8.3	5.6	207.1	108.5
3rd qtr.1993	−1.7	−6.4	5.9	194.9	111.5
4th qtr.1993	−5.4	−3.1	6.3	178.4	113.2
1st qtr.1994	0.3	0.0	6.5	193.3	116.4
June 1993	−3.2	−7.5	5.7	203.9	108.5
July	−3.3	−8.0	5.8	201.5	109.5
August	−0.4	−5.6	5.9	195.7	110.9
September	−1.5	−5.7	6.1	186.6	111.5
October	−3.4	−4.3	6.2	175.1	112.2
November	−4.7	−4.0	6.3	179.2	112.6
December	−8.1	−1.0	6.3	180.9	113.2
January 1994	0.5	−1.7	6.4	189.2	114.1
February	0.6	1.0	6.5	195.8	115.1
March	−0.2	0.7	6.5	195.8	116.4
April	−7.6	2.8	6.6	193.3	118.5
May		1.6		187.5	

■ UNITED KINGDOM

	Retail sales volume	Industrial production	Unemp- loyment rate	Vacancy rate indicator	Composite leading indicator
1985	100.0	100.0	11.2	100.0	102.3
1986	105.3	102.4	11.2	116.1	105.8
1987	110.7	106.5	10.3	141.2	110.3
1988	117.8	111.6	8.6	144.9	108.6
1989	120.1	114.0	7.2	124.7	106.2
1990	121.1	113.7	6.8	98.1	103.9
1991	119.6	109.2	8.8	68.9	107.9
1992	120.5	108.7	10.0	70.1	113.1
1993	124.6	111.3	10.3	77.2	120.3
2nd qtr.1993	3.0	2.4	10.3	74.8	116.5
3rd qtr.1993	3.8	2.5	10.4	77.4	119.3
4th qtr.1993	3.7	3.1	10.0	82.7	120.3
1st qtr.1994	3.4	3.9	9.8	84.1	120.6
June 1993	3.9	2.4	10.3	74.3	116.5
July	4.4	3.3	10.4	77.1	117.4
August	3.6	2.4	10.4	77.8	118.7
September	3.4	1.8	10.3	77.5	119.3
October	3.2	1.9	10.2	80.7	119.6
November	3.8	3.6	10.0	83.6	119.7
December	4.2	3.7	9.9	83.8	120.3
January 1994	3.9	4.3	9.9	83.9	120.9
February	2.8	3.7	9.8	84.0	121.2
March	3.5	3.7	9.7	84.2	120.6
April	4.1	5.6	9.6	87.1	119.9
May	3.9			87.7	

Figure 6.1: International economic indicators: production and employment (Germany and the UK)

electricity and water supply, except for Japan where they only cover mining and manufacturing, and the United Kingdom where they also include the construction industries.

- **Unemployment rate**: the percentages of the total national labour forces unemployed. These are OECD standardised rates that attempt, as far as is possible, to adjust for the different definitions of unemployment used by official sources, and allow meaningful comparisons.

- **Vacancy rate indicator**: national vacancy measures divided by total national civilian employment, expressed as indices. In the United States, the measure is of 'help wanted' advertising; in Japan, new vacancies; in Germany and France, all jobs vacant; in the United Kingdom, unfilled vacancies (see below); while in Italy, there are no data available.

- **Composite leading indicator**: end period values for indices that combine a number of different OECD data series. Cyclical fluctuations in these data usually precede cyclical fluctuations in general economic activity, hence the term leading indicator. For example, for the United States, a widely reported composite leading indicator includes average hours put in by manufacturing workers, manufacturers' orders for consumer goods, housing permits, producer price indices and the money supply.

All of these indicators can be used to assess the current state of the economy in each of these countries, as well as the patterns of their business cycles over the last few years. For example, the retail sales volume and industrial production indices are good leading indicators of the cycle. In this case, they show that the UK recovery is more advanced than the German one. At the same time, the much higher level of unemployment in the United Kingdom, compared to Germany, suggests deeper structural problems in the economy and its labour market that may not be solved by a return to more buoyant times.

INDUSTRY

National accounts provide a broad historic picture of the state of an economy, while the output data break it down by market and industrial sector. Figures for Economic Activity included in the FT's weekly UK

UK ECONOMIC INDICATORS

ECONOMIC ACTIVITY- Indices of industrial production, manufacturing output (1990=100); engineering orders (£bn); retail sales volume and value (1990=100); registered unemployment (excluding school leavers) and unfilled vacancies (000s)

	Indl. prod.	Mfg. output	Eng. order*	Retail vol.	Retail value*	Unem- ployed	Vacs.
1st qtr '92	95.0	93.4	28.5	98.7	99.5	2,625	117.9
2nd qtr.	94.9	93.8	28.5	99.4	104.5	2,712	117.6
3rd qtr.	96.0	94.2	27.9	99.6	104.8	2,806	116.4
4th qtr.	96.6	94.2	28.7	100.5	123.5	2,917	116.8
1st qtr '93	96.6	95.1	29.3	101.8	105.2	2,952	120.9
2nd qtr.	97.2	95.3	29.3	102.4	110.0	2,926	123.4
3rd qtr,	98.4	95.4	29.3	103.4	111.2	2,914	128.1
4th qtr.	99.6	95.7	28.5	104.3	132.2	2,812	138.9
April	96.3	95.0	29.3	101.8	110.9	2,942	123.7
May	98.2	96.6	29.2	102.0	109.3	2,920	124.1
June	97.1	94.3	29.3	103.3	109.9	2,915	122.5
July	98.4	95.6	29.1	103.1	111.3	2,917	127.5
August	98.4	95.2	29.7	103.4	111.0	2,922	128.7
September	98.4	95.4	29.3	103.7	111.3	2,902	128.2
October	99.5	95.6	28.3	104.0	115.7	2,851	135.6
November	99.9	95.8	28.4	104.4	124.9	2,813	140.4
December	99.3	95.6	28.5	104.4	151.4	2,771	140.8
1st qtr '94	100.4	97.1	30.4	105.3	110.9	2,754	141.2
January	100.2	97.0	30.3	105.4	110.0	2,791	140.9
February	100.8	97.4	30.9	105.0	108.8	2,753	141.1
March	100.3	97.0	30.4	105.5	113.3	2,719	141.5
April	101.9	98.1	30.4	106.0	113.7	2,682	146.4
May	102.0	98.4		106.0	114.4	2,661	147.4

Figure 6.2: UK economic indicators: economic activity

economic indicators table (see Figure 6.2) focus on key indicators of national economic performance that generally appear in advance of detailed GDP figures. Like the output data, these too are often leading indicators of the prospects for the UK economy. They cover various indices of manufacturing and retail performance, together with unemployment and unfilled vacancies over two years on a monthly or quarterly basis. All except engineering orders, unemployment and vacancies are indices based on 1990=100.

Reading the figures

- **Industrial production**: an index of the value added output of the production industries. This index excludes the service, agriculture, trade and finance sectors. Measuring value added avoids the double counting that would arise from valuing output of one industry that becomes input to another. Thus, value added output is the value of the output less the cost of raw materials and other inputs to its production.

- **Manufacturing output**: an index of the value added output of the production industries, excluding the production of the oil and gas industries. The index for manufacturing output can be broken down to show the performance of various sectors such as engineering, chemicals, textiles, food and drink, coke and oil refining, and metals, as shown below.

- **Engineering orders**: outstanding orders for output from the engineering industries in billions of pounds. These figures are the total value of the ordered output, not just its value added. Increases in orders, adjusted for inflation, are an indicator of future increases in economic activity, particularly if, as in this case, the demand is for capital goods.

- **Retail volume and value**: figures from the UK government's Central Statistical Office (CSO) that show the volume and value of retail sales over the previous month and over the previous quarter. The CSO breaks down the total by category of shops, such as food retailers or clothing and footwear.

Interpreting the information

Each month the CSO estimates the output of UK manufacturing industry and the level of energy production in the previous month. These come together as the index of output of the production industries. The two components are usually quoted separately because oil and gas output is often erratic and can easily distort the underlying performance of manufacturing industry. Repairs to oil installations in the North Sea, for example, can bring energy production sharply down in one month.

As well as assessing monthly rises in output, the CSO compares output with the level of a year ago and quarter to quarter, to give a better idea of underlying trends. This information is often presented by the FT in a chart, graphically representing the rises and falls of industrial and manufacturing production, as well as quarterly growth in particular sectors (see Figure 6.3).

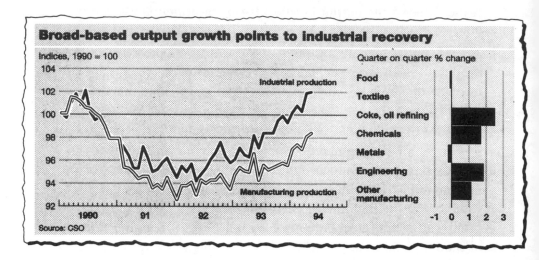

Figure 6.3: Industrial production

Industrial production is strongly indicative of the state of the business cycle. This is because the output of industries that produce capital goods and consumer durables, is reduced most during a recession, and increases most in a recovery. While the monthly net output of physical goods in the United Kingdom represents only a third of total output, industrial production is the principal monthly indicator of the overall level of activity in the economy.

Manufacturing output

A typical FT report on the industrial sector looks like this:

> A strong performance by the North Sea oil and gas sector boosted UK industrial production to record levels in the second quarter, indicating that the growth in output is gathering pace. Manufacturing output slowed slightly in June, providing further evidence that the pick-up in the manufacturing sector is steady rather than spectacular.
>
> The rise led the CSO to revise up its projection for annual economic growth to 5.5 per cent. This is considerably higher than the 3.3 per cent annual growth rate for overall gross domestic product in the second quarter of this year, and underlines the significance of the industrial sector in the overall recovery. The Treasury welcomed the figure as evidence that

the country was now seeing 'broadly based growth', and this upbeat verdict was echoed by City analysts. (*Financial Times*, 6/7 August 1994)

Reported figures like this provide very positive indications of the future development of the economy. Although the energy sector is erratic, strong increases of this kind reflect increased demand from the many industries that use its output. The figures also illustrate the importance of manufacturing in overall economic progress, and the way in which financial markets respond to such information.

Investors in energy and manufacturing industry stocks might be particularly encouraged by these figures, but the signs are good for almost all sectors of the economy that are dependent on domestic demand. Depending on the particular pattern of demand in their own industry, manufacturers might, as a result, invest in new plant and equipment; service sector companies, for whom human rather than capital resources might be more important, might respond by hiring more staff.

Orders and productive capacity

A number of surveys, produced by bodies such as the CBI, supplement the FT's regular reporting of UK industrial and commercial statistics. One of the most important is the CBI's quarterly industrial trends survey of manufacturers. The British Chamber of Commerce also carries out a quarterly economic survey of its members: unlike the CBI industrial trends survey, this includes the service sector.

The CBI survey gives a strong indication of future trends in manufacturing output by asking industrialists about the state of their order books. Surveying over 1,000 companies, it provides information on total new orders by sector (both actual and expected), and whether they are from domestic or export markets. It also covers corporate pricing and employment plans, as well as investment spending: on buildings, on plant and machinery, on product and process innovation, and on training and retraining. The CBI also conducts a monthly inquiry into the state of the distributive trades sector (wholesalers, retailers and motor vehicle traders) that supplements official information on retail sales (see below).

The CBI survey includes information on manufacturing industry's productive capacity and its use relative to orders. Productive capacity is a measure of the maximum sustainable output that could be produced by the industrial sector using the existing capital stock. Strong economic growth with high capacity use reflects possible inflationary pressures, though if demand remains strong and interest rates low, then further investment might be encouraged. Capital investment should indicate an increase in productive capacity, though some of the investment may be simply to replace old equipment that has been scrapped.

Orders for manufactured output, whether consumer or capital goods, are frequently volatile, but they can have a significant impact throughout the economy. An increase in orders is generally a positive sign, though it may indicate future rises in inflation if capacity use is high or unemployment low. Order backlogs or low inventories might also be worrying signs: bottlenecks in one industry create shortages of inputs in others, and managers should carefully watch capacity and orders data for industries that are their suppliers.

The structure of orders by industry of origin is also an important indicator. For example, within domestic orders by sector, increased orders for capital goods are a far more encouraging sign of continuing future demand than orders for consumer goods. They suggest that productive capacity is being increased, reducing the immediate dangers of bottlenecks and supply constraints. Rising orders for machine tools, for example, suggest new capital investment across a broad range of manufacturing industries. However, if those orders are primarily coming from overseas, prospects will be good for exports in the short-term, but not so promising for future domestic output.

Retail and wholesale sales

Indicators of national output of physical goods tend to pick out particular points along the chain of production and supply. They begin with the energy sector, the output of which is used by virtually everybody. Then they move to manufacturing industry: firstly the production of capital goods, and secondly the output of consumer goods that capital goods generate. Finally, they move to sales: once goods have been produced, they must be supplied to the end user.

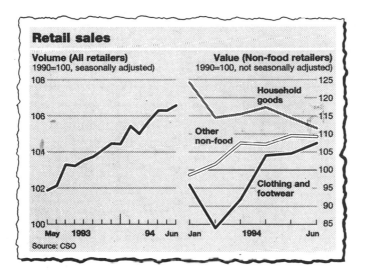

Figure 6.4: Retail sales

Wholesale sales are an important link in the chain of production and supply that connects companies with consumers and other business users. Wholesalers form the channel by which imports and domestic goods are supplied to end users, and figures on their sales and inventories are valuable rough and ready indicators of business and retail demand. For example, a rise in their sales or a fall in their inventories typically suggests a rise in demand. Hence their inclusion in the regular CBI survey of the distributive trades sector.

The level of retail sales is an even more important leading indicator, and one that receives considerable media attention. Encompassing up to a half of all consumer spending in the eventual figures for GDP (most of the rest is spent in the service sector and on accommodation), the volume and value of retail sales are key indicators of consumer confidence and demand (see Figure 6.4). For example, a significant upturn in retail sales will typically lead to higher wholesale sales, to more factory orders and eventually to increased production. Figures for retail stocks and retail orders will also give some indication of the pace of demand.

The pattern of retail sales is influenced by a wide range of factors, many of which affect different sectors in different ways, according to the

ANNUAL GROWTH IN SALES VOLUMES	Jun	Jul	Aug	Sep	Oct	Nov	Dec	Jan	Feb	Mar	Apr	May	Jun
Total retail	+30	+32	+31	+25	+26	+23	+34	+15	+10	+12	+22	+12	+27
Grocers	+43	+38	+37	+5	+25	+62	+60	+39	+40	+37	+33	+26	+38
Specialist food	+18	+13	+5	-14	-15	+10	+25	-26	-36	+4	+9	-44	+15
Off licences	-35	-23	-3	+23	-41	-61	-42	+15	+19	+4	+32	+36	+43
Clothing	+40	+55	+59	+14	+51	+32	+29	+19	+17	+19	+40	+28	+35
Footwear and leather	+43	+55	+37	+84	+59	+12	+48	+38	0	+11	+42	+75	+43
Durable household goods	+10	+12	+3	-16	+13	-21	+17	+20	+6	+29	+6	+17	+29
Furniture and carpets	+54	+31	+53	+17	+69	-29	+8	+18	+36	-38	+27	-2	+31
Hardware, china & DIY	-5	+10	+14	+23	+5	+10	+29	-5	+12	-13	-1	+29	-15
Confectionery	+3	+13	+30	0	-8	+36	+22	-10	-1	+36	+39	+18	+4
Booksellers & stationers	+37	+49	+22	+20	+50	+18	+48	+48	+17	+47	+2	-5	+42
Chemists	+44	+44	+37	+61	+16	+74	+83	+18	-8	-31	-53	-39	-5
Other retail	+8	+14	-3	+14	+19	+13	+25	-10	-38	-4	+7	+13	+28
Motor trade	-6	+8	+27	+15	+16	+14	-5	+50	+45	+22	+24	+16	+12

Source: CBI Distributive Trades Survey

Figure 6.5: Annual growth in sales volumes

microeconomic characteristics of the products. For example, seasonality is very important with some goods: off licences will expect to see sales volume jump at Christmas or during a long hot summer; grocers, on the other hand, can expect fairly consistent demand throughout the year.

Figures on retail sales should be examined very carefully by the companies that support and supply retailers. For example, the results of the CBI's distributive trades survey of over 500 retailers, wholesalers and motor traders will indicate whether consumer demand for their products is growing or declining (see Figure 6.5). Since the data are available relatively quickly, they enable supplying companies to adjust their output quite flexibly.

These CBI figures show annual growth in sales volume by sector to each month in the year, but suppliers will often want data covering shorter periods. New information is available monthly, but probably the best guide to use is the growth of sales on a three monthly rather than monthly basis: the former should give a better indication of short to medium term trends, in contrast to the very short-term fluctuations of the latter. Regularly published information from the British Retail Consortium, the main industry body, is also helpful for forecasting demand and planning production.

Value data shows changes in nominal demand, but volume data may reveal something about the nature of price competition in a sector, and how sensitive consumers are to price changes. Increases in volume will not necessarily be encouraging for some sectors if there is a divergence between volume and value: for example, heavy retail discounting in clothing and footwear, or price wars in supermarkets might leave retailers anxious about their profitability even if there have been considerable increases in volume.

Suppliers to the retail industries can read this information in different ways. For example, steady increases in volume sales might imply the need for a gradual expansion of output to meet this demand. However, if profitable opportunities look limited, or if export volumes seem to be rising faster, company managers may be encouraged to focus more of their efforts on export markets, particularly if the exchange rate means that their products are priced competitively in overseas markets (see chapter 9). Consumer price sensitivity might also be discouraging to producers of higher priced, higher quality products, though encouraging to producers of the 'pile 'em high, sell 'em cheap' variety of goods, or those whose low costs enable them to participate successfully in price wars.

Cyclical differences in demand among sectors are critical, hence the CSO chart's distinction between household goods (durables), other non-food goods, and clothing and footwear, and the CBI's sales breakdown into even more detailed categories. Durables, for example, are products for which demand shifts most in response to the business cycle. This is because they are frequently non-essential items, which can be cut first from consumers' budgets in a recession, but finally purchased in quantity when times look up. The fact that they are often relatively high priced products also affects this pattern.

Among particular sectors, the motor trade is an especially important indicator of the cycle of economic activity, and not only to businesses involved directly in the industry. As motor vehicles are both durables and relatively high priced products, the demand for them is very vulnerable to the business cycle. Demand also has a distinctly seasonal pattern, selling particularly strongly, for example, at the beginning of a new registration year. There are various measures of motor vehicle output, all of which are good leading indicators of the business cycle (see Figure 1.1 in chapter 1).

EMPLOYMENT AND THE LABOUR MARKET

The levels of employment and unemployment are some of the most contentious and widely reported economic indicators. Not only are they good indicators for investors and managers of the state of the business cycle, but they are also of wide interest to all participants in the labour market. In addition to covering jobs, employment data are an essential guide to personal incomes, wages and unit labour costs, as well as being the basis for measuring GDP by income, and for assessing inflationary pressures (see chapter 7). Furthermore, unlike data on industrial production and retail sales, they provide a broad picture of the economy, going beyond manufacturing and retail to encompass the service and agricultural sectors.

Information on the UK labour market appears frequently in the FT. The Economic Activity section of the weekly UK economic indicators table, for example (see Figure 6.2 above), includes two important indicators of the state of the market, in addition to its indicators for industry and commerce:

- **Registered unemployment**: the total number of people (in thousands, and excluding school leavers) that were out of work and claiming unemployment benefit in the previous period. The figure is seasonally adjusted to take account of annual fluctuations in the labour market, such as at the end of the academic year when school leavers flood the jobs market.

- **Unfilled vacancies**: vacancies (in thousands) notified to Department of Employment Job Centres, about one-third of the total vacancies in the economy. The change in the number of vacancies is seen as an important indicator of future employment trends.

The FT also regularly publishes figures and charts detailing levels of employment and unemployment elsewhere in the world. The level of employment in the United States, for example, is a critical indicator for many within and outside the country (see Figure 6.6). Financial markets, in particular, seem to view high levels of employment on US 'non-farm payrolls' (that is, excluding the agricultural sector) as indicative of upward pressure on inflation. Bond prices, for example, might fall on the announcement of growth in employment, as traders fear a tightening of monetary policy through a rise in interest rates.

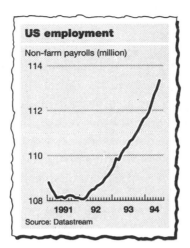

Figure 6.6: US employment

The unemployment rate in France might be of interest to a different set of investors and managers (see Figure 6.7). For example, rising unemployment might be discouraging to firms with substantial sales in that country. It might also lead to internal pressures for protection (perhaps especially in agriculture), and for slower progress on European union. These could have negative effects on all sorts of people with an interest in liberal trade and closer market integration. On the other hand, such pressures could have a positive impact on French companies, offering them easier access and less competition in domestic markets.

Unemployment and vacancies

Figures for unemployment and vacancies in the United Kingdom, as well as for average earnings and unit wage costs, are provided by the Department of Employment. The standard measure of unemployment, known as the claimant count, is often criticised for excluding large numbers of people who cannot find jobs, but who are not eligible for unemployment benefit. For example, women seeking to return to work, the self-employed and 16-and 17-year-old school leavers do not show up in the official count. Furthermore, the 1980s witnessed

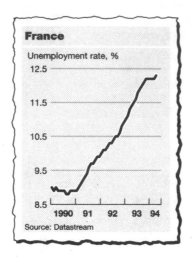

Figure 6.7 French unemployment

thirty changes to the definition of unemployment, all but one of which reduced the jobless total.

There are clearly more people unemployed than the official figures suggest. Every quarter, the Department of Employment carries out a survey of the labour force, designed to capture those unemployed people who are left out of the claimant count. The Labour Force Survey (LFS) uses the International Labour Office's measure of unemployment, an internationally recognised definition. It refers to people who were available to start work in the two weeks following their LFS interview and had either looked for work in the four weeks prior to the interview, or were waiting to start a job they had already obtained.

There is often a difference between the unemployment total revealed by the claimant count measure and the total arrived at by the LFS. The discrepancy between the two measures is usually greatest at a time of economic expansion when people feel encouraged to go out and look for work. But both measures miss people who have simply given up looking for work, and are not claiming or are not eligible for benefits: this group, which seems to be a growing feature of industrialised countries in the early 1990s, includes young people who have gone back to studying, women who have withdrawn from the labour force, and middle-aged men who have been made redundant

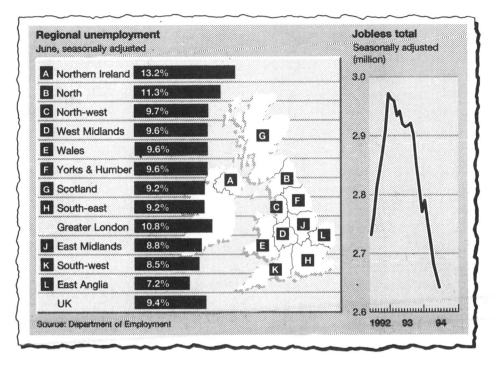

Figure 6.8: UK unemployment

by long-term employers and have, after long periods of searching, found themselves unwanted elsewhere.

Department of Employment statistics cover very detailed aspects of the labour market, for example, the breakdown of unemployment by region of the country (see Figure 6.8). Other analyses that are often reported in the FT include unemployment by age, sex, and length of time unemployed. These may be interpreted in various ways: for example, a fall in the number of young unemployed men is usually regarded as a sign of economic recovery. The figures also include information on employment which, it is important to note, is not exactly the opposite of unemployment: for example, unemployment might fall simply because fewer people are claiming benefits; that does not mean that they have gone into full-time employment.

The regional breakdown is valuable for managers in industries located in different parts of the country. For example, a multinational considering opening a new plant might consider basing it in an area of relatively high unemployment in order to take advantage of the substantial pool of workers available for hire. They may also benefit from a local wage level that is lower than in low unemployment regions. Managers in such a company will want to focus on critical microeconomic and supply side issues, such as whether a regional labour force contains workers with the right skills, or whether the workforce will need to be trained.

Mismatch between the skills demanded and the skills available in the local workforce is a frequent problem for companies. It is the reason why managers often find a trade-off between the rates of unemployment and inflation. If unemployment falls, the individuals who have found work may often be the ones that are most attractive to employers in terms of the skills they possess. The resulting skills shortages mean that managers have to raise the wage and salary levels they are willing to pay in order to attract the talent they need away from other companies. This can put pressure on inflation.

On the other hand, a decline in the unemployment rate is frequently good news for business. It gives a boost to personal disposable incomes, and invariably has a positive effect on consumer confidence, potentially increasing aggregate demand. At an individual level, fear of unemployment might be eased by a fall in unemployment throughout the economy. It could be the foundation for re-emergence of the 'feel good' factor, that intangible indicator of recovery and imminent boom.

The labour force

The labour force is the number of people employed, self-employed and unemployed but ready and able to work. Its size is determined by a variety of factors including the size of the population, the age structure (are there large numbers of people above or below working age?), the birth rate (is it at replacement level so that the population is constant?), migration (are there substantial inflows of foreign workers or outflows of skilled domestic workers, a 'brain drain'?) and participation rates (how many people of working age actually want to work?). As a percentage of the total population, the size of the labour force is affected by such factors as the average age of retirement, and the proportion of women who want to work in the recorded economy.

Employment and labour force growth in the OECD area	Total (000s) 1992	Annual percentage change		
		1992	1993	1994	1995
North America: Employment	129 835	0.5	1.4	3.0	1.9
Labour force	140 781	1.2	0.9	2.5	1.3
Japan: Employment	64 357	1.1	0.2	0.3	0.9
Labour force	65 779	1.2	0.6	0.7	0.8
Central & Western Europe:					
Employment	102 310	-1.3	-1.4	-0.5	0.6
Labour force	112 048	-0.2	-0.2	0.1	0.4
Southern Europe:					
Employment	60 231	-0.7	-2.5	-1.7	0.3
Labour force	67 952	0.2	-1.4	0.8	1.0
Nordic countries:					
Employment	11 070	-3.2	-3.4	0	1.1
Labour force	12 066	-0.8	-0.9	-0.3	0.6
Oceania:					
Employment	9 201	-0.3	0	2.2	2.5
Labour force	10 301	0.8	0	1.3	1.6

Source: OECD

Figure 6.9: OECD employment and labour force

The OECD publishes an annual *Employment Outlook* that surveys the prospects for the growth of the labour force and employment in its twenty-five constituent countries (see Figure 6.9). The outlook measures the overall size of the labour force and the numbers of people employed in the six regions in which OECD countries are located. It also forecasts the likely growth of these figures.

Labour force and employment data are very useful to companies in the planning of their future production over the medium to long-term. Though labour is often thought of as the variable factor of production, responding quickly and flexibly to changes in demand, this is rarely the case. For example, for large corporations with operations across a range of countries, it is vital to assess the pace of demand growth relative to the available factors of production in each location. Since, for such companies, capital is unlikely to be an issue, it is the availability of labour that concerns them. The rates of growth of local labour forces (and their productivity) will set the potential pace for growth in the company's output, in the same way that they do on a national scale.

When examining employment data, such companies will want to know exactly what kind of workers make up the pool of unemployed people, from which they might hire. Essentially, there are five types of unemployment. The first is residual unemployment, those people who do not want or are unable to work. The second is frictional unemployment, as workers change jobs: this is a sign of a healthy economy with labour being reallocated to more productive activities. The third is structural unemployment, where there is mismatch between available jobs and the skills of people who might fill them: this is where government supply side policy in such areas as education and training is essential.

The fourth type of unemployment is seasonal, and this will be of particular interest to companies involved in such seasonal industries as agriculture, construction and tourism. Managers of firms in these areas will need to monitor changes in the seasonal labour force carefully to ensure they have enough seasonal workers at the right time. Other firms might find it useful to take on temporary staff at any time of the year: in order to control their wage costs, but still hire good quality staff, they might decide to do so at the end of the academic year when there are often large supplies of students available to fill low paid temporary jobs.

The last type of unemployment is cyclical. Employment and unemployment are both very cyclical variables, though they do not respond to changes in demand quite as swiftly as output. When demand increases, companies tend first to increase overtime, and only then, if demand is strong and durable, to hire new staff. When demand turns down, hours are often cut first, and only then staff. Companies need to bear in mind total labour costs when they are hiring and firing. Taking on new staff costs more than just the extra wages; but, at the same time, reducing staff may lose the company far more than it has gained by the saving on wage costs. This might include the goodwill and productivity of all of their remaining staff.

CYCLICAL INDICATORS

The pattern of the business cycle in the United Kingdom is shown by cyclical indicators, produced once a month by the CSO. These monitor

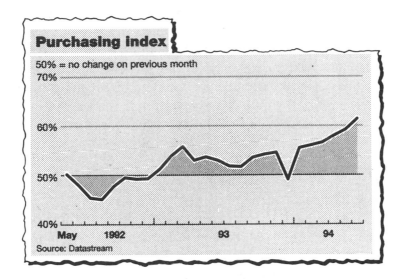

Figure 6.10: UK purchasing managers' index

and predict changes in the UK economy: based on series that are good leading indicators of turning points in economic activity (such as business and consumer confidence surveys), they provide early signs of when those turning points are coming. Composite indicators aim to smooth out trends and erratic fluctuations in the data, acting as a reasonably accurate guide to the cycle, usable by managers and investors as they attempt to plan for the future.

One example of a UK index of economic activity is that put together by the Chartered Institute of Purchasing and Supply and published monthly in the FT (see Figure 6.10). This index is constructed from various components of activity in the manufacturing sector, including new orders from both domestic and export markets, and employment. It surveys over 250 purchasing managers, measuring changes in economic performance between consecutive months.

A figure above 50 per cent indicates that activity has grown since the previous month, while a figure below indicates a fall. The figures collected by the institute also cover price data, and are able to discern impending supply bottlenecks in the event of a recovery and boom, and the price pressures they might cause. The impact of inflation on a business is discussed in chapter 7.

Indicators of this kind are based on a standard view of the business cycle. For example, in the first stages of a recovery, demand increases, company stocks are run down, and output rises as inventories are rebuilt. Next, firms hire unemployed workers who spend their incomes on consumer goods, creating more demand and employment through the multiplier (see chapter 2). Finally, capacity constraints lead to new investment and even more demand. Eventually though, output hits a ceiling as a result of bottlenecks and supply constraints, higher interest rates, and full employment. At this point, advancing inflation rates throw everything into reverse.

It is clearly valuable to know in advance whether a downturn or recovery is beginning. Hence the importance of the leading indicators discussed in this and other chapters of Part II. Indicators that turn in advance of GDP can be used to predict likely economic developments often up to a year ahead: in a standard cycle, very early ones might include interest rates, share prices, business confidence indices, and housing starts. Later, but still leading indicators often include consumer credit, car sales, manufacturing orders, and retail sales. Indicators that turn with GDP are known as coincident indicators; those that turn afterwards, lagging indicators.

Hundreds of private and public sector organisations produce forecasts for the UK economy, with varying degrees of accuracy. These forecasters range from City analysts to independent institutes to the Treasury's panel of independent forecasters, the 'wise men'. For example, Dun and Bradstreet, a business information group, conduct surveys of business expectations. This organisation aims to find the net percentage of business people expecting increased orders, sales, profits and employment in the next quarter, arriving at what it calls an 'optimism' index. The OECD and the IMF also produce forecasts for the UK economy and for many others. All of these public and private sector forecasts are discussed in more detail in chapters 10 and 11.

7

PRICES AND COMPETITIVENESS

Like employment, inflation is an economic indicator that affects everybody. In fact, it is probably the single economic indicator to which everyone responds: we see it in our living expenses, bid to make sure we get it in our wage increases, worry about it devaluing our savings and investments, and, as managers, attempt to ensure the prices of our products keep up with it. Decisions on consumption and saving are all influenced by changes in consumer goods prices. Decisions on investment and other matters by companies and investors are also affected by additional price indicators, as well as by the competitiveness of the national economy, itself often influenced by the rate of domestic inflation compared internationally.

Price indicators measure changes in the prices of particular sets of goods. Those for the UK economy feature in the Inflation section of the *Financial Times* weekly UK economic indicators table (see Figure 7.1). A number of different measures of UK inflation are published by the CSO, but by far the most popular and widely covered is the retail prices index (RPI). In addition to the RPI, indices are provided for inflation in earnings, and the prices of commodities and manufactured goods, as well as for the value of sterling. For earnings, materials and manufactured products, the indices are based on 1990=100; for retail and food indices, January 1987=100; for the Reuters index, 18 September 1931=100; and for sterling, 1985=100.

- **Earnings**: an index that measures the monthly level of earnings of employees in the United Kingdom. The index is compiled from a monthly sample survey of the gross wages and salaries paid to the employees of over 8,000 companies and organisations in the private and public sectors.

INFLATION-Indices of earnings (1990=100); basic materials and fuels; wholesale prices of manufactured products (1990=100); retail prices and food prices (Jan 1987=100); Reuters commodity index (Sept 18th 1931 =100); trade weighted value of sterling (1985=100)

	Earn-ings	Basic matls.*	Whsale. mnfg.*	RPI*	Foods*	Reuters cmdty.*	Sterling*
1st qtr. '92	113.4	97.6	107.3	136.2	129.0	1,599	90.6
2nd qtr.	113.7	96.5	108.8	139.1	129.1	1,598	92.3
3rd qtr.	114.9	94.7	108.9	139.0	127.3	1,542	90.9
4th qtr.	116.4	100.7	109.7	139.6	127.7	1,648	79.8
1st qtr. '93	118.0	104.2	111.2	138.7	130.1	1,740	78.5
2nd qtr.	117.9	102.7	113.1	140.9	131.5	1,667	80.2
3rd qtr.	118.7	100.1	113.5	141.3	131.2	1,647	81.0
4th qtr.	119.6	100.1	113.9	141.8	129.5	1,622	81.1
April	117.6	103.3	112.9	140.6	130.8	1,672	80.5
May	118.3	102.7	113.2	141.1	132.2	1,669	80.5
June	117.8	102.1	113.3	141.0	131.4	1,661	79.6
July	118.3	101.1	113.5	140.7	131.3	1,690	81.3
August	118.9	100.3	113.5	141.3	131.5	1,636	81.0
September	118.8	99.0	113.6	141.9	130.9	1,616	80.8
October	119.4	98.7	113.7	141.8	130.0	1,584	80.4
November	119.7	100.1	113.7	141.6	129.1	1,619	81.0
December	119.6	101.6	114.3	141.9	129.4	1,661	81.7
1st qtr.'94	122.9	101.1	114.9	142.0	130.8	1,763	81.3
January	121.2	100.5	114.7	141.3	130.0	1,690	82.4
February	123.5	101.3	114.9	142.1	130.8	1,780	81.0
March	124.0	101.3	115.1	142.5	131.6	1,819	80.5
April	121.7	102.0	115.4	144.2	131.9	1,822	80.0
May		102.7	115.5	144.7	133.2	1,924	79.9
June						2,005	80.1

Figure 7.1: UK economic indicators: inflation

- **Basic materials and fuels**: an index that tracks the prices of raw materials and fuels used by UK industries. These indicators are often referred to as producer input prices.

- **Wholesale prices of manufactured products**: an index that tracks the prices of manufactured goods as they leave factories. These indicators are often referred to as producer output prices or 'prices at the factory gate'.

- **Retail prices index**: an index of the average change in the prices of millions of consumer purchases represented by a 'basket' of goods. This is the most widely quoted index of inflation, sometimes referred to as the headline rate of inflation. The essential element to note is the change in the RPI year to year: if inflation is 4 per cent, this means that the RPI has risen by 4 per cent since the same month of the previous year; the average basket of goods is 4 per cent more expensive.

- **Food prices**: an index that tracks the prices of foods.

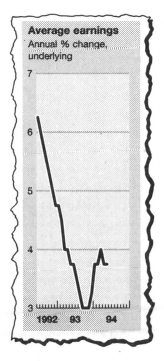

Figure 7.2: UK average earnings

- **Reuters commodity index**: an index of the prices of raw materials, calculated from sterling prices for seventeen primary commodities, weighted by their relative importance in international trade. This acts as a guide both for businesses using commodities in their production processes, and for investors in commodities.

- **Trade-weighted value of sterling**: a measure of the strength or weakness of the pound against the currencies of UK trading partners weighted by the volume of trade with each of those partners.

EARNINGS

The UK Department of Employment's monthly labour market statistics for growth in average earnings cover the whole economy, including both the service and manufacturing sectors (see Figure 7.2).

In addition to basic wages, earnings also include overtime payments, grading increments, bonuses and other incentive payments. For this reason, earnings increases usually exceed settlement increases and wage claims.

Because the earnings figures are affected by special factors such as back pay and changes in the timing of pay settlements, the Department also publishes its estimate of the underlying trend in earnings. Other figures published on the same day include hours of work and employment; hours of overtime worked; productivity (output per head); days lost through industrial disputes; and unit wage costs (wages per unit of output). Unit wage costs are an important indicator of inflationary pressures in an economy. If wages increase faster than productivity, then unit wage costs rise.

The rate of growth of average earnings is of concern to many people: from employees who want to make sure their pay is at least keeping up with the pack, or need a benchmark against which to set their latest wage claim; through investors in the financial markets who often view it as the most powerful indicator of future inflation; to managers in manufacturing industry, for whom in the United Kingdom, labour typically accounts for up to 40 per cent of their total costs of production.

Average earnings figures are also essential to managers in the retail sector. For example, fast food store managers need to know what the relevant pay scales are for the 'McJobs' they are offering. Average earnings, both at the national and local level, are essential inputs to management (cost) accounting, to production planning, to calculations of the likely profitability of potential new ventures, and many more business decisions.

The distribution of income

Differences in earnings can be enormous, and in the United Kingdom, the pattern in recent years has been for what is called the earnings gap to widen dramatically (see Figure 7.3). This chart shows the trends in earnings over the past twenty-five years for three percentiles, male wage earners at the top of the bottom 10 per cent, in the middle, and at the bottom of the top 10 per cent. It demonstrates the extent to which the 1980s have witnessed large and widening disparities in earnings.

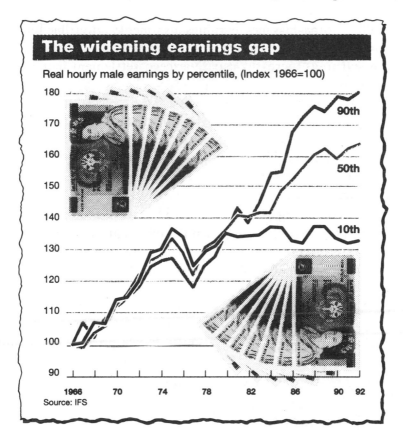

The widening earnings gap

Real hourly male earnings by percentile, (Index 1966=100)

Figure 7.3: UK earnings gap

Earnings have powerful effects on the distribution of income, and this too has widened in the 1980s. Both events have primarily been a result of government policies, based on beliefs in the virtues of lower taxation for higher earners (see chapter 2), weakness in the representatives of employees, and 'trickle down' economics whereby the success of people in higher income brackets will eventually percolate down to the poor, by raising the level of incomes throughout the economy.

Most of these ideas are of somewhat questionable empirical value, but there remains the issue of how to reduce the earnings gap. Suggestions include the need for more education and training, elimination of taxation on low wage jobs by raising the thresholds for income tax, making the benefit system more job-promoting, and generally improving the incentives for people to take low paid jobs.

Such schemes should encourage employers to price people into work without them being forced into poverty. They can thus address concerns about unemployment as well as inequality.

PRODUCER PRICES

Labour costs are one part of industry's costs; the capital costs of interest payments on debts are another. Lastly, there are the costs of the basic raw materials and fuels used in conjunction with labour and capital to produce output. These are referred to as producer input prices, and come under the general description of producer prices. This term also encompasses the prices at which industry sells its output to wholesalers, producer output prices or 'prices at the factory gate'.

Commodities

Commodities are basic raw materials, primary products and foodstuffs that are homogeneous and generally traded on a free market. Not only are they of interest to companies that use them in their production processes; they are also traded in asset contracts by investors and speculators. Commodity contracts may represent cash transactions for immediate delivery, or, more commonly, forward contracts for delivery at a specified time in the future. The bulk of such contracts are bought and sold on a commodities exchange by dealers and commodity brokers or traders. Their homogeneity, coupled with fast communications and an efficient system of quality grading and control, means that they can be traded without an actual transfer of the goods. This allows enormous scope for hedging and speculative activity as traders buy and sell rights of ownership in spot and futures markets.

The prices of commodities are determined in the normal market way by the forces of demand and supply. Because of the nature of the conditions of demand and supply for commodities, their prices tend to swing more violently than prices of manufactured goods. A small but persistent surplus in the supply of, say, tin, over demand can cause a dramatic slump in prices; similarly, disastrous weather conditions and a poor harvest can drive up a crop price.

```
LONDON SPOT MARKETS
■ CRUDE OIL FOB (per barrel/Sep)          +or-

Dubai                     $16.03-6.08w    -0.40
Brent Blend (dated)       $17.37-7.39     -0.62
Brent Blend (Sep)         $17.37-7.39     -0.40
W.T.I. (1pm est)          $19.40-9.42     -0.395
■ OIL PRODUCTS NWE prompt delivery CIF (tonne)

Premium Gasoline          $185-187        -1
Gas Oil                   $149-151        -3
Heavy Fuel Oil            $96-98          -1
Naphtha                   $166-168        -2.5
Jet fuel                  $164-166        -4
Petroleum Argus Estimates
■ OTHER

Gold (per troy oz)♣       $386.50         +1.3
Silver (per troy oz)♣     528.5c          +5
Platinum (per troy oz.)   $416.75         +6.50
Palladium (per troy oz.)  $147.30         +1.05
Copper (US prod.)         116.0c
Lead (US prod.)           37,75c
Tin (Kuala Lumpur)        13.85m          +0.11
Tin (New York)            253.5c
Zinc (US Prime W.)        Unq.
Cattle (live weight)†     N/A
Sheep (live weight)†♠     N/A
Pigs (live weight)        N/A
Lon. day sugar (raw)      $305.0          +7.7
Lon. day sugar (wte)      $345.0          +1.5
Tate & Lyle export        £307.0          +4.0
Barley (Eng. feed)        £99.50t
Maize (US No3 Yellow)     $143.5
Wheat (US Dark North)     £180.0
Rubber (Aug)♥             87.50p          +2.0
Rubber (Sep)♥             85.50p          +2.0
Rubber KL RSS No1 Aug     321.5m          +1.5
Coconut Oil (Phil)§       $590.0z         +5.0
Palm Oil (Malay.)§        $065.0q         +5.0
Copra (Phil)§             $405.0          +5.0
Soyabeans (US)            £177.0q
Cotton Outlook 'A' index  80.70c
Wooltops (64s Super)      421p
```

Figure 7.4: Commodities: London spot markets

The FT's Commodities and Agriculture page appears from Tuesday to Friday with the upper section devoted to reports on the commodity markets, and the lower section to a presentation of the previous day's trading and price data from markets in London, New York and Chicago. The lower section also appears on Saturday with a separate review of the week in the markets. For business users of commodities, the prices in the London spot markets will be of most interest (see Figure 7.4).

The table records prices and price changes for the full range of commodities: the principal crude oils, oil products, metals, meat, sugar, grains, rubber, vegetable oils and oilseeds, cotton and wool. The term spot markets means that these commodities are available on the spot, or at least for delivery within two days. The prices represent the cost of the actual physical materials, in contrast to the paper markets for commodity futures.

Commodities are primarily of interest to industrial users. Oil is the one with the most widespread potential impact since almost all businesses have some energy needs, but there are plenty of other examples. Prospective cocoa prices, for instance, are critical to chocolate makers, while certain metal prices will affect such companies as producers of cars, ships and manufactured goods, as well as the construction industry.

Companies whose profitability is partly dependent on the cost of their raw materials will naturally seek protection from potential surges in primary commodity prices. It is this need to hedge that gives rise to the futures markets. They are used by companies to avoid the risks of adverse price movements during the periods between contracting purchases and receiving deliveries. This hedging involves the opening of parallel but opposite futures contracts when physical orders are made, so that physical 'profits' or 'losses' made by the time the commodity is delivered will be cancelled out by losses or profits on the futures markets.

Alternatively, a company might buy commodities forward on the futures markets for actual physical materials. Buying a contract for delivery of physical materials at some specified point in the future allows a manufacturing manager to plan production more effectively, knowing the prices of these inputs and locking into them. Speculators take on the risk companies wish to avoid in the hope of accruing the potential profits the latter have relinquished.

Companies may also track commodity prices as a leading indicator of inflation. Most obviously, this is because higher prices are likely to feed through to prices, as firms pass on the extra costs to their customers: for example, cocoa prices eventually push up the price of chocolate. It typically takes about a year for price rises to feed through to the underlying rate of RPI, since manufacturers first use up their stocks bought when prices were lower.

Commodity prices are also a good inflation indicator since the markets in which they are bought and sold are very flexible, responding instantly to changes in demand and supply. Hence a rise in aggregate demand will show up earlier in commodity prices than it does in consumer prices. Of course, many of these price movements are responding to large scale speculative demand. Price rises do not necessarily mean, therefore, that raw materials will soon be in short supply: when temporary investors decide to park their money elsewhere, prices may well come down again. Companies need to watch carefully to understand what exactly is causing price movements.

From the point of view of investors, the commodity market is very high risk, and its data need to be studied carefully. Not only are price swings often dramatic, but, for non-US investors, they are also affected by exchange rate movements since commodity contracts are usually priced in dollars (see chapter 9). Investors in companies that are dependent on commodities may also want to check commodity price data carefully. For example, rising metal prices may squeeze the profit margins of companies that process ores, manufacture metal packaging, or sell tinned food.

Inputs and outputs

Both producer input and output prices are expressed in terms of an index and are regarded as important forward indicators of retail price inflation (see Figure 7.5). For example, a big leap in raw material prices may be absorbed by manufacturers for a while, but, in the past at least, they have been likely, at some stage, to raise prices to restore their profit margins. When they do, retailers eventually respond by raising shop prices.

During the recession of the early 1990s, prices of raw materials and fuels used by UK manufacturers began to fall, reflecting depressed economic conditions abroad and domestically, as well as the strength of sterling. This trend was reversed suddenly in September 1992 when sterling left the exchange rate mechanism of the European Monetary System (EMS) and devalued. Input price inflation leapt from being flat in September to a year to year growth rate of over 4 per cent in November, reflecting the higher cost of imported raw materials as a result of the weaker pound.

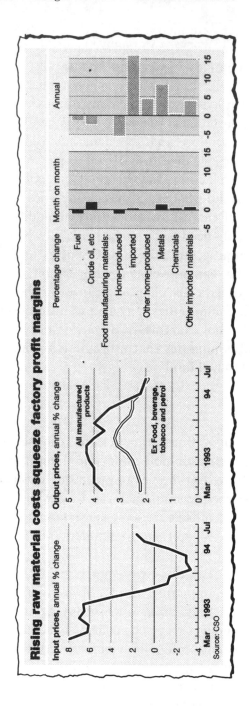

Figure 7.5: Producer prices

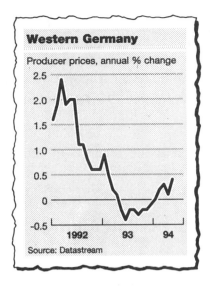

Figure 7.6: Western German producer prices

The FT regularly publishes charts of producer price indices in various important economies of the world (see Figure 7.6). Western German producer prices, for example, may be an important indicator of inflationary prospects in that country. This may have implications for the Bundesbank's next decision on interest rates, which is always watched closely by financial markets around the world. Indeed, it was the Bundesbank's relentless pursuit of low inflation, in conjunction with the costs of German unification, that led to sterling's ejection from the EMS (see chapter 3).

Trends in input prices like those of commodities are vital data for the manufacturing manager who is planning production. They are also useful to the cost accountants: commodities typically make up about 5 per cent of total costs. Most importantly, though, they ask sales and marketing staff the question of whether input price rises can be passed on to their customers. This tends to depend on the degree of price competition in the industry, either domestically or from overseas. A highly competitive industry could see input prices rising, but output remain flat, as firms absorb the rises and reduce their profits.

Retailers are in a particularly difficult position: theirs is a structurally competitive industry, often with a certain amount of consumer price sensitivity. In such an environment, it is sometimes hard to pass on costs, especially when inflation is low, and customers can see no reason for such actions. In such times, both retailers and manufacturers have to consider whether to accept a new business environment where sales volume not profit margins separates winners and losers. Such decisions will affect the future rate of inflation, and whether a low inflation psyche can be established. Inflationary expectations certainly need to be reduced in order to achieve a low inflation economic recovery.

CONSUMER PRICES

Earnings, commodity and other producer input prices ultimately affect the prices of consumer goods. It is rises in these prices that most people understand as inflation. In the United Kingdom, it is most eagerly monitored in the retail prices index: the CSO says it gets more queries from the public about the RPI than any other statistic, a reflection of the influence inflation has on everyone's life. For example, inflation determines the real value of savings, affects increases in pensions and other state benefits, and plays an important part in wage bargaining.

The retail prices index

The RPI is compiled by tracking the prices of a 'basket' of goods, which represents spending by the 'typical' UK family. All types of household spending are represented by the basket (see Figure 7.7) apart from a handful of exceptions, including savings and investments, charges for credit, betting and cash gifts. Indirect taxes such as value added tax (VAT) are included, but income tax and national insurance payments are not: as indicated below, direct taxes are accounted for in a separate index, the tax and price index.

The average change in the price of the RPI basket is calculated from the findings of government price collectors. Each month, they visit or telephone a variety of shops, gathering about 130,000 prices for different goods and services. They go to the same places and note the prices of the same things each month so that over time they

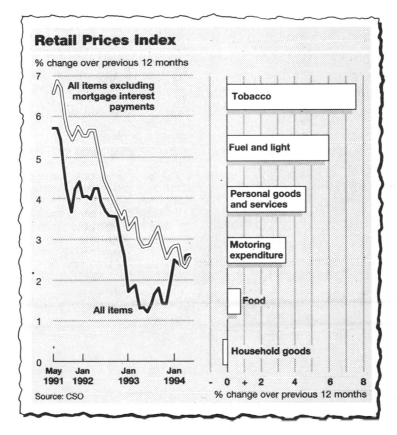

Figure 7.7: Retail prices index

compare like with like. Information on charges for gas, water, newspapers, council rents and rail fares are obtained from central sources. Some big chain stores, which charge the same prices at their various branches, help by sending information direct from their headquarters to the CSO.

The components of the RPI are weighted to ensure that the index reflects average household spending. Thus housing expenditure has a much greater weighting than cinema tickets; the biggest weightings currently go to housing, food and motoring (see Figure 7.8). The weights are obtained from a number of sources but mainly from the CSO's Family Expenditure Survey. For this, a sample of 7,000 households across the country keep records of what they spend over a fortnight plus details of big purchases over a longer period.

Inflation rate: +2.6%		RPI: 144.7 in June
Food (seasonal) (20)	+8.9%	
Food (non-seasonal) (142)	+0.1%	
Catering (45)	+3.8%	
Alcoholic drink (76)	+2.2%	
Tobacco (35)	+7.5%	
Housing (158)	+4.1%	
Fuel & light (45)	+6.4%	
Household goods (76)	+0.3%	
Household services (47)	+1.2%	
Clothing & footwear (58)	+0.7%	
Personal goods & services (37)	+3.5%	
Motoring expenditure (142)	+2.4%	
Fares & travel costs (20)	+2.1%	
Leisure goods (48)	-0.3%	
Leisure services (71)	+3.9%	Source: CSO

Figures in brackets are weights in retail prices index in parts of 1,000
Percentages represent annual % change to June 1994

Figure 7.8: Inflation rates

The spending patterns of two groups of people are excluded on the grounds that they are significantly different from most people's: families with the top 4 per cent of incomes and low income pensioners who mainly depend on state benefits.

Every year the components and the weightings of the RPI are reviewed to take account of changing spending habits. Over the past few years, microwave ovens, video recorders and compact discs have been introduced, while black and white televisions were dropped when sales declined.

In addition to the 'all items' index (the headline rate of inflation), the CSO publishes the RPI excluding mortgage interest payments (RPIX or the underlying rate of inflation), a measure favoured by the Treasury. It does this because a cut or rise in interest rates automatically influences mortgage interest payments. These have a higher weighting than any other component of the RPI and, as a result, have a strong bearing on the direction of the index. Excluding mortgage interest payments from the standard index prevents interest rate changes obscuring the underlying pattern of price changes.

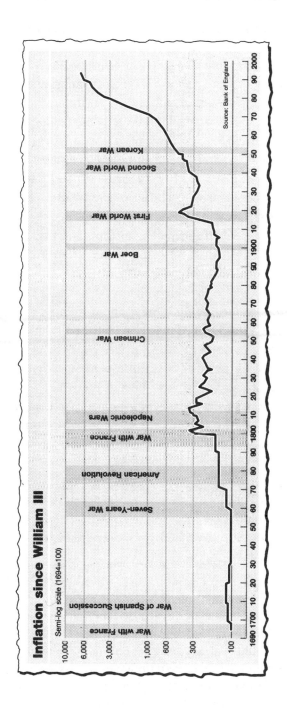

Figure 7.9: Inflation since William III

The Bank of England's preferred measure of inflation is known as 'core' inflation (RPIY). This excludes local authority and indirect taxes as well as mortgage payments. It is useful for clarifying the sometimes seasonal impact of changes in local and central government tax changes. These often occur in April, making it an important month for price increases, but also obscuring what is really happening with inflation.

A further index, the tax and price index (TPI) shows how much taxpayers' gross incomes need to change in order to maintain their spending power after taking account of deducted tax as well as changes in prices. It was introduced after the government budget of 1979 when VAT was increased but income tax reduced, shifting the burden from direct to indirect taxation. The rise in VAT, a component of the RPI, was duly reflected in the inflation figures, but the fall in income tax was not. The TPI was introduced to show the balancing effect of the cut in income tax.

Inflation is by no means a new phenomenon, though a continuously rising general level of prices is historically unusual. Prior to the end of the war, periods of rising prices over the centuries were quite often followed by periods of falling prices or deflation (see Figure 7.9). Although it now seems to be accepted that a low level of inflation is a natural and necessary condition of a healthy economy, this was perhaps not the case in the United Kingdom for at least 250 years up to 1945.

The causes of inflation

A typical FT report on inflationary prospects looks like this, a reflection of the latest version of UK monetary policy:

> The Bank of England yesterday warned that unless base rates are increased in the next few months the government could fail to meet its target of reducing underlying inflation to a 1-2.5 per cent range by the end of this parliament. In its quarterly inflation report, the Bank forecast that underlying retail price inflation, which excludes mortgage interest payments, would peak at over 3 per cent in the first quarter of 1996.
>
> The Bank added three more inflationary risks to the three outlined in its May inflation report – money supply growth, a rise in average earnings, and inflationary expectations in the financial markets. The report says that new dangers are recent rises in commodity prices, the prospect

of a rebound in corporate profit margins and the risk that the economy is closer to its full growth potential than previously thought. (*Financial Times*, 3 August 1994)

As chapter 2 mentioned in discussion of the causes of inflation and the UK government's policy to control it, the Bank of England publishes a quarterly inflation report, designed to convey its opinion of the inflationary outlook and appropriate policy responses. The one reported in this extract covers an extensive range of potential causes of inflation, including rises in some of the company costs and prices discussed above: average earnings, commodity prices, and the maintenance of constant profit margins in response to rising input prices by raising producer output prices. It also alludes to the output gap (see chapter 2), to growth of the money supply (see chapter 8) and to expectations of inflation, especially reflected in the bond markets (also see chapter 8).

Whatever the causes of inflation, it is very difficult for it to be wrung out of the system. Though rising consumer prices reduce the value of personal disposable incomes and savings, and encourage wage earners to demand higher pay to maintain their purchasing power, the fact is that many people are fond of inflation. For managers, for example, it might make company wage structures less rigid, enabling greater scope for using pay incentives; it might also misleadingly indicate increases in company sales and profits.

Inflation might be less objectionable at first sight to other people as well. For house owners, it gives them the pleasure of seeing their property prices go up and erodes the real value of their debts. For governments too, it erodes the real burden of debt, allowing the raising of revenues without raising tax rates: with a large budget deficit, for example, there is a strong temptation to let inflation loose. Lastly, for wage earners, reasonably sized percentage annual increases in pay might seem like a good thing, even if they are just keeping up with inflation.

COMPETITIVENESS

A monthly table of international economic indicators covering the six major economies of the OECD focuses on Prices and

■ FRANCE

	Consumer prices	Producer prices	Earnings	Unit labour costs	Real exchange rate
1985	100.0	100.0	100.0	100.0	100.0
1986	102.5	97.2	104.5	101.5	103.4
1987	105.9	97.8	107.8	103.0	104.8
1988	108.8	102.8	111.1	104.0	102.2
1989	112.6	108.4	115.4	105.3	99.8
1990	116.5	107.1	120.6	109.5	103.6
1991	120.2	105.8	125.8	113.8	102.2
1992	123.1	104.0	130.3	115.8	105.8
1993	125.6	101.1	133.7		108.5
2nd qtr.1993	2.0	–3.3	n.a.	2.6	109.7
3rd qtr.1993	2.2	–3.4	n.a.		106.5
4th qtr.1993	2.1	–2.2	n.a.		107.7
1st qtr.1994	1.7	–1.5	n.a.		107.5
June 1993	1.9	n.a.	2.6	n.a.	109.0
July	2.1	n.a.	–	n.a.	106.7
August	2.2	n.a.	–	n.a.	105.4
September	2.3	n.a.	2.3	n.a.	107.5
October	2.2	n.a.	–	n.a.	107.4
November	2.2	n.a.	–	n.a.	107.0
December	2.1	n.a.	2.2	n.a.	108.5
January 1994	1.9	n.a.	–	n.a.	107.5
February	1.8	n.a.	–	n.a.	106.9
March	1.5	n.a.	2.0	n.a.	107.9
April	1.7	n.a.	–	n.a.	106.6
May	1.8	n.a.	–	n.a.	107.4

■ ITALY

	Consumer prices	Producer prices	Earnings	Unit labour costs	Real exchange rate
1985	100.0	100.0	100.0	100.0	100.0
1986	106.1	100.2	104.8	102.7	101.3
1987	111.0	103.2	111.6	105.6	102.0
1988	116.5	106.8	118.4	109.7	100.2
1989	124.2	113.1	125.6	112.3	103.6
1990	131.8	117.8	134.7	118.8	106.2
1991	140.3	121.7	147.9	131.3	105.5
1992	147.7	124.0	155.9	136.8	101.9
1993	153.9	128.7	161.2	139.4	87.3
2nd qtr.1993	4.1	3.9	3.1	2.6	88.4
3rd qtr.1993	4.3	4.3	4.1	2.1	87.9
4th qtr.1993	4.1	3.9	3.8	–1.4	85.7
1st qtr.1994	4.2			n.a.	85.1
June 1993	4.2	4.1	4.1	n.a.	90.1
July	4.4	4.2	4.1	n.a.	88.7
August	4.4	4.4	4.2	n.a.	87.9
September	4.2	4.3	3.9	n.a.	87.0
October	4.3	4.1	3.9	n.a.	86.6
November	4.2	3.9	3.6	n.a.	85.6
December	4.0	3.7	3.6	n.a.	84.7
January 1994	4.2	3.5	4.0	n.a.	85.1
February	4.2	3.6	4.3	n.a.	85.5
March	4.2			n.a.	84.8
April	4.1			n.a.	87.5
May	4.0			n.a.	87.8

■ UNITED KINGDOM

	Consumer prices	Producer prices	Earnings	Unit labour costs	Real exchange rate
1985	100.0	100.0	100.0	100.0	100.0
1986	103.4	101.4	107.7	104.1	94.2
1987	107.7	104.9	116.3	106.6	94.6
1988	113.0	108.7	126.2	109.5	102.3
1989	121.8	113.9	137.2	114.4	101.3
1990	133.3	121.0	150.1	122.7	102.8
1991	141.2	127.5	162.4	131.3	106.5
1992	146.4	131.5	173.1	134.0	103.5
1993	148.7	136.7	180.9	134.3	95.7
2nd qtr.1993	1.3	4.0	5.0	–0.5	95.3
3rd qtr.1993	1.6	4.3	4.4	1.1	97.1
4th qtr.1993	1.6	3.9	3.9	1.7	97.1
1st qtr.1994	2.4	3.3	4.8	2.0	98.5
June 1993	1.2	4.0	4.9	1.2	95.1
July	1.4	4.2	5.0	0.7	97.4
August	1.7	4.3	3.6	0.8	97.2
September	1.8	4.3	4.5	1.7	96.6
October	1.4	4.0	3.8	2.0	96.2
November	1.9	3.6	4.0	1.9	97.1
December	1.9	4.0	4.0	1.2	97.9
January 1994	2.5	3.7	4.8	1.7	99.8
February	2.4	3.4	4.0	1.9	98.2
March	2.3	2.8	4.4	2.5	97.4
April	2.6	2.2	5.2		97.0
May		2.0			96.8

Figure 7.10: International economic indicators: prices and competitiveness (France, Italy and the UK)

Competitiveness (see Figure 7.10). This gives details of indices for consumer prices, producer prices, earnings, unit labour costs and the real exchange rate in each of these countries, in this case France, Italy and the United Kingdom. Yearly figures are shown in index form with the common base year of 1985=100. The real exchange rate is an index throughout; the other quarterly and monthly figures show the percentage change over the corresponding period in the previous year.

Reading the figures

- **Consumer prices**: indices of consumer prices that are not seasonally adjusted. These are equivalents of the UK RPI.

- **Producer prices**: indices of producer prices that again are not seasonally adjusted, and use varying measures of output: for the United States, those of finished goods; for Japan, manufactured goods; for Germany, industrial goods; for France, intermediate goods; for Italy, total producer goods; and for the United Kingdom, manufactured products, corresponding to the wholesale prices of manufactured products in the UK economic indicators series, though with a different base year.

- **Earnings**: indices of non-seasonally adjusted earnings. These refer to wage rates in manufacturing, except for France and Italy, where they cover rates in industry. The earnings rates are hourly, except for Japan, where they are monthly, and the United Kingdom, where they are weekly.

- **Unit labour costs**: seasonally adjusted indices of labour costs per unit of output, measured in domestic currencies. For Germany, they cover mining and manufacturing; for the others, just manufacturing. Unit labour costs reflect labour costs and productivity.

- **Real exchange rate**: calculated by JP Morgan as indices of relative national costs or prices expressed in a common currency. These real effective exchange rates are calculated against a composite of fifteen industrial countries' currencies, adjusted for changes in the relative wholesale prices of domestic manufactures (a measure of inflation). A fall in the index indicates improved international competitiveness.

Interpreting the information

National competitiveness is a difficult concept to define. One attempt is that it is the degree to which a country can produce goods and services that meet the tests of international markets while simultaneously maintaining and expanding the real incomes of its people over the long-term. This depends on changes in costs and prices relative to comparable changes in countries with which trade is conducted, adjusting for movements of the exchange rate. It is generally accepted that greater competitiveness of a country's output can be achieved through some combination of reasonable productivity growth and an appropriately valued exchange rate.

Each of these indicators gives some guide to national competitiveness. The first two are measures of domestic rates of inflation: for each country, they can be used to assess changes in the general price level, and inflationary prospects. In effect, they can be interpreted in the same way as all the above figures for inflation in the United Kingdom. However, when they are compared internationally, they become indicative of countries' ability to sell their exports abroad; they show relative consumer and producer prices. For example, if, as in this example, UK consumer prices are rising faster than French ones, without compensating movements in the franc-sterling exchange rate, UK exports to France are more expensive than they were, and hence less competitive.

Earnings and unit labour costs focus on the relative costs side of comparisons of international competitiveness. Earnings measure total labour costs; unit labour costs measure labour costs divided by output, and are therefore a function of productivity. For each country, as discussed with regard to UK inflation, earnings and unit labour costs are an important indicator of inflationary pressures in an economy: if labour costs increase faster than productivity, then unit labour costs rise. Used to compare countries, they reveal cost competitiveness: higher unit labour costs, without compensating movements in the exchange rate, make it harder for companies to price their goods competitively on the international market and maintain their profit margins.

Real exchange rates are effective exchange rates between countries' currencies that have been adjusted to take account of differential

Unit labour costs (at present exchange rates)			
UK=100	1990	1992 (Average)	1992 (Post ERM exit)
Belgium	97.8	NA	NA
Canada	98.6	94.1	99.7
France	101.3	102.5	114.0
Germany	107.9	115.7	128.8
Greece	115.0	NA	NA
Ireland	NA	NA	NA
Italy	92.5	93.1	93.2
Japan	81.8	99.3	113.0
Netherlands	93.1	98.7	112.5
Portugal	236.6	NA	NA
Spain	124.3	NA	NA
UK	100.0	100.0	100.0
US	79.0	75.4	83.3

Source: National Institute of Economic and Social Research

Figure 7.11: Unit labour costs

rates of inflation. The inflation indicator might be wholesale prices as in the table or unit labour costs. Either way, the real exchange rate is an excellent indicator of national competitiveness, incorporating changes in the exchange rate, the relative rates of inflation and the relative growth of productivity. An example of its importance is illustrated by the particularly decisive shift in the value of this indicator for the United Kingdom in the last quarter of 1992 (see Figure 7.11: unit labour costs at present exchange rates is an equivalent concept to the real exchange rate). This was the point when the pound left the EMS and devalued against the currencies of most UK trading partners in the EU.

The combination of devaluation and productivity give the United Kingdom a strong low cost advantage over other EU countries, though not against North America or Japan. For companies exporting to the EU, competing with EU imports, or considering either of these options, this should be good news. They will be able to price their goods very competitively, and still earn quite attractive profits. Thus competitiveness on a national scale and as a corporate concern become intertwined.

Relative unit labour costs will also be of great interest to managers in multinationals responsible for setting compensation levels across a range of operations. They will be naturally concerned with patterns of national productivity and labour costs; they will also want to maintain some sort of comparability of pay scales across their organisation, all relative to changing exchange rates among the currencies of the countries in which they are located. Data on unit labour costs, adjusted or unadjusted for currency movements, might offer some kind of standards, both national and global against which to assess their internal salary structures. More detail on currencies, as well as further issues for companies involved in international markets to consider are discussed in chapter 9.

8

MONEY AND FINANCE

Real economic activity is about output, production and employment, while nominal activity builds in changes in the prices of goods, services, and labour over time. Two intertwined elements complete the picture of the domestic economy: finance and the markets that determine the price of capital, the other essential factor of production; and money, the force that lubricates the whole economic system, connecting real and nominal values, and the value of which in itself, determined by inflation, can have serious repercussions for the real economy. Indicators of finance and money are of great interest to all investors and managers.

Monetary and financial indicators for the UK economy appear in the Financial section of the *Financial Times* weekly UK economic indicators table (see Figure 8.1). These cover measures of the money supply, credit and interest rates. Similar indicators for five other leading economies appear monthly in the FT, and are discussed below (see Figure 8.2).

- **M0**: the annual percentage change in this measure of the money supply, also known as 'narrow money' or the monetary base. This measure consists almost entirely of notes and coins in circulation, plus banks' deposits at the Bank of England.

- **M2**: the annual percentage change in this broader and more recently introduced measure of the money supply, covering M0 plus sterling retail deposits in banks and cash. By UK definitions, this is a narrower measure than M4; its definition in some other countries is broader, their M2 being known as 'broad money'.

- **M4**: the annual percentage change in what is known in the United Kingdom as 'broad money', a measure comprising M0 plus bank and building society retail and wholesale deposits.

FINANCIAL-Money supply (annual percentage change), M0, new M2 (retail deposits and cash), M4; bank sterling lending to private sector; building societies' net inflow; consumer credit†; Clearing Bank base rate (end period).

	M0 %	M2 %	M4 %	Bank lending £m	BS inflow* £m	Cnsmer. credit† £m	Base rate %
1st qtr '92	1.9	7.6	5.7	+ 6,099	266	+155	10.50
2nd qtr.	2.3	5.8	5.2	+ 9,468	77	+ 13	10.00
3rd qtr.	2.5	5.3	5.1	+ 5,461	-262	- 18	9.00
4th qtr.	2.8	5.0	4.5	+ 4,088	214	+211	7.00
1st qtr '93	4.4	4.9	3.4	+ 5,137	820	+446	6.00
2nd qtr.	4.2	5.6	3.3	+ 5,140	1,713	+556	6.00
3rd qtr.	5.4	5.4	3.5	+ 6,161	-69	+909	6.00
4th qtr.	5.5	5.5	4.3	+ 5,776	-263	+1119	5.50
April	4.3	5.5	3.3	+ 2,150	1,069	+199	6.00
May	3.5	5.8	3.5	+ 1,953	700	+130	6.00
June	4.9	5.5	3.2	+ 1,037	-56	+227	6.00
July	5.0	5.4	3.4	+ 2,064	-61	+199	6.00
August	5.6	5.1	3.6	+ 2,334	-132	+244	6.00
September	5.5	5.6	3.5	+ 1,763	124	+466	6.00
October	5.4	5.5	3.7	+ 1,711	258	+300	6.00
November	5.1	5.8	4.5	+ 1,044	-400	+302	5.50
December	5.9	5.2	4.8	+ 3,021	-121	+517	5.50
1st qtr '94	5.4	5.6	5.4	+ 4,515	-1,322	+1110	5.25
January	5.2	5.4	5.1	+ 283	-265	+241	5.50
February	5.5	5.5	5.4	+ 1,488	-404	+351	5.25
March	5.6	5.9	5.7	+ 2,744	-653	+518	5.25
April	5.9	5.4	5.6	+ 739	385	+412	5.25
May	6.9	4.5	5.4	+ 1,495	370	+203	5.25
June	6.8						5.25

Figure 8.1: UK economic indicators: financial

- **Bank lending**: bank and building society lending to the private and corporate sectors in millions of pounds, also known as M4 lending.

- **Building societies' net inflow**: the difference between the amount building societies have deposited with them and the amount they have lent in millions of pounds.

- **Consumer credit**: a measure of net changes in how much consumers have borrowed from retailers, finance houses, building societies and on the main bank credit cards in millions of pounds. It does not cover mortgages or bank loans and thus accounts for only around 15 per cent of total private sector debt.

- **Clearing bank base rate**: the lowest interest rate at which high street banks will lend money at the end of the period. This is close to the rate paid by a floating rate mortgage payer.

Every month, the Bank of England publishes figures showing the amount of money in circulation in the UK economy, and the year to year percentage changes. The total value of money in circulation depends on the definition of the money supply. In the United Kingdom there are two main measures, one broad and one narrow. Frequently, monetary authorities choose to target growth in the money supply as part of an anti-inflationary strategy. Rapid growth in the amount of money circulating in the economy is often taken to be a sign that inflationary pressures are building up (see below).

M4 growth is the broad money measure, and an indicator of short term to medium term trends in the economy. For example, sluggish growth in M4 lending indicates that consumers and companies are reluctant to borrow, while brisk M4 growth is indicative of a stronger economy. On the same day that the Bank of England publishes the M4 lending figures, the British Bankers Association puts out its own monthly statement about lending by the main retail banks. These will also be scrutinised by companies and the financial markets for indications of likely future trends in output, inflation and interest rates.

Mo is a shorter term money supply measure. Growth of Mo indicates that consumer spending is buoyant; a contraction in Mo suggests consumers are behaving more cautiously. It is a valuable guide to the trend of retail sales, and one of the inflationary indicators monitored by the government. Consumer credit is also a useful snapshot of general consumer behaviour; building society net inflow is indicative of consumer activity in the more specific, but vital housing market. For example, the lower or more negative the figure for building society net inflow, the more encouraging the signs for house purchases. As indicated in chapter 5, the housing market frequently leads recovery and recession.

INTERNATIONAL MONEY AND FINANCE

Monthly FT figures for Money and Finance appear in the newspaper's international economic indicators table. These cover the six leading economies of the OECD, in this case, the three most dominant economies of the world, the United States, Japan and Germany (see Figure 8.2). The figures focus on the most widely followed measures of narrow and broad money, representative short and long-term interest rates and average equity market yields. All figures are percentages: growth rates, interest rates and yields.

INTERNATIONAL ECONOMIC INDICATORS: MONEY AND FINANCE

This table shows growth rates for the most widely followed measures of narrow and broad money, a representative short- and long-term interest rate series and an average equity market yield. All figures are percentages.

	■ UNITED STATES					■ JAPAN					■ GERMANY				
	Narrow Money (M1)	Broad Money (M2)	Short Interest Rate	Long Interest Rate	Equity Market Yield	Narrow Money (M1)	Broad Money (M2-CDs)	Short Interest Rate	Long Interest Rate	Equity Market Yield	Narrow Money (M1)	Broad Money (M3)	Short Interest Rate	Long Interest Rate	Equity Market Yield
1985	9.0	8.9	8.00	10.59	n.a.	5.0	9.3	6.62	6.51	n.a.	4.4	4.1	5.45	6.94	n.a.
1986	13.5	8.3	6.49	7.67	3.43	6.9	8.2	5.12	5.35	0.84	9.9	-2.1	4.64	5.90	1.79
1987	11.6	6.5	6.82	8.39	3.12	10.5	11.5	4.15	4.64	0.55	9.0	7.3	4.03	6.14	2.21
1988	4.3	5.2	7.65	8.84	3.61	8.4	10.4	4.43	4.77	0.54	9.8	6.4	4.34	6.46	2.61
1989	1.0	3.9	8.99	8.49	3.43	4.1	10.6	5.31	5.22	0.48	6.3	5.7	7.11	6.94	2.22
1990	3.7	5.3	8.06	8.54	3.60	2.6	8.5	7.62	6.91	0.65	4.5	4.5	8.49	8.71	2.11
1991	5.9	3.3	5.87	7.85	3.21	5.2	2.0	7.21	6.37	0.75	5.1	5.6	9.25	8.44	2.38
1992	12.4	2.4	3.75	7.00	2.95	4.5	-0.4	4.28	5.25	1.00	7.0	8.2	9.52	7.77	2.45
1993	11.6	1.1	3.22	5.86	2.78	3.0	1.4	2.83	4.18	0.87	9.4	7.9	7.28	6.44	2.11
2nd qtr.1993	11.9	1.0	3.18	5.98	2.80	3.2	1.4	3.09	4.55	0.83	9.5	8.6	7.68	6.73	2.24
3rd qtr.1993	12.2	1.4	3.18	5.61	2.76	3.3	1.9	2.83	4.25	0.80	9.9	8.1	6.82	6.34	2.01
4th qtr.1993	10.5	1.3	3.34	5.59	2.73	3.5	1.4	2.14	3.57	0.84	8.6	7.5	6.34	5.83	1.79
1st qtr.1994	9.8	2.2	3.52	6.06	2.75	4.7	1.9	2.05	3.68	0.82	11.1	11.6	5.88	5.93	1.75
June 1993	12.8	1.5	3.25	5.94	2.80	3.4	1.4	3.10	4.58	0.82	10.1	8.5	7.60	6.77	2.22
July	12.7	1.5	3.20	5.79	2.80	3.8	1.6	3.11	4.40	0.81	10.1	8.7	7.24	6.57	2.09
August	12.2	1.3	3.18	5.68	2.76	3.5	1.7	2.93	4.27	0.79	10.1	8.3	6.62	6.34	1.98
September	11.7	1.3	3.16	5.35	2.73	2.6	1.9	2.46	4.09	0.79	9.5	7.3	6.63	6.12	1.96
October	10.9	1.1	3.26	5.32	2.71	3.7	1.8	2.30	3.85	0.80	9.2	6.4	6.64	5.93	1.86
November	10.4	1.3	3.40	5.70	2.74	3.3	1.5	2.22	3.64	0.84	8.4	7.3	6.31	5.86	1.82
December	10.1	1.5	3.35	5.74	2.74	3.4	1.4	1.90	3.25	0.89	8.1	8.8	6.11	5.71	1.69
January 1994	9.7	2.0	3.20	5.71	2.72	4.2	1.6	1.96	3.34	0.85	11.8	11.4	5.90	5.63	1.71
February	10.0	2.1	3.49	5.97	2.74	4.8	1.5	2.05	3.60	0.80	11.0	11.9	5.91	5.87	1.77
March	9.8	2.5	3.84	6.47	2.80	5.2	1.9	2.13	4.08	0.79	10.5	11.4	5.84	6.27	1.76
April	9.0	2.6	4.05	6.94	2.91	5.9	2.2	2.13	4.03	0.80	11.6	10.8	5.61	6.43	1.68
May	7.1	1.9	4.54	7.17	2.91	5.1	1.7	2.08	3.90	0.78	11.2	10.8	5.20	6.63	1.67

Figure 8.2: International economic indicators: money and finance (the US, Japan and Germany)

Reading the figures

- **Narrow money (M1)**: measures of the money supply, commonly defined as notes and coins in circulation plus bank deposits that are available on demand. Unlike the UK money supply figures which show annual percentage changes, these figures show monetary growth rates as percentage changes over the corresponding period in the previous year. All are seasonally adjusted except for Japan and Italy; the data is derived from central bank sources.

- **Broad money (M2, M2 plus CDs, M3 or M4)**: much more variable definitions of the money supply, these generally include M1 plus time and savings deposits as well as foreign currency deposits of foreigners. Variations in broad money definitions include Japan's addition of certificates of deposit (CDs) and Germany's M3 (see below).

- **Short interest rate**: rates of interest at which banks in these countries lend wholesale to each other short-term. Each one is a standard, universally recognised three-month rate. For example, the UK rate is the three-month LIBOR or London Interbank Offered Rate, how much banks charge for lending to other banks, their 'offer' or selling price for money lent for three months. Equivalent rates for Germany and France are three-month FIBOR in Frankfurt and three-month PIBOR in Paris. The standard rate for Italy is that payable on three-month Eurolira; for the United States, ninety-day commercial paper, bills issued by large, creditworthy institutions; and for Japan, three-month CDs.

- **Long interest rate**: average yields on ten-year benchmark government bonds over the period. Bonds are debt instruments, securities sold by governments (in this case), companies or banks in order to raise capital. They normally carry a fixed rate of interest, known as the coupon, have a fixed redemption value, the par value, and are repaid after a fixed period, the maturity. The maturity on these bonds is ten years; the current yield is the coupon as a percentage of their current price; and they are benchmarks for long-term rates of interest throughout the economy.

- **Equity market yield**: period averages of gross dividend yields on the FT-Actuaries world index covering each individual market, that is, the total dividends payable on the stocks included in each index as a percentage of the total value of the index. The indices aim to cover a significant proportion of the stocks listed on each market rather than concentrating merely on the largest companies. Companies are only included where a timely and reliable source of daily price movements is available, and in which there are liquid markets.

Interpreting the information

The figures for the growth of the money supply can be read in the same way as those for the United Kingdom: as indicators of the buoyancy of consumer spending, the enthusiasm of consumers and companies to borrow for consumption or investment purposes, the prevalence of inflationary pressures, and the likely future prospects for interest rates, output, and actual inflation. Interest rates are themselves indicators of possible output and inflation trends, influencing both the strength of demand for goods and services, and the supply of money. For example, a rise in short-term rates will check money supply growth, while a rise in long-term rates will probably restrain demand for funds for investment.

Short-term interest rates are determined to some extent in the markets, but are also manipulated by government monetary policy. LIBOR, for example, is influenced by the rate at which the Bank of England lends to the discount houses (see chapter 2). It is at the heart of the UK interbank market, which is in turn the core of the money markets (see chapter 1). The interbank market allows banks to lend and borrow surplus liquidity in substantial amounts: LIBOR is a measure of short-term swings in rates, a constantly changing indicator of the cost of money in large amounts for banks themselves. It is a major reference point for the international financial markets, as are its equivalents in other major financial centres. For example, very large company depositors should be able to deal at or near interbank rates when they are placing money in the market.

Intimately related to interest rates, both short and long-term, are the prices of bonds. The relationship between bond prices and interest rates is an inverse one: as one goes up, the other goes down. This is because a bond pays a fixed amount which, when calculated as a percentage of its market price, is the yield, equivalent to the rate of interest. If rates go up, the relative attractiveness of a deposit account over a bond increases. Since the coupon is fixed, for the yield on the bond to rise to offer an interest return once again comparable to that on the deposit account, the price of the bond must fall. Some bonds carry little or no interest, rewarding the buyer instead through a substantial discount from their redemption value and, hence, the prospect of a sizeable capital gain.

As discussed in chapter 2, the government of a country finances many of its activities through borrowing, by issuing bonds and bills. Maturity periods for longer term bonds (known as gilts in the United Kingdom) vary, but ten years is generally taken to be a standard. The benchmark yields on these bonds indicate how much the government is obliged to offer on new issues, and are a reflection of the cost of borrowing money long-term. Investors in gilts will use them as benchmarks for the returns on their asset portfolios; company treasurers will use them to estimate their likely cost of capital, the interest they will have to pay on new loans, or the coupon they will have to offer on corporate bonds.

Interest rates are the returns on debt; the equivalent for equity is the dividend yield, dividends as a percentage of the share price. The figures for equity market yields are designed to represent global equity markets and the increased interest in cross-border equity investment, particularly from the United States and Japan. Their primary function is global equity performance measurement (hence it is essential that shares that make up the index can be purchased and sold readily), but they are also being used for the creation of derivative products, such as stock index funds. These serve hedging and speculative purposes for investors and companies.

THE MONEY SUPPLY

Money is variously defined as a measure of value, a store of wealth and a medium of exchange. For the purposes of measuring the money supply, it is the last definition that is crucial: money is anything that is accepted as a medium of exchange, essentially notes, coins, and bank deposits. The number of times it changes hands over a period is known as the velocity of circulation.

Multiplying the money supply and its velocity together gives the total amount of money spent over a period, equivalent to the real level of national output multiplied by the level of prices. This set of relationships is at the heart of monetary policy: essentially, if the velocity of circulation is fixed, there is a positive relationship between the money supply and both the level of real output and the rate of inflation. Depending on the direction of causation, controlling the money supply might be a way to affect these two key policy targets.

As explained in chapter 2, monetary policy is a key element of government economic policy. Control of the money supply is generally conducted by the national monetary authorities through a variety of techniques: management of interest rates, bank reserve asset ratios, credit controls and open market operations. The degree of central bank intervention in the markets, as well as the issuing of new government securities, are frequently viewed as guides to the authorities' economic policy intentions.

Gilts and Treasury bills

Chapter 2 explained how the government borrows money through the issue of financial securities called gilts, and uses the sale and repurchase of these instruments (open market operations) to influence the money supply. The means by which this is done in the United Kingdom, the public offering of stocks where a minimum price is set and tenders invited, is most easily illustrated through the way the government's shortest term debt securities are issued, Treasury bills.

Treasury bills are bills of exchange issued by the Bank of England on behalf of the UK government. They have a three month maturity, but carry no interest, the yield being the difference between the purchase and redemption prices. The bills are issued by tender each week to the discount houses in units of between £5,000 and £100,000, and on Monday, the FT contains a table with details of the tender (see Figure 8.3). How this is described in the newspaper's reports is shown in an extract below (see page 156).

- **Bills on offer, total of applications, and total allocated**: the value of the bills on offer is £100 million, and the value of the total applications to buy those bills is a measure of market enthusiasm for them. In this example, the later tender was more oversubscribed than the

BANK OF ENGLAND TREASURY BILL TENDER

	Aug 5	Jul 29		Aug 5	Jul 29
Bills on offer	£500m	£500m	Top accepted rate	5.3747%	5.7558%
Total of applications	£3012m	£1368m	Ave. rate of discount	5.3747%	5.6029%
Total allocated	£500m	£500m	Average yield	5.4477%	5.6823%
Min. accepted bid	£98.660	£98.565	Offer at next tender	£500m	£500m
Allotment at min. level	100%	74%	Min. accept. bid 182 days	-	-

Figure 8.3: Bank of England Treasury bill tender

earlier one. Since there is almost invariably oversubscription, naturally the total allocated is the same as that offered.

- **Minimum accepted bid and allotment at minimum level**: the former is the lowest bid price accepted, in the later case here, £98,660 for every bill with a face value of £100,000. The bid is lower than the redemption price so that the purchaser can make money on the difference. The allotment is simply the proportion of the bills sold at the minimum price; the rest would have been sold for higher prices (lower discounts).

- **Rates of discount and yield**: the top accepted discount rate is the other side of the minimum accepted bid, with the average rate calculating in the discount on the bills sold for higher prices. The discount rates do not correspond exactly to the actual discount since they are presented as annual rates even though the bills mature in three months. Loosely speaking, these are the rates a buyer would earn for purchasing four consecutive bills. The discount rate is calculated as the difference between the purchase and redemption prices as a percentage of the latter. In contrast, the yield is the difference as a percentage of the former.

The link to inflation

Monetary authorities take different attitudes to the targeting of the money supply, depending on their view of which measure is the most accurate representation of the actual money supply, which can be measured effectively, and which has the most direct link to inflation. For example, the Bundesbank insists that M3 is the most reliable indicator of possible inflation, as well as being one it can carefully define and measure (see Figure 8.4).

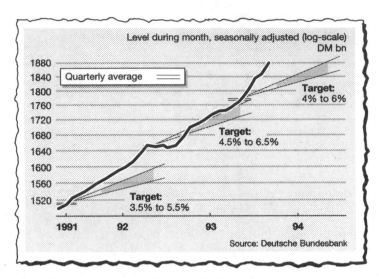

Figure 8.4: German money supply growth (M3)

The German monetary authorities continue to view the M3 components of cash and easily accessible short-term savings as a potential threat to monetary stability. They are uneasy that much of this so-called monetary capital is not safely locked up in long-term bonds or other instruments. But, at the same time as this reaffirmation of German faith in broad monetary targets, such goals have been dropped in many other leading industrial countries. This is because, in most countries, the money supply has proved a fickle guide to inflation: its relationship to total spending has broken down.

Goodhart's law, named after a former Bank of England economist, states that once a measure of money becomes a policy target, it begins to lose its connection to inflation and economic activity. This may have happened with a number of measures of broad money: for example, in the United States, broad money has contracted with the recovery; while, in Germany, M3 growth soared as the economy went into recession and inflation slowed. Similarly, M0 or the monetary base has been a recent target of UK monetary policy, but now seems to have lost its connection to inflation (see Figure 8.5).

- **M0 and inflation**: the chart indicates that annual growth in M0 was a leading indicator of the annual inflation rate (the retail price index excluding mortgage interest payments, RPIY) during the late

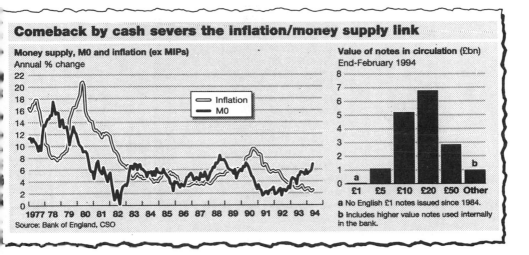

Figure 8.5: Inflation and the money supply

1970s; a coincident indicator through much of the 1980s, tracking RPIY; and once again a leading indicator at the turn of the decade. Since then, the relationship seems to have become unhinged.

CREDIT AND INTEREST RATES

Money supply figures should still be tracked by investors and company managers keeping an eye on prospects for inflation, but it is more important and more valuable to consider movements of interest rates. These can have far more dramatic effects on the values of share and bond portfolios, on the costs of corporate borrowing, and on the outlook for the economy's progress through the business cycle.

Interest rates tend to rise and fall in line with the level of economic activity. In a recession and the early stages of a recovery, they will generally be low and falling to encourage borrowing; while in the subsequent boom, they will rise as the demand for money exceeds the supply. For bond investors, therefore, a recession is likely to be good for their portfolios, and a recovery less positive. For companies, the rising interest rates of a boom might be disadvantageous, but the growing economy itself should offer numerous opportunities for enhanced profitability. This should benefit investors in equities.

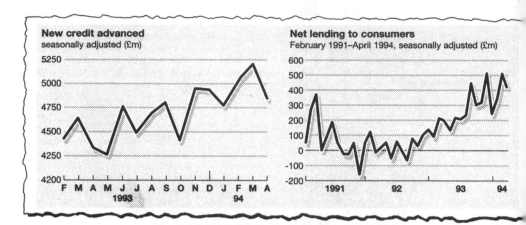

Figure 8.6: Net credit advanced and net lending to consumers

The relationship between equity prices and interest rates is more complicated and less predictable than that between bond prices and interest rates. As with bonds, if interest rates rise, the relative dividend yield of shares will be less attractive than the interest rate on a deposit account. The yield will also be less attractive than that on the bond with its adjusted price. Furthermore, the yield may become even less desirable because the rate rise will raise the company's interest costs, reduce its profitability and perhaps lead it to cut the dividend. However, much of the return sought on shares is from their potential for capital growth and an interest rate rise need not affect that. In the long-term, the prospects for corporate profitability tend to have far more of an influence on share prices than interest rates.

Shorter term, however, it is vital for managers to track the costs of borrowing, as reflected in real interest rates. In theory, these should be measured by subtracting expected inflation from nominal interest rates, but because expectations cannot be measured directly, it is common to use actual inflation instead. In making new investments, companies will naturally want to take advantage of low interest rates and protect themselves against potentially unwelcome rises in the future. In a recovery, they will aim to assess when rates have bottomed out, and, at that point, try to lock into fixed rate mortgages and loans. If they are unable to do that, and are only able to raise floating rate funding, they will need to plan for increasing capital costs as recovery continues and interest rates rise further.

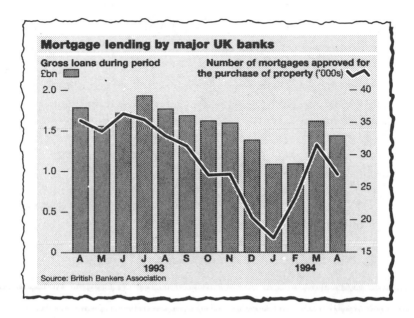

Figure 8.7: UK bank mortgage lending

Even firms without substantial existing or planned debts need to monitor rates, for example, those in sectors where business is highly sensitive to changes in interest rates, such as banks and life assurance companies. In these industries, revenues and a substantial proportion of costs are directly affected by rate changes. Firms in industries dependent on household expenditure, such as the retail sector and breweries, will be less directly affected but still experience important changes in demand, as consumers shift their spending in responses to the accessibility and cost of credit (see Figure 8.6).

The housing market and associated industries are particularly susceptible to movements in interest rates, which feed instantly through into mortgage rates (see Figure 8.7). A slight rise in long-term interest rates, or expectations that they will rise in the near future, can drastically reduce both the number of mortgages approved for the purchase of property, and their gross value. Since the housing market is an important leading indicator as well as a driving force of recovery, too early a rise in interest rates, perhaps in response to bond market fears of inflation, might choke off increasing demand.

A typical FT report on the interest rate, its impending movements, and the reactions of financial markets, looks like this:

Financial markets yesterday signalled their expectation of an imminent rise in UK interest rates. This was based on Bank of England dealings in the money market which persuaded many traders that a half percentage point increase was likely. Anxiety about a rise in rates prompted selling in the futures market. By the close last night, short sterling, the futures market's medium for speculating on interest rate changes, pointed to short-term rates of over 6 per cent by September compared with base rates currently at 5.25 per cent.

The Bank yesterday accepted bids for Treasury bills at rates of up to 5.75 per cent. That was interpreted by some traders as a sign that base rates would rise shortly. In its daily operations, however, the Bank dealt at unchanged rates. These activities are the Bank's traditional method of signalling its desired level of base rates. (*Financial Times*, 30/31 July 1994)

In this extract, the government's regular Treasury bill auction appears to give an indication of its intentions towards the interest rate. The financial markets' reaction to such hints could have implications for company borrowing, for consumer demand, for inflation and for bond and equity prices.

Bond markets

As the extract suggests, the bond markets are moved by economic and financial news. Most important are the movements of interest rates and inflation. For example, the threat of higher inflation (perhaps driven by the prospect of higher earnings and higher commodity prices feeding through to producer and retail prices) implies returns, in terms of both interest and capital appreciation, that are eroded in value. It also suggests the likelihood of higher interest rates: though promising for income, these imply the prospect of falling bond prices. Since the rate of interest typically goes up in a time of economic buoyancy, bond prices tend to fall on the upswing of the business cycle.

Exchange rates and relative interest rates also play an important role in the bond market. For example, a weak dollar or fears of inflation in the United States might mean that the US authorities decide to raise local interest rates, leading to falling US bond prices.

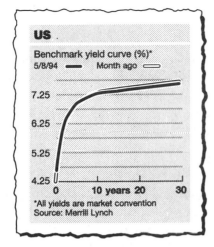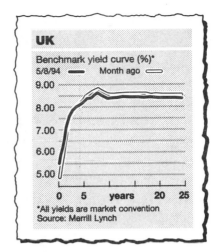

Figure 8.8: US and UK benchmark bond yield curves

Given the extensive interconnections of global bond markets, these movements are likely to push rates and prices elsewhere in the world in the same direction. For example, lower bond prices and higher yields in the United States than in the United Kingdom might tempt international bond investors to move out of UK gilts and into US bonds, pushing down the prices of the former.

Long-dated gilt prices tend to move most in response to expectations of inflation and interest rate changes. Since their maturity value is fixed, they are a good indicator of expected trends in the rates of interest and inflation. The relationship between long and short-term rates, shown in the yield curve, is a means of comparing rates on bonds of different maturities, as well as assessing the relative tightness of monetary conditions. Longer term yields are usually higher because of the greater degree of risk of owning them. When short-term rates are higher, there is a negative yield curve.

Monday's FT includes a chart of the latest yield curves for benchmark US and UK government bonds (see Figure 8.8) as well as of the yield curve for national government bonds in Frankfurt and Tokyo. These indicate the yields on typical bonds for each possible time to maturity. In this example, yields on longer term bonds are higher up to a point but then flatten out, suggesting either that monetary conditions are about to tighten with the government increasing short-term rates, or that they are at least expected to tighten.

Corporate bonds

If corporate borrowers consider long-term interest rates to be at or nearing their lowest point in the business cycle, it might be a good time to lock into them by issuing very long-term fixed rate corporate bonds, or attempting to secure fixed rate loans. In making the decision when to go to the market for funding, corporate financial managers face something of a trade-off: they want the lowest available interest rates, but at such times, there may not be the encouraging signs of increasing demand for their products. The ambition will be to find the point at which the product market is once again becoming a seller's market, while the capital market is still a buyer's market.

For investors, the yields on corporate bonds are generally higher and the prices lower, reflecting the more variable creditworthiness of their issuers and a greater risk of default. These bonds are often classified by rating agencies such as Standard & Poor's and Moody's, which rate bonds according to the risk they carry (ranging from high-quality AAA to below-grade D). Low-grade corporate bonds, rated as being below investment quality, offer very high yields. Known colloquially as junk bonds, these essentially unsecured, high-yield debt securities peaked in popularity in the late 1980s, and financed a significant portion of the merger and acquisition boom in the United States.

The international bond markets offer an alternative method of raising money for companies that do not want to issue stock or accept the conditions of a bank loan. They also offer opportunities for interest rate and currency swaps: for example, when a company that can easily raise money in sterling because of local reputation needs dollars to fund an acquisition or expansion, it may find an American company in the opposite position and swap its debt. Such transactions can also be designed to protect companies against the interest and exchange rate risks they take on, both in their financing arrangements and in their actual business operations.

STOCK MARKETS

Indicators of the state of equity markets are another important area where investors and managers need information, and in this, they are well served by the FT. For example, major share price movements

Chief price changes yesterday

FRANKFURT (DM)			
Rises			
Heidelb Zem	1210	+	14
Volkswagen	488	+	12.2
Falls			
Altana	589	–	12
Asko	1020	–	11
Leifheit	690	–	10
Linde	923	–	12
NEW YORK ($)			
Rises			
Microsoft	50¼	+	1 5/16
Motorola	50	+	1⅛
Nationsbank	55⅛	+	⅝
Upjohn	30½	+	½
Falls			
US West	40⅜	–	1½
Synergen	4½	–	4⅜

PARIS (FFr)			
Rises			
Canal Plus	919	+	49
Credit Foncier	995	+	49
Credit Local	415.5	+	29.5
Dollfus Mieg	458	+	27
Unibail	529	+	29
Falls			
Geophysique	547	–	21
TOKYO (Yen)			
Rises			
Kitazawa Sangyo	755	+	45
Misawa Resort	1250	+	110
Nippon Shindo	445	+	30
Yamagata Bank	594	+	34
Falls			
Fanuc	4190	–	300
Unitika	375	–	15

LONDON (Pence)			
Rises			
BWD Securities	110	+	5
British Borneo	218	+	8
Division Group	133	+	28
Eidos	350	+	20
Evans Halshaw	454	+	11
Forte	230	+	8½
Geest	225	+	17
Jones Stroud	288	+	10
Leslie Wise	66	+	4
M & G Group	879	+	37
Mercury Asset	588	+	26
National Express	320	+	16
Pearson	660	+	22
Perpetual	1023	+	44
Sharelink	278	+	25
Tams (John)	79xd	+	7½
Falls			
Betterware	79	–	6
Boots	538	–	11
Hickson	169	–	7
OIS Intl	36	–	18
Sketchley	105	–	5

Figure 8.9: Daily share price changes

around the world are highlighted in a feature on the front of the FT's second section. This gives chief price changes on the previous day for equities not only in the United Kingdom, but also in Frankfurt, New York, Paris and Tokyo (see Figure 8.9). For each quoted stock, the daily table presents its closing price in the local currency, and the change on the previous trading day's price. The prices shown are not necessarily those involving the greatest percentage change in the various markets, since this often applies to relatively small companies with only a narrow market in their shares. The FT's table generally concentrates on the most interesting price movements among large companies.

The price movements of individual stocks are influenced by a range of factors specific to the business. Common ones include company profits, the growth of those profits, dividends, and takeover bids.

These are the fundamentals of corporate life, and fundamental analysis aims to uncover the truths about a company behind the figures to determine whether its shares are over or underpriced. The way changes in company fundamentals actually cause price movements is not always obvious because of the market's capacity to discount future events. These are news events, the core of the forces that move individual stock prices, but expectations of future news events can be just as powerful.

The fact that prices move on account of expectations of the future, as well as being determined by historic and current knowledge of a company's performance, suggests that they incorporate all known information about the value of shares. This is the foundation of one of the most powerful theories of asset valuation, the efficient market hypothesis. The predictions of this theory are that no one can forecast future price moves consistently and that, over the long-term, without inside information, no one can beat the market. The corollary is that stock prices follow what is called a random walk: at any point in an equity's price history, it is impossible to predict whether its next move will be up or down. Hence, investment strategies based on technical analysis, chartism or the study of past price trends, will not perform dependably.

From the point of view of a senior manager in a quoted company, monitoring the share price and its relation to the progress of the overall market are as important as for an investor. Firstly, a high and rising share price means that the company is attractive to investors, and it is likely to be possible to raise funds for new investment (either debt or new equity) relatively easily and at reasonable cost. Secondly, good capital market performance makes a firm relatively well protected from potential hostile takeover bids, as well as allowing it to contemplate making its own acquisition with 'paper' offers (its own shares swapped for those of the target). Lastly, and most importantly, managers have a responsibility to their shareholders to manage the company with the primary goal of corporate value creation, offering an appealing rate of return in terms of both dividends and share price appreciation, and one that, if at all possible, consistently outperforms the market.

Figure 8.10: Key UK stock market indicators

Market movements

A snapshot of recent price and trading activity throughout the whole UK equities market is provided by the graphs and key indicators published daily on the back page of the FT's second section (see Figure 8.10). These data, together with the daily share price table, are a valuable checklist for the key moves in the major markets of the world. Much more detailed data, as well as reports on the markets and commentary on the main forces influencing them, are available throughout the rest of the newspaper. The companion volume to this book, *The Financial Times Guide to Using the Financial Pages*, provides an accessible route map to this information and how it may be used by investors and managers.

- **FT-SE-A All-share index**: this index provides investors with an instant overview of movements in the UK equity market over several months. It moves more sluggishly than the better known 'Footsie' (FT-SE 100) index because it has a large number of comparatively inactive constituents which lag behind the market leaders. Graphs featuring the performance of individual share prices relative to the All-share index also appear frequently in the FT, usually linked to a news item.

- **Equity shares traded**: the volume of shares traded over the same period, excluding intra-market and overseas turnover.

- **Key indicators**: an easy reference point for a number of leading market indices and ratios, plus the five best and worst performing sectors.

Discussions above have indicated how changes in interest rates affect the prices of equities and bonds (chapter 9 examines their effects on currencies), but what other factors move the prices of individual assets and of whole markets? Obviously, supply and demand are the basic influences at an individual asset level, but what are the underlying determinants of these economic forces, and what causes substantial broad market moves? These are questions surrounded in controversy, especially related to the stock market, and it is important to differentiate between various kinds of price movement.

In the stock market, there are essentially three kinds of moves: the long-term trend of the overall market as reflected in the indices; short-term moves around the trend; and the movements of individual shares and sectors. For the most part, individual sectors broadly follow overall market trends, though some may be growth industries, some may be mature or declining industries, or some may simply be the beneficiary or victim of a particular event with ramifications peculiar to that industry (for example, the oil industry and the Gulf War, or the computer, media and telecommunications industries and the hype surrounding the 'information superhighway'). In those cases, sector values can diverge from the market trend.

News about particular companies can have a powerful impact on the market, as well as causing individual equity price movements. This is especially the case with blue chip companies, the most highly regarded companies in the market and usually ones with substantial assets, a strong record of growth, and a well-known name. Moves in response to blue chip news are typically short-term, affected by such intangibles as sentiment, investor psychology, and how the market is 'feeling'! Medium term moves seem to be influenced by supply and demand factors, such as the weight of money moving into or out of stocks: for example, the market tends to expect a certain level of growth in overall corporate earnings. If it does not materialise, money might leave the market.

It is probable that long-term moves depend on fundamental economic and political factors. The market often follows the broad patterns of economic activity, and certainly news about inflation, productivity, growth and the government's fiscal and monetary stance can have major effects on the level of the market. Hence the importance of understanding what the economic indicators mean and how they relate to the markets.

On occasion, stock prices can plummet in a way that appears to bear no relation to fundamentals, supply and demand or even, at least in its early stages, to market sentiment. Such an occasion was Black Monday and the stock market crash of 1987, when prices fell by record amounts in markets throughout the world. Much analysis of this event has been conducted, and there is still no agreement on its root causes. Certainly, fundamental economic forces do not appear to have been critical, since most economies continued to grow reasonably well in its aftermath, and the downturn did not come until the very end of the decade. Part of this was due to the prudent economic policies of key governments, who avoided some of the disastrous policy mistakes made after the last major market meltdown, the crash of 1929.

9

TRADE AND EXCHANGE RATES

Output, employment, inflation and interest rates can all be considered in terms of a single economy cut off from the outside world. In reality, of course, almost all countries have numerous economic contacts with others, and, though these relationships may appear complex, they are just like any other economic transaction. Opening up markets and economies to cross-border flows of goods, services and capital merely adds a new dimension and scale to economic activity. As chapter 3 suggested, it is helpful to grasp the essentials of international trade and foreign exchange in order to understand the global environment in which you are making business and investment decisions.

A national economy's interaction with the rest of world can be simply tracked through two basic groups of economic indicators: the balance of payments, an accounting record of international trade and financial flows between countries; and exchange rates, values of the local currency in terms of other currencies. A monthly table of the *Financial Times* international economic indicators covers Balance of Payments (and exchange rates) for the six main economies of the OECD, in this example, the United States and France (see Figure 9.1). It provides values for these countries' exports, visible trade and current account balances, and their currencies' exchange rate with the ecu and effective exchange rates.

- **Exports**: the values of national exports of merchandise (that is, trade in physical goods, not services) in billions of ecus. These and the next two sets of trade figures are seasonally adjusted, except for the Italian series and the German current account. German data up to and including June 1990 refer to the former West Germany, prior to reunification.

INTERNATIONAL ECONOMIC INDICATORS: **BALANCE OF PAYMENTS**

■ UNITED STATES

	Exports	Visible trade balance	Current account balance	Ecu exchange rate	Effective exchange rate
1985	279.8	−174.2	−162.5	0.7623	100.0
1986	230.9	−140.6	−152.7	0.9838	80.2
1987	220.2	−131.8	−145.0	1.1541	70.3
1988	272.5	−100.2	−107.5	1.1833	66.0
1989	330.2	−99.3	−92.2	1.1017	69.4
1990	309.0	−79.3	−72.1	1.2745	65.1
1991	340.5	−53.5	−6.7	1.2391	64.5
1992	345.9	−65.2	−51.4	1.2957	62.9
1993	397.3	−98.7	−88.8	1.1705	65.6
2nd qtr.1993	96.0	−24.7	−21.2	1.2069	64.3
3rd qtr.1993	99.6	−27.5	−24.3	1.1443	65.4
4th qtr.1993	106.9	−25.0	−26.9	1.1388	66.4
1st qtr.1994	106.9	−28.9	−28.4	1.1244	66.8
June 1993	32.1	−9.6	n.a.	1.1833	64.5
July	32.8	−9.5	n.a.	1.1349	65.9
August	33.9	−8.9	n.a.	1.1251	65.7
September	32.9	−9.0	n.a.	1.1728	64.7
October	34.5	−9.3	n.a.	1.1597	65.5
November	35.5	−8.8	n.a.	1.1282	66.6
December	36.9	−6.9	n.a.	1.1287	67.0
January 1994	35.2	−9.7	n.a.	1.1139	67.5
February	34.1	−10.8	n.a.	1.1184	66.7
March	37.5	−8.4	n.a.	1.1410	66.1
April	36.1	−10.6	n.a.	1.1385	66.0
May	35.5	−10.9	n.a.	1.1622	65.3

■ FRANCE

	Exports	Visible trade balance	Current account balance	Ecu exchange rate	Effective exchange rate
1985	133.4	−0.6	−0.2	6.7942	100.0
1986	127.1	0.0	3.0	6.7946	102.0
1987	128.3	−4.6	−3.7	6.9265	103.0
1988	141.9	−3.9	−3.4	7.0354	100.8
1989	162.9	−6.3	−3.6	7.0169	99.8
1990	170.1	−7.2	−7.2	6.9202	104.8
1991	175.4	−4.2	−4.9	6.9643	102.7
1992	182.5	4.6	2.9	6.8420	106.0
1993	177.8	13.9	8.9	6.6281	108.3
2nd qtr.1993	44.5	3.1	1.4	6.6118	109.7
3rd qtr.1993	45.0	3.9	3.5	6.6508	106.4
4th qtr.1993	45.8	4.5	3.5	6.6431	107.3
1st qtr.1994	46.1	2.4	2.3	6.5881	108.0
June 1993	14.7	0.73	−0.42	6.5842	108.9
July	15.1	1.56	1.27	6.6299	107.0
August	14.6	0.73	1.27	6.6761	105.3
September	15.3	1.57	1.00	6.6465	107.0
October	14.9	1.28	1.17	6.6631	106.9
November	15.0	1.22	0.02	6.6637	106.8
December	15.8	2.02	2.38	6.6025	108.2
January 1994	15.1	0.30	2.44	6.5956	107.9
February	15.0	0.78	−0.64	6.5905	107.6
March	15.8	1.36	0.51	6.5782	108.3
April	15.7	1.18	0.07	6.6240	107.1
May	16.3	1.15		6.5972	107.9

Figure 9.1: International economic indicators: balance of payments (the US and France)

- **Visible trade balance**: differences between the values of merchandise exports and imports in billions of ecus, or net exports. The value of imports can be derived by subtracting the visible trade balance from exports. Export and import data are calculated on the FOB basis (free on board), except for German and Italian imports which use the CIF method (including carriage, insurance and freight charges).

- **Current account balance**: trade balances in goods, services and short-term financial flows in billions of ecus. A current account balance is calculated as follows: net exports of goods (visible trade or merchandise balance), plus net exports of services or 'invisibles' (the combination of which is known as the balance of trade in goods and services), plus net rent, interest, profits and dividends, plus net current transfers, such as remittances, pensions paid abroad, and aid. Net rent, interest, profits, dividends and transfers are together known as net income from abroad.

- **Ecu exchange rate**: the number of national currency units per ecu. The ecu is a 'currency basket', made up of a predetermined amount of a number of different currencies. It is the currency in which transactions of the European Monetary System are frequently administered. Its composite character as a currency substitute means that it is less volatile than the individual units, and, as a result, it is increasingly being used for commercial purposes.

- **Effective exchange rate**: nominal average exchange rates against a trade-weighted basket of currencies, presented as an index based on 1985=100. Effective exchange rates do not take account of differential rates of inflation, and are therefore not a useful guide to national competitiveness. They are, though, a valuable way of expressing the equivalent of a currency's movements against all other key currencies in one figure.

BALANCE OF PAYMENTS

Balance of payments figures for the United Kingdom are covered in more detail in the FT. Each month the CSO publishes figures showing

UK ECONOMIC INDICATORS

EXTERNAL TRADE- Indices of export and import volume (1990=100); visible balance (£m); current balance (£m); oil balance (£m); terms of trade (1990=100); official reserves (end period)

	Export volume	Import volume	Visible balance	Current balance	Oil balance	Terms of trade*	Reserves US$bn
1st qtr '92	101.7	97.1	-2,770	-2,383	+412	101.1	44.31
2nd qtr.	103.2	101.1	-3,060	-2,937	+340	102.6	45.70
3rd qtr.	103.0	101.9	-3,366	-2,081	+328	103.0	42.68
4th qtr.	105.6	103.4	-4,210	-2,566	+407	98.8	41.65
1st qtr '93	106.1	104.5	-3,595	-3,105	+415	103.8	40.90
2nd qtr.	105.2	102.0	-3,330	-3,226	+613	103.1	41.90
3rd qtr.	107.2	104.1	-3,176	-1,775	+712	104.0	43.04
4th qtr.	107.1	106.8	-3,579	-2,564	+700	103.7	42.93
April	102.8	101.3	-1,277		+201	102.5	41.66
May	104.6	100.9	-1,042		+315	103.5	41.73
June	108.1	103.8	-1,011		+ 97	103.1	41.90
July	104.9	104.2	-1,372		+274	103.5	43.32
August	110.3	100.3	- 387		+246	103.8	43.16
September	106.4	107.9	-1,417		+192	104.5	43.04
October	109.8	106.5	- 911		+228	103.5	43.55
November	104.5	104.9	-1,256		+208	104.0	43.60
December	107.0	108.9	-1,412		+264	103.6	42.93
1st qtr '94	111.6	107.6	3,069		+937	104.6	42.92
January	112.3	108.7	-1,013		+279	104.6	43.45
February	111.6	105.5	- 874		+333	102.9	43.41
March	111.0	108.7	-1,182		+325	106.3	42.92
April							43.45
May							43.46
June							43.37

Figure 9.2: UK economic indicators: external trade

how much the country imported and exported in the previous month, and consequently how much the country is in deficit or surplus with the rest of the world. These are reported in the External Trade section of the FT's weekly UK economic indicators table (see Figure 9.2).

Reading the figures

- **Export volume**: a volume index of the level of exports of goods from the United Kingdom, based on 1990=100.
- **Import volume**: a volume index of UK purchases of goods from abroad, based on 1990=100.
- **Visible balance**: also known as the (merchandise) trade balance,

this is the net balance in the value of exports and imports of goods in millions of pounds.

- **Current balance**: the balance of trade in both goods and services plus net interest, profits, dividends, rents and transfer payments flowing into the United Kingdom from countries overseas in millions of pounds.

- **Oil balance**: the balance in the value of trade in oil in millions of pounds.

- **Terms of trade**: a price index, based on 1990=100, that shows UK export prices in relation to import prices. An improvement in the terms of trade occurs when export prices rise at a faster rate than import prices.

Interpreting the information

The volume of exports is determined by the demand from overseas, which in turn depends on the state of the importing economies (their national income levels and stages of the business cycle), the price of the exports (a function of relative inflation levels and the exchange rate) and, of course, the quality of the products. In terms of value, exports are always measured FOB, at the point they leave the country.

Like export volume, import volume depends on relative prices arising from relative inflation and exchange rates, as well as the state of the UK economy. When the economy is growing, imports generally increase: this may be beneficial if it offsets domestic inflationary pressures when the economy is close to full capacity. But if the level of import penetration is high, and import prices rising, inflation may be affected adversely.

The CSO's monthly figures are mainly concerned with trade in visible items or merchandise goods. This is partly because they are generally the most reliable and the most readily available. Trade in visible items is presented both in current values and in volume terms with adjustments made for 'erratic items', such as aircraft and precious stones, that are likely to distort the underlying trend.

Visible trade is simpler to measure than invisible trade in services, and financial transactions such as transfer payments, interest payments, profits, dividends and rents. When the United Kingdom

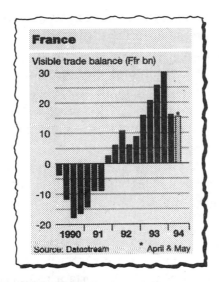

Figure 9.3: French visible trade balance

imports more visible items than it exports, a perennial national problem, it is said to have a 'trade gap'. This may be of no particular concern provided it is offset by surpluses elsewhere on the balance of payments, such as in invisible items.

The FT frequently presents charts of countries' visible trade balances (see Figure 9.3), graphically depicting the relative export performance of their companies and those of their trading partners. The newspaper also covers countries' balance of trade in oil, another item for which production and trade are highly erratic. The generally positive balance for the United Kingdom reflects the continuing production of North Sea oil.

By bringing together the balances in visible and invisible trade, and net income from abroad, the CSO provides the current account. Adding in the capital account produces a complete statement of the United Kingdom's trade and financial transactions with the rest of the world, the full balance of payments, published every quarter. By definition, for the balance of payments to balance, a deficit on the current account balance must be made up in the capital account, through net investment into the country, loans from abroad or depletion of the official reserves.

A persistent deficit on the current account puts pressure on the currency (as discussed in chapter 3). In a fixed exchange rate system, this encourages devaluation to increase the price competitiveness of exports, decrease that of imports, and bring the account back into balance; in a floating rate system, the currency will decline automatically in response to market forces. Currency movements of this kind can have a variety of effects on investors and companies involved in international trade (see below).

The terms of trade are a handy guide to the relationship between export and import prices. The fall in the terms of trade indicated by the table in the fourth quarter of 1992, was a result of the ejection of sterling from the exchange rate mechanism of the EMS. The fall in the value of the pound against the currencies of many trading partners meant that UK exports were relatively lower priced while imports were higher priced. It is important to note that an 'improvement' in the terms of trade is actually disadvantageous for many parts of the economy, since exports become more expensive and perhaps uncompetitive, and imports cheaper and perhaps more competitive with domestic goods.

Such effects on trade reveal the importance of these indicators for companies assessing the strength of foreign competition. This competition might be in the home market, in the foreign company's domestic market, or on third markets. More detailed information is required than these broad figures (notably, sectoral trade indicators), but it is nevertheless valuable to understand the overall patterns of trade. A country with rising imports might be worth exploring for new markets; one with rising exports might need to be evaluated as a source of potential competitors. All kinds of considerations of entering markets, making acquisitions, and developing competitive strategies will be affected by trade figures.

Trading partners

Countries typically have a range of trading partners, based on their import needs, the markets that demand their firms' output, geographical proximity, and historical connections. In the United Kingdom, these break down into two broad categories: countries within the European Union (EU), the United Kingdom's partners in

TRADE WITH COUNTRIES INSIDE AND OUTSIDE THE EU
Balance of payments basis (£m seasonally adjusted)

	Exports			Imports			Visible balance			Invisibles balance	Current balance
	European Union	Countries outside the EU	Whole world	European Union	Countries outside the EU	Whole world	European Union	Countries outside the EU	Whole world		
1992	60,365	46,682	107,047	64,022	56,431	120,453	-3,657	-9,749	-13,406	2,867	-10,539
1993	63,510	57,329	120,839	67,730	66,789	134,519	-4,220	-9,460	-13,680	2,799	-10,881
Q2	15,502	14,158	29,960	16,681	16,309	32,990	-1,179	-2,151	-3,330	-126	-3,456
Q3	16,188	14,441	30,629	16,924	16,881	33,805	-736	-2,440	-3,176	1,191	-1,985
Q4	15,496	15,161	30,657	17,353	16,883	34,236	-1,857	-1,722	-3,579	1,525	-2,054
1994 Q1	16,922	15,303	32,225	17,954	17,429	35,383	-1,032	-2,126	-3,158	2,402	-756
1993 Dec	5,107	5,057	10,164	5,872	5,704	11,575	-765	-647	-1,412	n/a	n/a
1994 Jan	5,684	5,065	10,749	5,928	5,848	11,776	-244	-783	-1,027	n/a	n/a
Feb	5,501	5,173	13,674	5,762	5,830	11,582	-261	-657	-918	n/a	n/a
Mar	5,737	5,065	10,802	6,264	5,751	12,015	-527	-666	-1,213	n/a	n/a
Apr	5,885	5,206	11,091	6,195	5,699	11,894	-310	-493	-803	n/a	n/a
May	n/a	5,080	n/a	n/a	5,847	n/a	n/a	-767	n/a	n/a	n/a

Source: CSO

Figure 9.4 UK trade balances

the single market; and countries outside the EU, including the United States, Japan and the Commonwealth (see Figure 9.4).

Trade balances between countries are frequently affected by barriers to trade such as tariffs and quotas. These influence companies' abilities to export their products. Export success is also influenced by the bureaucratic procedures and regulations involved in trading, as well as by trade disputes between firms' home countries and their export markets. Such disputes might be general, raising broad questions about the openness to imports of national markets, such as Japan's; or they might relate to specific sectors, such as agriculture or fisheries.

One of the powerful motivating forces of the EU's common market is to remove many of these obstacles to trade between its members, to make it very much easier for companies to sell their products (and buy inputs) in all EU countries. For example, if trade within the EU is made easier, the purchasing department for a chain of clothing shops might switch its choice of suppliers to EU manufacturers, rather than lower cost suppliers in the developing world. Taking into account the total costs of doing business, the EU clothing might become competitive, and quite possibly be of higher quality and fashion value. Easier intra-EC trade might be indicated by its increase as a proportion of total trade, though, for the United Kingdom at least, non-EU trade remains very important (see Figure 9.5).

A typical FT report on UK trade figures looks like this:

> Record trade figures and strong car production data provided further evidence yesterday that the UK economic recovery is spreading through the industrial sector. The CSO said exports to countries outside the European Union rose to record levels in the second quarter of this year, as UK companies benefitted from rising demand in the US and other economies.
>
> Exports to non-EU countries – which represent almost half of all UK trade – rose to a seasonally adjusted £15.57 billion. Imports, by contrast, fell 1 per cent, resulting in a steady reduction in Britain's trade deficit with non-EU countries. The trade deficit figures were better than the City had expected, and analysts said they showed Britain's recovery was expanding without yet sucking in large quantities of imports. (*Financial Times*, 22 July 1994)

This extract illustrates the impact of overseas markets on two key domestic economic targets, the level of national income (both as a trend and on the business cycle), and the balance of payments. Increasing

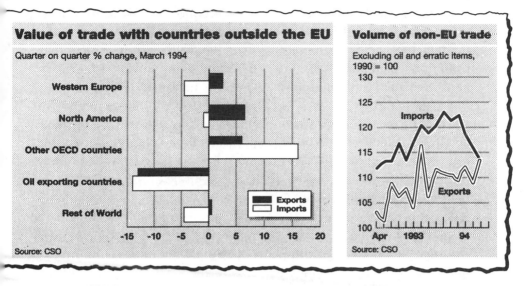

Figure 9.5: UK non-EU trade

exports, for example, will boost a recovery; they may themselves be boosted by recovery and increased demand overseas. This indicates the significance of trading patterns in the unusually unsynchronised business cycles of the industrialised countries in the recession of the early 1990s. The United States went into recession first, but, as it is first to recover, its rising demand is helping to pull the United Kingdom out of recession; in turn, the UK recovery and rising demand for EU imports might fuel recovery in France, Germany, and so on.

The extract also refers to a common pattern of the UK business cycle, that it is not sufficiently export-led and that it sucks in too many imports too soon, causing drastic trade and current account deficits in the balance of payments. These effects can ripple through the economy, affecting the extent of the recovery, the prospects for inflation, and the value of the currency. As a result, trade figures are critical indicators for investors, for companies involved in importing and exporting, and for virtually all businesses.

The service sector

Services are becoming an increasingly important part of trade in the global economy, as well as facilitating trade in physical goods. Four particularly key areas are science and technology, telecommunications, transport, and financial services. Science and technology is the fundamental factor in the recent, dynamic development of the other three: this sector is at the heart of innovation, a crucial factor in boosting future economic competitiveness and productivity.

Technological progress affects trade patterns and the comparative advantages of individual nations or whole regions in making particular products. The recent, rapid growth of telecommunications, for example, is largely due to interaction with this trend, particularly technological innovation in microelectronics. Telecommunications, in turn, spur the expansion of trade and commercial services, chiefly by facilitating contact between producers and consumers.

Similarly, transport, one of the most traditional of service sectors, provides the essential environment for the actual physical conduct of merchandise trade. Advances in transport technology, and falling freight charges, can give powerful encouragement to the expansion of international trade. Banking and financial services are also important, not solely for their links to trade, but also for the key role they play in financing development and economic growth.

From the point of view of managers in the service sector, national trade patterns are very important indicators of potential markets. For example, if a country is rapidly increasing its levels of exports and imports, it is likely there will be increasing demand for transport, telecommunication and financial services there. Similarly, growth of a service infrastructure in a developing country will encourage exporters of goods to that market: export levels are likely to increase if it is becomes easier to deal with overseas markets in terms of transport, communication and financing.

OFFICIAL RESERVES

In addition to the figures on the balance of payments, the External Trade table of the FT's UK economic indicators has a column of data for the country's official reserves:

- **Official reserves**: Treasury figures for the United Kingdom's official gold and foreign currency reserves held by the Bank of

England. The data show the total reserves in billions of US dollars at the end of the period. The decline from the second to the third quarter of 1992 is a reflection of the Bank's failed intervention in the market on and around Black Wednesday: effectively, these reserves were transferred to the speculators who were short selling the pound.

Data on official reserves act as a guide to the extent of Bank of England intervention on the foreign currency markets to support or undermine the value of the pound. It is difficult to get an exact picture of this intervention because of other Bank transactions, including new borrowing and repayment of debt by the public sector, and official transactions for government departments and foreign central banks. However, it may be assessed as an indicator of the government's intentions for the national currency, and the implications that might have for an investment portfolio or an international business.

At the end of 1993, Japan had more official reserves than any other country, including foreign exchange, Special Drawing Rights (a currency basket, made up of five currencies, in which some global transactions are made) and its reserve position at the IMF, but excluding gold. During the year, this jumped from $71 to $99 billion as Japan's current account surplus exceeded net outflows of capital. It is an indication of the effectiveness of Japanese exporting, and of the difficulties other countries' exporters face in penetrating Japanese markets. It might imply future general appreciation of the yen, making Japanese exports less competitive, and its imports more competitive. This would be advantageous to companies aiming to sell to the Japanese market, or competing with Japanese companies on third markets.

CURRENCY VALUES

Currencies are measured in terms of one another or of a trade-weighted index, a basket of currencies. The value of a currency in a trade-weighted index is assessed on a basis which gives a value appropriate to the volume of trade conducted in that currency (see Figures 9.6 and 9.7). A trade-weighted figure for sterling appears in the Inflation section of the FT's UK economic indicators, reflecting its

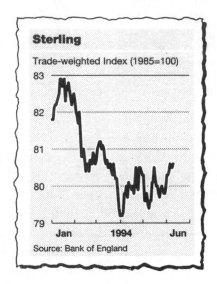

Figure 9.6: Trade-weighted sterling index

impact on national prices and competitiveness. FT figures for effective exchange rates of other leading OECD countries feature in the international economic indicators table (see Figure 9.1 above).

A trade-weighted or effective exchange rate is the best measure of the strength or weakness of a country's currency, an index of the average of all its bilateral rates weighted by the pattern of its trade with other countries. For example, trade-weighted sterling is a measure of the strength or weakness of the pound against the currencies of UK trading partners weighted by the volume of trade with each of those partners.

For a company that relies on imports of overseas goods as inputs to its production processes, or on export markets for the sale of its own output, exchange rates such as these are a valuable indication of overall relative prices. For an importer, a rise in the value of the domestic currency will be beneficial, since its imports will be cheaper; for an exporter, this will be less good news, since the prices of its exports will rise, perhaps making them uncompetitive with goods produced domestically in foreign markets or imported from elsewhere. For information on specific exchange rates between pairs of countries, and notably rates between the domestic economy and their main markets overseas, importers and exporters need more detailed data.

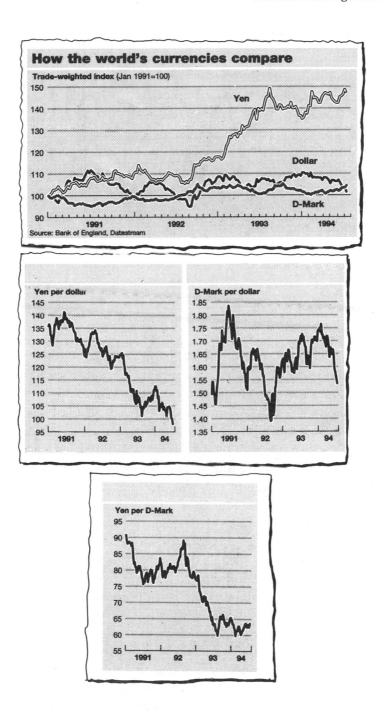

Figure 9.7: Major world currencies

Primary currencies

With actual bilateral exchange rates, the FT provides detailed information on two primary currencies in the world: the pound and the dollar. A large number of international contracts are struck in these currencies and the dollar particularly is used globally as a reserve currency. The dollar has long been the dominant currency in world trade and the United States has often been able to pay for its imports with dollars. Given that fact and the persistent twin deficits of the current account and government budget, the United States is consistently exporting dollars which then move around world markets and economies.

The other two primary currencies are the D-Mark and the yen, and the FT regularly tracks their movements against each other and against the dollar (see Figure 9.7). Half-yearly, the FT shows current and six month earlier values for sixteen currencies in terms of dollars, D-Marks and yen. The chart here tracks the past four years' movements of trade-weighted indices for the dollar, the yen and the D-Mark, as well as rates between them. It indicates the extent to which the yen has risen against the other two currencies, making Japanese exports less competitive and furthering that country's recession.

The FT's Currencies and Money page is given over largely to recording dealing rates and brief reports of trading in the foreign exchange, as well as the money markets discussed in chapter 8. The page is headed by a brief report describing the major events in the foreign exchange markets during the previous day's trading. In addition, there are more detailed descriptions of the experiences of individual major currencies, both on the previous day and over a rather longer time-span. These items generally discuss the main factors affecting exchange rates (see chapter 3).

The FT table for the primary currency exchange rates is published daily (see Figure 9.8). It is possible that by the time the rates are consulted the markets may have moved quite sharply. The rates in the newspaper cannot guarantee to be up to the minute; what they do provide is a daily record of the market's activities for reference purposes.

The table shows the reciprocal values of sixteen of the world's principal trading currencies plus the ecu, quoted in a grid displaying each currency's value in terms of the others. Monday's FT carries a further exchange rate table, covering virtually every currency of the world.

EXCHANGE CROSS RATES

Jul 18		BFr	DKr	FFr	DM	IE	L	FI	NKr	Es	Pta	SKr	SFr	£	C$	$	Y	Ecu
Belgium	(BFr)	100	19.08	16.65	4.851	2.038	4863	5.442	21.24	500.0	400.9	24.16	4.092	2.010	4.331	3.143	309.3	2.542
Denmark	(DKr)	52.42	10	8.729	2.543	1.068	2549	2.853	11.13	262.1	210.2	12.66	2.145	1.053	2.270	1.648	162.1	1.333
France	(FFr)	60.05	11.46	10	2.913	1.224	2921	3.268	12.76	300.3	240.8	14.51	2.457	1.207	2.601	1.888	185.7	1.527
Germany	(DM)	20.61	3.932	3.432	1	0.420	1002	1.122	4.379	103.1	82.64	4.979	0.843	0.414	0.893	0.648	63.75	0.524
Ireland	(IE)	49.07	9.362	8.172	2.381	1	2387	2.671	10.42	245.4	196.7	11.85	2.008	0.986	2.125	1.542	151.8	1.248
Italy	(L)	2.056	0.392	0.342	0.100	0.042	100.	0.112	0.437	10.28	8.244	0.497	0.084	0.041	0.089	0.065	6.360	0.052
Netherlands	(FI)	18.38	3.506	3.060	0.891	0.374	393.6	1	3.903	91.88	73.67	4.439	0.752	0.369	0.796	0.578	56.83	0.467
Norway	(NKr)	47.08	8.981	7.839	2.284	0.959	2289	2.562	10	235.4	188.7	11.37	1.926	0.946	2.039	1.480	145.6	1.197
Portugal	(Es)	20.00	3.816	3.330	0.970	0.408	972.7	1.088	4.248	100.	80.18	4.331	0.818	0.402	0.866	0.629	61.86	0.508
Spain	(Pta)	24.94	4.758	4.153	1.210	0.508	1213	1.357	5.298	124.7	100.	6.025	1.021	0.501	1.080	0.784	77.14	0.634
Sweden	(SKr)	41.40	7.898	6.894	2.008	0.844	2013	2.253	8.794	207.0	166.0	10	1.694	0.832	1.793	1.301	128.0	1.052
Switzerland	(SFr)	24.44	4.663	4.070	1.186	0.498	1189	1.330	5.192	122.2	97.99	5.304	1	0.491	1.058	0.768	75.59	0.621
UK	(£)	49.76	9.493	8.266	2.414	1.014	2420	2.708	10.57	248.8	199.5	12.02	2.036	1	2.155	1.564	153.9	1.265
Canada	(C$)	23.09	4.405	3.845	1.120	0.471	1123	1.257	4.905	115.5	92.58	5.578	0.945	0.464	1	0.726	71.42	0.587
US	($)	31.82	6.070	5.298	1.543	0.648	1547	1.731	6.758	159.1	127.6	7.685	1.302	0.639	1.378	1	98.40	0.809
Japan	(Y)	323.3	61.68	53.84	15.69	6.589	15724	17.60	68.68	1617	1296	78.10	13.23	6.498	14.00	10.16	1000.	8.220
Ecu		39.34	7.504	6.550	1.908	0.802	1913	2.141	8.356	196.7	157.7	9.502	1.609	0.791	1.704	1.236	121.7	1

Yen per 1,000; Danish Kroner, French Franc, Norwegian Kroner, and Swedish Kroner per 10; Belgian Franc, Escudo, Lira and Peseta per 100.

Figure 9.8: Exchange cross rates

Their values are shown in terms of four key currencies: sterling, the dollar, the D-Mark and the yen. The rates given are usually the average of the latest buying and selling rates. Many of these currencies are pretty obscure in terms of their role outside their countries of origin; many of them are fixed against the dollar or tied to important international or regional currencies; and many of them are very strictly controlled by the local monetary authorities, and are not openly dealt on world foreign exchange markets.

One last daily table headed 'Other currencies' gives sterling and dollar buy and sell rates for a handful of second-rank currencies in which some sort of free market exists or which are politically sensitive. In some of these cases, there may be a considerably higher degree of official exchange rate control than with front rank currencies. Any or all of these of these data will, of course, be immensely important to any company or investor trying to do business in or with these countries.

Currency transactions

Business in the international currency markets is conducted twenty-four hours a day by telex, telephone and computer screen. As the London markets close in the evening, business is handed over to New York, which overlaps with Tokyo for a couple of hours each afternoon. Thus, there are no official closing rates in these international markets. The FT takes a representative sample of rates from major participants in the London markets at around 5 p.m. local time each trading day.

The currency markets are particularly influenced by interest rates. Exchange rates are in part determined by the relative rates across countries. If these change, by one country perhaps raising its rates, deposits in that country will become more attractive. To make the deposits, its currency will be bought and others sold, pushing up its price in terms of the other currencies. The higher value of a country's currency might also make its stocks and bonds more attractive to investors, relative to other international assets.

On the other hand, a higher currency value makes exports more expensive, weakening the country's competitive position and potentially reducing exporters' profits. This may lead to equity price

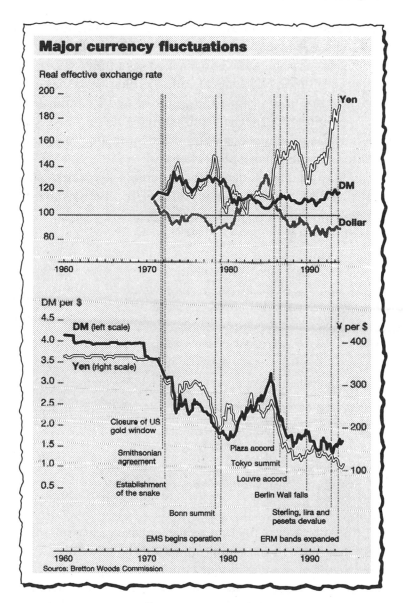

Figure 9.9: Major currency fluctuations

declines. At the same time, a strengthening currency is less attractive to foreign investors, since outlays are higher and returns lower. This may be counterbalanced if the currency is strengthening as a result of very favourable economic conditions, which will overcome the potential effects of higher export prices. For example, a strong yen has rarely prevented Japanese companies from continuing to sell their products effectively in overseas markets.

The rates are frequently used by exporters and importers striking contracts in more than one currency at an agreed published rate. Businesses also frequently need to hedge against currency risk. For example, a UK business with significant dollar income might sell dollars forward at a particular rate. This protects it against the pound weakening (though it also means gains from it strengthening would be missed), but more importantly makes the exchange rate predictable for that company to aid planning.

Currency fluctuations

Since 1973 and the start of the period of global floating exchange rates, there have frequently been dramatic fluctuations between the major currencies of the world. The EU has limited this through its own system of fixed rates (see below and chapter 3), but there have remained serious fluctuations between the big three (see Figure 9.9).

- **Real effective exchange rate**: these are relative costs or prices expressed in a common currency, measures of overall national competitiveness. The lower the index, the more competitive the country.

- **D-Marks and yen per dollar**: the patterns of these currencies' exchange rates against each other, and how they have been influenced by major political and economic developments.

The fall of a country's currency is potentially good news for its companies: if they are exporting, their relative prices are more competitive; if they are competing with imports on domestic markets, likewise. However, if currencies are fluctuating, it is very hard to be able to predict and to take advantage of those price changes. Similarly, if a currency repeatedly and continually declines against others, business planning is made difficult. It may suggest fundamental weaknesses in the domestic economy, particularly in the form of high inflation, discouraging new capital investment in production of output to compete with imports.

Business managers must carefully track the fortunes of the currencies in which they do business. They should also pay close attention

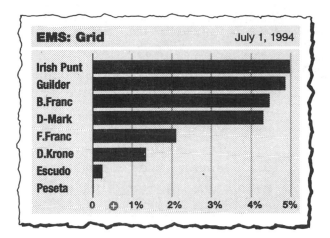

Figure 9.10: EMS grid

to pronouncements by politicians on the way they would like to see
their currency go. For example, at a time of a dramatically weakening
dollar in the middle of 1994, the US Treasury secretary, Lloyd
Bentsen, tried to 'talk it up': 'we believe a stronger dollar is better for
our economy and better for the world's economy. The dollar is not a
tool of our trade policy.' This was an attempt to convince financial
markets that the US government did not regard yen appreciation
against the dollar as a way of opening Japanese markets to imports.
Such statements have unpredictable effects on currency values.

EMS, EMU and ERM

Of particular interest to the many companies doing business within
the European Union are the relationships between the currencies of
its twelve countries and their prospects for economic and monetary
union (EMU) in a single currency (see chapter 2 for details). The state
of the exchange rate mechanism (ERM) of the EMS is published in
grid form on the front page of Monday's FT (see Figure 9.10).

- **EMS grid**: the member currencies of the ERM measured against
  the weakest currency in the system. The currencies are in descending order of relative strength. Most of the currencies can fluctuate

EMS EUROPEAN CURRENCY UNIT RATES

Jul 18	Ecu cen. rates	Rate against Ecu	Change on day	% +/- from cen. rate	% spread v weakest	Div. ind.
Netherlands	2.19672	2.14758	−0.00249	−2.24	4.97	-
Belgium	40.2123	39.4663	−0.0532	−1.86	4.57	14
Germany	1.94964	1.91482	−0.00275	−1.79	4.49	-
Ireland	0.808628	0.803842	+0.002458	−0.59	3.24	4
France	6.53883	6.57431	−0.00559	0.54	2.07	−5
Denmark	7.43679	7.53017	−0.00759	1.26	1.35	−9
Portugal	192.854	197.291	−0.125	2.30	0.32	−15
Spain	154.250	158.300	−0.061	2.63	0.00	−18
NON ERM MEMBERS						
Greece	264.513	289.637	−0.396	9.50	−6.28	−
Italy	1793.19	1920.61	+12.83	7.11	−4.18	−
UK	0.786749	0.793615	+0.002618	0.87	1.74	−

Ecu central rates set by the European Commission. Currencies are in descending relative strength. Percentage changes are for Ecu; a positive change denotes a weak currency. Divergence shows the ratio between two spreads: the percentage difference between the actual market and Ecu central rates for a currency, and the maximum permitted percentage deviation of the currency's market rate from its Ecu central rate.
(17/9/92) Sterling and Italian Lira suspended from ERM. Adjustment calculated by the Financial Times.

Figure 9.11: EMS European currency unit rates

within 15 per cent of agreed central rates against the other members of the mechanism. The exceptions are the D-Mark and the Dutch guilder which move in a narrow 2.25 per cent band.

The daily FT Currencies and Money page includes a further table of figures for the EMS, particularly in relation to the ecu (see Figure 9.11). The value of the ecu is calculated as a weighted average of a basket of specified amounts of EU currencies.

- **Ecu central rates**: the basic rates of national currencies against the ecu around which they may fluctuate. These rates are set by the European Commission. As with the EMS grid, the currencies are in descending order of relative strength.

- **Rate against ecu and change on day**: the current market rates of the national currencies against the ecu, and the changes in those rates from the day's starting rates.

- **Percentage deviation from the central rate**: percentages by which the current market rates are above or below the central rates. The percentage differences are for the ecu against the national currencies: a positive difference indicates that the currency has weakened against the ecu.

- **Percentage spread over the weakest currencies**: percentages by which currencies are spread against the weakest currency in the system, numerical equivalents of the graphic display of the EMS grid.

- **Divergence index**: ratios between two spreads, the percentage deviation of actual market rates from ecu central rates, and the maximum permitted percentage deviation of currencies' market rates from their ecu central rates. This is an indicator of how close to their new permitted floors currencies have fallen. In this example, since the Dutch and German currencies are tied closer together than the rest, there is no divergence index for the D-Mark.

- **Non-ERM members**: the Italian and UK currencies have still not sought re-entry to the ERM and the Greek currency has never been involved as yet, but for the purpose of tracking convergence between all countries of the EU, the FT calculates their currency rates against the ecu.

The performance of the currencies of the twelve EU members, and the pronouncements of European politicians on the prospects for EMU are of vital importance to all investors and companies in these countries. A single currency will remove at a stroke all uncertainties about foreign exchange, making European investment, exports and imports much easier. Some companies have already moved in this direction to some extent by arranging many of their sale and purchase contracts in ecus. For them, movements of the EMS and of the ecu against their domestic currencies must be watched carefully. Hence the prominence given to them in the FT's international economic indicators table and in the weekly front page chart of the EMS.

Part III

FORECASTING AND POLICY

10

GOVERNMENTS AND GLOBAL ORGANISATIONS

As the previous chapters should have made clear, the huge quantity of economic data reported by the *Financial Times* is not intended to be simply a historical record of national, regional and global economies. That is certainly part of their function, but, much more importantly, these economic indicators are a basis for approaching the future. In revealing the current state of the economy, they provide foundations for forecasting its future progress, an essential activity for governments, company managers and investors alike. It is through forecasts, which can be very simple or quite complex, that these parties are able to make the policy decisions that may lead to the achievement of their individual goals.

Economic forecasts derive from models. These might be models of overall developments in the aggregate national or global economy: such models can be used to forecast shifts in demand across different markets, growth in total world trade, or changes in inflation, interest rates, or unemployment. Or they might be models of parts of the economy: disaggregated forecasts may relate to developments in particular industrial sectors or regions of the world; while even more specific forecasts may relate to a single product or the reactions of a key business competitor to certain business decisions. In each case, forecasting is of great importance in setting economic policies (or business and/or investment strategies) within the context of a clearly defined view of the present and likely future developments.

Basic approaches to forecasting simply extrapolate the past; they are merely a way of articulating present indications. More sophisticated models attempt to understand the source of past changes and build it into their forecasts. This requires a detailed knowledge of economic history and economic principles, though, even then, fore-casting is by no means an exact science. But, while the accuracy of economists' predictions is frequently a target of jokes about the pro-fession, forecasting remains an essential pursuit. As conducted at its most general level, by national governments and by global organisa-tions on behalf of groups of countries, it drives all aspects of their economic policy.

GOVERNMENT FORECASTS

Government forecasts are primarily concerned with forecasting the movement over time of key macroeconomic variables: output, infla-tion, unemployment, interest rates, and so on. They derive from large-scale macroeconomic models of the economy, and are usually produced every three to six months. In the United Kingdom, for example, the Treasury produces a central forecast at the time of its annual budget in November, which is then published again in revised form six months later (see Figure 10.1). In this case, the chart shows key elements of the Treasury's 1994 summer forecast: the govern-ment's expectations for the growth of gross domestic product (GDP), the percentage of money GDP taken up by taxation (with and with-out North Sea oil taxes), and the rate of retail price index inflation excluding mortgage interest payments.

Treasury forecasts also cover the public sector borrowing require-ment (PSBR), the balance of payments, and the levels of employment and unemployment. Developed within the context of the outlook for the world economy, they include each component of the economy that contributes to overall growth: retail sales, manufacturing output, changes in consumer spending in response to tax changes, disposable income growth and the personal savings ratio, car registrations, the housing market, investment in the corporate sector, the visible and current account balances, and so on. For a manager or investor, one of these indicators might be enough of a hint as to an appropriate strategy; for governments, all influences on demand must be consid-ered in formulating policy.

FT writer Samuel Brittan's reflections on this particular forecast are an interesting observation on the practice of forecasting: 'The

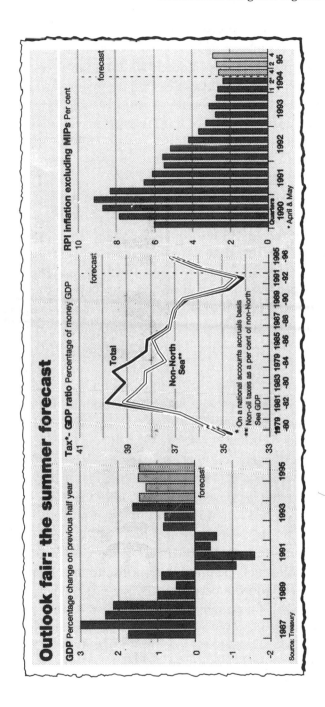

Figure 10.1: Treasury forecasts

golden rule for economic forecasters is: forecast what has already happened and stay at the cautious end. The British Treasury's summer economic forecast obeys both these rules: like other forecasts it tells us more about the present and the recent past than about the future.' Even models as detailed as that of the Treasury are more systems of managing information than accurate representations of real economies. Thus, while they can be expected to describe the present reasonably accurately, they cannot be relied upon to forecast the future and get it right.

Nevertheless, government forecasts are very much tied to the levers of economic policy, as well as the government's underlying beliefs about the way the economy works. And there can often be conflict between the ideas on which forecasts and policy are based. For example, in this case, the government's fiscal policy doctrine is that the budget should balance and that demand cannot be managed by spending more or taxing less. These beliefs appear to be in contradiction to the ideas implied by the forecast and driven by its underlying model.

Central banks

A country's monetary authorities also typically produce an economic forecast, though it is not always published. The United Kingdom's Bank of England, for example, is currently barred from publishing its full forecast in case it clashes with that of the Treasury. However, as explained in chapters 2 and 7, it does publish a quarterly inflation report with its prognostications on current and future inflationary pressures. The considerably more independent Federal Reserve ('the Fed') in the United States presents a twice-yearly report to the US Congress containing its economic projections (see Figure 10.2).

This table features the Fed's predictions for percentage changes in nominal US GDP, real GDP, and the consumer price index, plus the average level of the civilian unemployment rate. These indicators reflect the Fed's central goals of low inflation and robust growth, policy targets over which it has considerable control relative to the US government, through its management of interest rates. Often accompanying the projections are detailed rationale for the Fed's monetary policy as well as comments on the financial markets.

The Fed's economic projections		
	1994	1995
Percentage change:		
Nominal GDP	5.50 - 6.00	5.00 - 5.50
Real GDP	3.00 - 3.25	2.50 - 2.75
Consumer price index	2.75 - 3.00	2.75 - 3.50
Average level:		
Civilian unemployment rate	6.00 - 6.25	6.00 - 6.25

Figure 10.2: Federal Reserve forecasts

Central bank forecasts may well derive from models of the economy that are a little biased towards the levers of monetary policy,
those over which the banks hold most sway. Such forecasts are sometimes criticised for being based on a view of the economy that focuses
on a symptom (inflation) of poor economic performance, rather than
deeper structural weaknesses, and that relies on monetary policy
alone as a cure.

ECONOMIC POLICY

Treasury and central bank forecasts represent governments' views of
the future. In conjunction with their stated economic goals, these
form the basis for the planning and execution of economic policy.
For example, the essence of the present UK government's ambitions
can be encapsulated in the phrases 'a low tax, low inflation economy', and 'free markets, free trade, and free enterprise'. The
macroeconomic means by which it pursues these goals are monetary,
fiscal and exchange rate policy, while the actual levers used to intervene in the economy are interest rates and decisions on taxation and
public spending (see chapter 2). These policies can have as important
implications for the private sector as the forecasts.

The budget and short-term economic forecasting are intimately
related, forming a central plank of overall economic policy. The
macroeconomic task of the budget is to get the level of the PSBR
right: firstly, in terms of its effects on demand (will reduced taxes or
increased spending boost demand and output?); and secondly, in

terms of its effects on real interest rates (will an excessive debt ratio raise rates, 'crowding out' private investment?). The two sets of effects are closely linked: a high PSBR might tempt the government to tolerate high inflation to erode the real value of the debt, but it also might restrict the government's ability to use fiscal policy in a recession, making it difficult for taxes to be pushed lower or spending higher.

Monetary and exchange rate policy relate more to inflation and international competitiveness. They too are intimately related in that interest rates, the primary tool of both, can be used to target either the money supply or the exchange rate, but not both. From a manager's point of view, both goals are important, one in terms of the rate and predictability of inflation, the other in terms of the level and predictability of the exchange rate. An acceptable balance of inflation, interest and exchange rates may be pursued through a policy such as participation in the exchange rate mechanism (ERM), but this can easily come unstuck (see chapter 3).

On the supply side of the economy, government policy can have direct effects on corporate and investor behaviour. For example, in the product markets, competition and regulatory policy, through government departments and such institutions of market regulation as the UK Monopolies and Mergers Commission and the Securities and Investments Board, can be important in the provision of a stable business environment and the improvement of industrial performance. In the labour markets, tax incentives, education and training, and a host of other policies might boost productivity and competitiveness.

Credibility and the political business cycle

Economic policy is typically put together with a set of national objectives in mind: low inflation, full employment, no new taxes, and so on. Certainly, these goals are the slogans by which governments get themselves elected, or otherwise. For example, since 1979, the UK Conservatives have found that they can win elections by focusing on tax and inflation, and without a great deal of concern for unemployment. Elections have been won and lost on the basis of actual or distorted economics, such as the 'Labour's tax bombshell' claim of the 1992 campaign.

But elections are also won and lost over the government's perceived management of the economy and its actual delivery on election pledges. The 1992 Clinton campaign's frequent reminder to itself, 'it's the economy, stupid', for example, was a reflection of public perceptions of the failure of the Bush administration to ameliorate the recession, and the breaking of its promise not to raise taxes. Failure to deliver is often a result of politicians omitting to explain how difficult the fulfilment of economic ambitions might be when they are campaigning for office. This is most conspicuously the case in the former communist states where the fruits of market economic success will not be immediately shared by a large section of the population, as a result of which they may hanker for the old days.

Government economic credibility can also be strained when its policies are blown apart by events, as happened to the UK government with sterling's exit from the ERM in late 1992 (see chapter 3). In this case, the government's primary objective was low inflation, and the means by which was pursued, exchange rate policy through the ERM. Although inflation targets became the focus of different means (see chapter 2) and relatively low inflation maintained, Black Wednesday saw a sharp collapse in public confidence in the government's ability to handle the economy, a loss of credibility that is extremely damaging to its re-election prospects.

The importance of the economy to the electoral process has led to what is called the political business cycle, as governments attempt to achieve favourable economic circumstances at election time. For example, in engineering a boom before an election they might set the business cycle in motion, so that expansionary policies to boost incomes, reduce unemployment and maintain power, must be followed by contractionary policies to limit inflation. For the present UK government, lower taxes and continuing low interest rates might be the preferred option, but these could cause longer term problems for the PSBR and inflation. Electoral success also requires the elusive 'feel good' factor, and, most importantly, restoration of government credibility.

Credibility extends importantly to business and financial market confidence in the government's ability to achieve its objectives. For example, in the United Kingdom, Treasury forecasts are often criticised for being as much an expression of what the government would like to see happen, as what they expect to happen; they are sometimes seen to be more akin to some companies' annual budgets, incorporating desirable rather than necessarily achievable targets. There is an element here of using forecasts as means to the goal, perhaps trying to talk inflation down. Nevertheless, the Treasury's forecasting record in the late 1980s boom and the early 1990s recession is poor. In particular, it is often more optimistic of inflationary prospects than the City, something managers and investors should bear in mind.

WORLD ECONOMIC INSTITUTIONS

A number of international forums exist to discuss global economic issues, and the FT reports on most of their activities. One of the main ones is the Group of Seven (G7), a grouping that dates back to 1975 when French president, Valèry Giscard d'Estaing invited the leaders of the United States, West Germany, Japan and the United Kingdom to discuss economic problems following the first oil price shock. Since then, the summits have grown to include political and foreign issues: these form the subject of a political declaration issued on the penultimate day of talks. The sixth and seventh members are Italy and Canada. Since the disintegration of the Soviet Union, Russia has also participated in some of the discussions.

The OECD has been referred to repeatedly in previous chapters as the umbrella group for most of the countries for which the FT provides detailed economic data. Sometimes referred to as the 'rich countries' club', this organisation's membership consists of the twenty-five industrialised nations of the world, with Mexico being the most recent new member. The OECD goes back to the end of the war when it was set up as the Organisation for European Economic Cooperation to organise US aid to Europe's recovery; it took on its present form in 1960, promoting economic cooperation between industrial economies.

The OECD is a particularly valuable source of publications and forecasts. Its annual surveys of the member countries and twice yearly *Economic Outlook* provide a useful overview of prospects for the industrialised world. Affiliated to it are the International Energy Agency, and centres for advising former communist economies and research on economic development. The June 1994 annual meeting of the organisation raised the prospect of South Korea becoming a member by the end of 1996. It also prepared the way for negotiations with the Czech Republic, Hungary, Poland and Slovakia, for a policy dialogue with Russia, and the possible entry further down the line of other 'dynamic non-member economies'. Next in the queue are Chile, Argentina, Brazil and China.

An organisation that has received a substantial amount of FT coverage is the European Bank for Reconstruction and Development (EBRD). This is a development bank set up in 1990 to help the countries of eastern Europe develop market economies. A European Union initiative, it resembles existing multinational regional development banks, such as the African Development Bank, and was the first institution specifically designed to coordinate western economic help for eastern Europe in the wake of the collapse of its communist regimes.

EU states and institutions have a 53.7 per cent stake in the EBRD; most other European countries are also shareholders and the United States has the biggest single stake of 10 per cent. Japan's 8.5 per cent shareholding matches those of the United Kingdom, Germany, France and Italy.

The Bretton Woods twins

1994 marked the fiftieth anniversary of the conference at Bretton Woods that created the framework for post-war international economic relations. In particular, that conference saw the founding of two powerful institutions, the International Monetary Fund (IMF) and the World Bank. The IMF was established to encourage international cooperation on monetary issues. Its primary purpose is to tide members over temporary balance of payments difficulties, which it does by making them hard currency loans while trying to enforce structural adjustment of their economies.

The Fund has more than 140 members who pay subscriptions according to the size of their economies. They pay 75 per cent of the quota in their own currency and 25 per cent in international reserve assets. Members are then given borrowing rights with the Fund which they can use to help finance a balance of payments deficit. Countries in difficulty can also negotiate standby credit on which they can draw as necessary. Members are required to repay their drawings over a three to five year period.

The IMF's Bretton Woods twin is the World Bank, established at the same time, and originally intended to finance Europe's post-war reconstruction. This institution has subsequently concentrated on loans to poor countries to become one of the largest single sources of development aid. The Bank has traditionally supported a wide range of long-term investments, including infrastructure projects such as roads, telecommunications and electricity supply. The World Bank's funds come mainly from the industrialised nations, but it also raises money on international capital markets. The Bank operates according to business principles, lending at commercial rates of interest only to those governments it feels are capable of servicing and repaying their debts.

Discussions surrounding the fiftieth anniversary of the Bank and the IMF particularly focused on the former's future role. In the light of the increased international availability of investment capital (see chapter 3), the Bank intends to put more emphasis on advice to client governments and less on lending, acting as a catalyst and facilitator of private sector investment in the developing world and the ex-communist countries.

GLOBAL FORECASTING

Every six months the IMF publishes its *World Economic Outlook*, forecasting developments in world output and trade for the next two to three years (see Figure 10.3). The outlook also covers inflation in consumer prices in groups of countries. The IMF forecasts divide the world into three groups of countries: industrialised, developing, and the former communist states in transition to market-based economies. Each group faces different sets of problems, and in recent IMF forecasts, quite contrasting immediate futures. For example, in this case, 1995 growth in world output is forecast at 3.7 per cent, but breaks down into 2.6 per cent for the industrial countries, 5.8 per cent for those in the developing world, and only 1.4 per cent for the countries in transition.

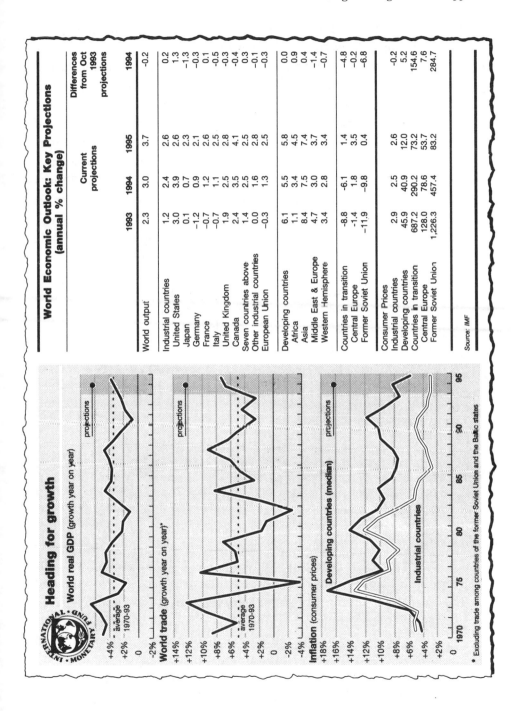

World Economic Outlook: Key Projections
(annual % change)

	Current projections			Differences from Oct 1993 projections
	1993	1994	1995	1994
World output	2.3	3.0	3.7	-0.2
Industrial countries	1.2	2.4	2.6	0.2
United States	3.0	3.9	2.6	1.3
Japan	0.1	0.7	2.3	-1.3
Germany	-1.2	0.9	2.1	-0.3
France	-0.7	1.2	2.6	0.1
Italy	-0.7	1.1	2.5	-0.5
United Kingdom	1.9	2.5	2.8	-0.3
Canada	2.4	3.5	4.1	-0.4
Seven countries above	1.4	2.5	2.5	0.3
Other industrial countries	0.0	1.6	2.8	-0.1
European Union	-0.3	1.3	2.5	-0.3
Developing countries	6.1	5.5	5.8	0.0
Africa	1.1	3.4	4.5	0.9
Asia	8.4	7.5	7.4	0.4
Middle East & Europe	4.7	3.0	3.7	-1.4
Western Hemisphere	3.4	2.8	3.4	-0.7
Countries in transition	-8.8	-6.1	1.4	-4.8
Central Europe	-1.4	1.8	3.5	-0.2
Former Soviet Union	-11.9	-9.8	0.4	-6.8
Consumer Prices				
Industrial countries	2.9	2.5	2.6	-0.2
Developing countries	45.9	40.9	12.0	5.2
Countries in transition	687.2	290.2	73.2	154.6
Central Europe	128.0	78.6	53.7	7.6
Former Soviet Union	1,226.3	457.4	83.2	284.7

Source: IMF

Heading for growth

World real GDP (growth year on year)
+4%
+2%
0
-2%
average 1970-93
projections

World trade (growth year on year)*
+14%
+12%
+10%
+8%
+6%
+4%
+2%
0
-2%
-4%
average 1970-93
projections

Inflation (consumer prices)
+18%
+16%
+14%
+12%
+10%
+8%
+6%
+4%
+2%
0
Developing countries (median)
Industrial countries
projections

1970   75   80   85   90   95

* Excluding trade among countries of the former Soviet Union and the Baltic states

Figure 10.3: IMF forecasts

The IMF has definite views on the right strategies for economic growth and development. Invariably, or at least over the most recent recession, it urges all countries to work hard to stay competitive and participate in the economic revival. Within that context, however, it dispenses very varied advice. In the developed world, for example, open markets, especially in Japan, are seen as fundamental, as is the use of periods of economic expansion to reduce budget deficits and push through fundamental labour market reforms. The IMF also believes that the continuing US structural budget deficit impedes business investment, job creation, future growth and improvement of the country's trade deficit.

The developing nations are divided into two camps by IMF analysis: the fast-growing and successful majority built on macroeconomic stability, good governance, market-oriented policies and dynamic mutual trade; and the laggards which suffer high and variable inflation, overvalued currencies, excessive fiscal deficits and import controls, and the lack of a stable environment for economic decision-making. The latter are closer to a number of the transition states, which have pursued expansionary fiscal and monetary policies at times of large output declines. These policies have fueled hyperinflation and the flight of domestic capital, as well as deterring foreign investment.

Despite the presently bleak position of most of the countries in transition and some of the developing countries, most recent IMF forecasts have been encouraging about the future. However, the accuracy of its forecasting does not have quite such a positive record. Like many government forecasts, the institution often has a tendency to try to talk up a recovery. This may have beneficial short-term effects, but longer term, can damage the credibility of its forecasts. Certainly, investors and managers using the forecasts should treat them with a degree of caution.

The OECD too produces regular forecasts for its members (see Figure 10.4). For example, the June 1994 report forecasts growth across all OECD member countries of 2.6 per cent in 1994, followed by 2.9 per cent in 1995, and 2.6 per cent again in 1996. The forecasts also include projections for world trade, inflation, unemployment, budget deficits, current account balances, and national debts as a proportion of nominal GDP.

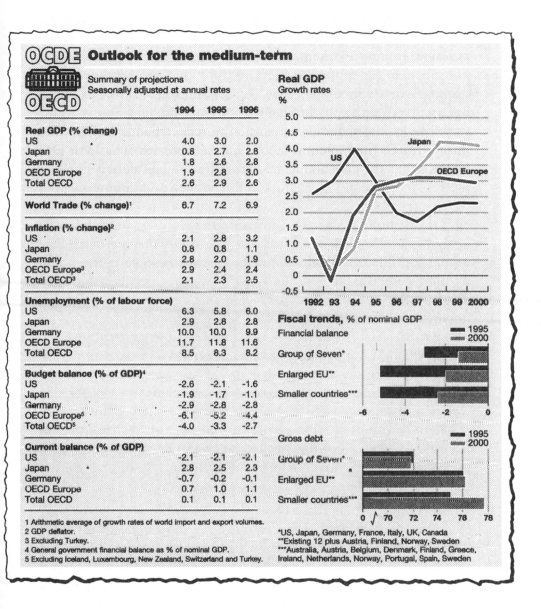

OCDE Outlook for the medium-term

OECD

Summary of projections
Seasonally adjusted at annual rates

	1994	1995	1996
Real GDP (% change)			
US	4.0	3.0	2.0
Japan	0.8	2.7	2.8
Germany	1.8	2.6	2.8
OECD Europe	1.9	2.8	3.0
Total OECD	2.6	2.9	2.6
World Trade (% change)[1]	6.7	7.2	6.9
Inflation (% change)[2]			
US	2.1	2.8	3.2
Japan	0.8	0.8	1.1
Germany	2.8	2.0	1.9
OECD Europe[3]	2.9	2.4	2.4
Total OECD[3]	2.1	2.3	2.5
Unemployment (% of labour force)			
US	6.3	5.8	6.0
Japan	2.9	2.8	2.8
Germany	10.0	10.0	9.9
OECD Europe	11.7	11.8	11.6
Total OECD	8.5	8.3	8.2
Budget balance (% of GDP)[4]			
US	-2.6	-2.1	-1.6
Japan	-1.9	-1.7	-1.1
Germany	-2.9	-2.8	-2.8
OECD Europe[5]	-6.1	-5.2	-4.4
Total OECD[5]	-4.0	-3.3	-2.7
Current balance (% of GDP)			
US	-2.1	-2.1	-2.1
Japan	2.8	2.5	2.3
Germany	-0.7	-0.2	-0.1
OECD Europe	0.7	1.0	1.1
Total OECD	0.1	0.1	0.1

1 Arithmetic average of growth rates of world import and export volumes.
2 GDP deflator.
3 Excluding Turkey.
4 General government financial balance as % of nominal GDP.
5 Excluding Iceland, Luxembourg, New Zealand, Switzerland and Turkey.

Real GDP
Growth rates
%

Fiscal trends, % of nominal GDP
Financial balance
Group of Seven*
Enlarged EU**
Smaller countries***

Gross debt
Group of Seven*
Enlarged EU**
Smaller countries***

*US, Japan, Germany, France, Italy, UK, Canada
**Existing 12 plus Austria, Finland, Norway, Sweden
***Australia, Austria, Belgium, Denmark, Finland, Greece, Ireland, Netherlands, Norway, Portugal, Spain, Sweden

Figure 10.4: OECD forecasts

In the 1960s and 1970s, the OECD dominated the market for international macroeconomic forecasting, though it is now in competition with a number of often equally inaccurate private sector forecasters.

But the organisation is not just a forecaster; it also produces valuable comparable economic and social statistics, covering, for example, education, labour markets, taxes and welfare reform from a global perspective. Many of these are used in policy, further encouraging the collection of good comparable data. The OECD is also one of the few places where senior government officials can talk openly about economic issues of mutual interest. Its annual meeting involves the finance, foreign and trade ministers of each of its member countries.

International economic policy

Global organisations such as the OECD and the G7 are important institutions for the encouragement of international economic policy coordination. Indeed, as the following FT extract suggests, this is one of their key functions:

> The principal purpose of international economic institutions is to reconcile the politics of nation states with their international interests and obligations. With this in mind, the international economic regime of the future should ideally cover five areas; monetary and financial stability; economic development; trade and investment; the environment; and migration. In each case, the aim should be to try to minimise government and maximise the play of the market. This is not just a question of ideology. It is a practical matter. The capacity to cooperate is limited. It should be hoarded just like any other globally scarce resource. (*Financial Times*, 26 July 1994)

One short-term issue that frequently requires policy coordination is relative exchange rate shifts driven by the financial markets. For example, the rapid depreciation of the dollar in the summer of 1994 could have been as damaging to growth in Europe and Japan (where competitiveness would have been endangered), as to the United States itself, where the threat to growth arose from falling bond and share prices in response to expected interest rate rises. In such circumstances, concerted intervention by monetary authorities in both appreciating and depreciating currency countries, should be able to retrieve some governmental powers from the financial markets. But the authorities have to be prepared to intervene multilaterally and massively, not half-heartedly in such a way as to give speculators hope of even greater gains.

Longer term, governments almost certainly need to coordinate policy on such issues as environment and migration. In addition, they should probably compare notes on the pressing problem of unemployment, as suggested in the 1994 OECD *Jobs Study*. This research reports that, over the past two decades, Europe has experienced weak employment growth but high productivity, while the United States has succeeded in creating large numbers of jobs, but that most are low skilled and low productivity. Neither is a desirable pattern of job creation, a situation the study ascribes to a long-running failure to adapt labour markets, education and training to changes in the world economy, such as globalisation and the spread of new technologies.

Neither the pace of technological change nor imports from relatively low wage countries are to blame, the study argues, but high unemployment can only be tackled by restoring the capacity of economies and societies to adapt to change. Primarily addressing governments, but with important implications for businesses and investors, the study specifically recommends: enhancing the creation and diffusion of technological know-how; increasing working time flexibility; nurturing an entrepreneurial climate; increasing wage and labour cost flexibility; reforming employment security provision; expanding and enhancing labour market policies; improving labour force skills; and reforming unemployment and related benefit systems.

11

MANAGERS, INVESTORS AND ACADEMICS

In addition to the 'official' economic forecasts prepared by governments and supranational organisations, there are a range of forecasts published by private sector bodies. In the United Kingdom, many of these are produced by the independent and generally non-profit sector: university departments, such as London Business School's (LBS) Centre for Economic Forecasting (CEF); research institutes, such as the National Institute for Economic and Social Research (NIESR); and specialist forecasting companies like Oxford Economic Forecasting (OEF).

There are also forecasts by the research departments of large financial institutions like Goldman Sachs; and from the broader business community, both at the level of the individual corporation like Shell, and of corporate organisations like the Confederation of British Industry (CBI). The balance of forecasts, in terms of their sources, varies across countries. For example, in the United States, almost all macroeconomic models are commercial, while in the United Kingdom, the leading models are based at academic institutions.

INDEPENDENT ECONOMIC MODELS

Official forecasts of the UK economy are made by using the macroeconomic models of the Treasury and the Bank of England. Four more academic models are indirectly supported by the government, through the Warwick University-based Macroeconomic Modelling Consortium of the Economic and Social Research Council (ESRC). These are the models at LBS, NIESR, Strathclyde University and the

National Institute forecast

	Real GDP†		Manu.	UK Economy Job-		▼Ex-	Curr		World Economy Real	Cons	World
	Total	Non-oil	output	less♠	RPI▼	m'gage	bal♣	PSBR♦	GNP*	prices*Trade★	
1993	1.9	1.6	1.8	2.8	1.5	2.7	-11	46	1.0	2.9	3.9
1994	2.9	2.6	2.5	2.7	3.3	2.9	-12	35	2.2	2.4	6.3
1995	2.6	2.6	3.2	2.6	3.9	3.4	-15	27	2.4	3.0	5.4

*All figures are percentage change, year on year, except where stated. †Average measure; ♠ millions, fourth quarter; ▼ fourth quarter; ♣ £bn; ♦ Fiscal year, £bn; * OECD countries percentage change, year on year, ★ Volume*

Figure 11.1: National Institute forecasts

Warwick Bureau itself. For example, the NIESR global econometric model (GEM) produces quarterly forecasts of key variables in the UK economy (real gross domestic product (GDP), manufacturing output, unemployment, inflation, the current account balance and the public sector borrowing requirement) as well as output, inflation and trade in the world economy (see Figure 11.1).

Other independent macroeconomic models that produce forecasts include three university-based ones which have had their ESRC funding withdrawn: the Cambridge Economic Policy Group (CEPG), City University Business School, and Liverpool University. In addition there are private sector offshoots of academic forecasts, also generally considered to be more reliable and more independent than official forecasts: OEF, Cambridge Econometrics (derived from the Cambridge Growth Project), and the Henley Centre. The equivalents in the United States are Data Resources Inc. (DRI) and WEFA, spun off from the University of Pennsylvania's Wharton School, the pioneer of macroeconomic modelling and forecasting.

These models are all based on the kinds of information discussed in chapters 5 to 9: the main economic indicators, such as the rates of unemployment and inflation; survey data, such as the CBI distributive trades survey; trade data, such as the figures for car sales produced by the Society of Motor Manufacturers and Traders; and market data, such as interest and exchange rates, and equity market indices.

Macroeconomic models and forecasts are to some extent dependent on the macroeconomic theory and related political ideology that drive them. For example, monetarist models like the Liverpool model typically have fewer equations than Keynesian models: they are based on a view of the economy with rather simpler relationships, such as the money supply being the direct and exclusive determinant of inflation (see chapter 2). They are related to new classical models, the main propositions of which are that economic agents behave as if they know the correct model of the economy, and that markets normally clear without surpluses or shortages.

Models are frequently used to analyse the outcome of various alternative government economic policy choices. As a consequence, at least in the United Kingdom, forecasters do not produce their output solely for the sake of making accurate predictions, but often as a means to convey their policy analysis and recommendations. Typically, any forecaster who is fundamentally critical of policy will produce forecasts with less favourable outcomes than official forecasts.

At the same time, despite differences in models and forecasts, no forecaster operates in a vacuum, and all are influenced by the others. Indeed, this is sometimes a source of criticism of UK academic forecasts, where more iconoclastic models have had their funding withdrawn, and the outcomes of funded ones can bear close resemblance to official forecasts. Of course, if the official and funded academic forecasts were consistently accurate, no one could complain.

Gurus in government

Following the ejection of sterling from the exchange rate mechanism (ERM) in the summer of 1992, with Treasury credibility at an all-time low, the UK government decided to co-opt a number of distinguished forecasters into an advisory role. The Treasury's panel of independent forecasters consists of Andrew Britton from NIESR, Tim Congdon of City firm Lombard Street Research, David Currie of the CEF at LBS, Gavyn Davies of Goldman Sachs, Wynne Godley of King's College, Cambridge and the CEPG, and Patrick Minford of Liverpool University and Cardiff Business School. An original member who has subsequently left to work with David Currie is Andrew Sentance, then of the CBI.

The panel publishes a regular report on the British economy, in which its members' sometimes very different forecasts are averaged.

The Treasury also regularly surveys thirty-two independent forecasts and presents the consensus. This form of forecasting has been criticised as the substitution of crystal ball gazing for thought: the Treasury uses the panel to show how its predictions on output and inflation are near to or slightly more pessimistic than the average of the independents. In practice, this is of little use since when the forecasters have made the most harmful errors, they have erred together. Aiming to match the consensus is not a policy, unless it is designed to show that panel forecasts are as fallible as those of the government.

Such undermining of the 'guru' status and authority of the panel is furthered by their press labelling as 'wise men'. But, despite such comment, the lack of economic policy expertise in government frequently leads to the use of scholars and semi-scholars from economics departments, schools of government, management consultants and financial institutions in some kind of advisory role. The position of gurus in government ranges from the formalisation of the economist's job in the US government's Council of Economic Advisers; through the quasi-autonomous and now extinct National Economic Development Office (NEDO), an agency set up in the 1960s to analyse the reasons for the United Kingdom's relatively poor economic performance, and to encourage dialogue and cooperation between employers, the government and trade unions; to the freelance (and usually free market) economic troubleshooters, bringing 'ideas from within the walls of North American universities' to beleaguered governments across eastern Europe and the former Soviet Union.

FINANCIAL MARKETS

Macroeconomic forecasts are not confined to the academic world, though that is certainly where modelling can be conducted free of the constraint of producing quick and usable data on a regular basis. In the City of London, for example, forecasts are required to be done 'early and often'. A relatively short-term outlook is normally the limit of their aspirations (what will happen to interest rates within the next month?), but decision-makers in financial institutions understandably demand rapid output that is directly relevant to their immediate problems.

Much of the output of financial market models is naturally closely guarded in the hope that it may bring advantage to its owners and their clients. But, at the same time, City economists like to maintain a public profile for marketing purposes, and are often called upon by the media to give their opinion on the latest macroeconomic developments. Their interpretations of inflation data, for example, may give some clues as to how the financial markets will react, though more often than not, they are explaining why the markets have already reacted as they did. Invariably, too, there are disagreements about what various indicators mean, depending on different underlying beliefs about the economy, and whether the firm is taking an optimistic or pessimistic view of the markets.

Each month *The Economist* newspaper polls a group of City forecasters and calculates the average of their predictions for real GDP growth, consumer price inflation and current account balances in fifteen countries. The institutions involved are BZW, EIU, Goldman Sachs, Hoare Govett, James Capel, Kredietbank, Lehman Brothers, Long-term Credit Bank, Merrill Lynch, JP Morgan, Morgan Stanley, Nomura, Nordbanken, Paribas, Royal Bank of Canada, Salomon Brothers, Scotiabank, UBS, and SG Warburg. In addition, once a quarter, *The Economist* publishes consensus forecasts of exchange rates based on polls of twenty to thirty banks and blue chip companies. These predict averages and ranges for the dollar for three, six and twelve months ahead against the yen, D-Mark, franc, lira, pound, Canadian dollar, peseta, Australian dollar, Swedish krona and Swiss franc.

Investment strategy

Forecasting is a key task in financial institutions because of the profound effects economic developments can have on potential profits. And while leading economic indicators might provide a hint as to what the economic future holds, such forecasts are unconditional: they do not anticipate what the additional effects of powerful economic agents like government policy and the financial markets themselves might be. To try to get ahead of the competition, companies will aim to model more accurately, and with more consideration of possible discontinuities in the markets, such as the collapse of the ERM or substantial changes in tax policy.

But financial institutions also use other types of models, microeconomic theories of investment decision-making such as option pricing, and techniques of forecasting asset price movements such as technical analysis. Indeed, these models are at the heart of financial market behaviour. Fundamental analysis, in which investors study the performance of a company and its place in the overall economy, is just one among many means of trying to achieve superior returns on investments. Financial forecasters use all kinds of methods of predicting the future, ranging from examining the patterns of past share price movements to the exploration of market inefficiencies.

In contrast to macroeconomic modelling, in financial economics, the relationship between theory and data is very close. Financial data are easily obtainable, very precise and correspond directly to the theoretical concepts. As a result, theory is of great practical relevance: if it does not fit the facts, it is rapidly discarded; if it does, it might find itself sweeping the dealing rooms. Fischer Black and Myron Scholes' option pricing formula, for example, was first published as a recondite piece of theory, but within a few years became standard apparatus in every financial institution that deals in derivatives.

BUSINESS FORECASTS

Like financial market forecasting, business forecasts can be divided into general assessments of the national or global macroeconomy, and specific microeconomic forecasts related to markets in which a company is active. Published macroeconomic forecasts typically come from industry organisations such as the CBI, the Society of Business Economists, or, in the United States, the Conference Board, which has a closely followed index of consumer confidence. A forecast that is widely followed in the United Kingdom is one published by the Item (Independent Treasury Modelling Group) Club, the only private sector UK forecast to use the Treasury model (see Figure 11.2).

An extract from the FT interprets the club's forecast for growth in UK GDP and underlying inflation, the rate that excludes mortgage interest payments:

> The Treasury's upbeat forecast for the economy, published last week, is today described as 'complacent' by a research group, the Ernst & Young

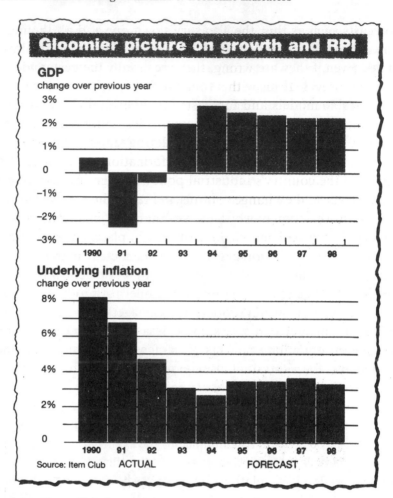

Figure 11.2: Item Club forecasts

Item Club. The Item Club predicts that next year inflation will be higher, and growth lower, than the Treasury expects. The club's summer report says: 'The key risk facing growth prospects in the UK is a loss of confidence in the private sector. The threat is not so much the large tax increases but the impact of the steepest three-month rise in bond yields since earlier this century.' The rise in bond yields signals 'a substantial deterioration in inflation expectations' according to the report. 'If the financial markets are right about inflation, as a result of a commodity price shock or a smaller amount of slack in the economy than thought, then the economy could be in a problem in the pre-election years of 1996-97.' (*Financial Times*, 4 July 1994)

Forecasts such as this, the Treasury's own one and all the independent forecasts are widely used, if widely disparaged, in business circles. Even if they are wrong, they are usually the best guides available, and provide firms with a framework for their planning exercises. Comparable models and forecasts for other national and regional economies are also essential for companies doing business internationally. For example, when considering entering new overseas markets, multinationals need basic information on the overall economy, and the country's industrial policy, foreign investment policy, foreign trade and exchange controls and tax regime, as well as indications of the direction in which each of these is going.

Once the macroeconomic forecasts are in place, companies require detailed analysis and forecasting of the particular markets in which they are operating. For this purpose, they will often employ econometricians to track information in the relevant product and labour markets, and to interpret it for senior managers. For example, corporate economists might use survey data from market research to estimate the quantitative effects of changes in price and other factors on demand for a product. Regression analysis, forecasting techniques, and microeconomic theory will all play a role (see chapter 1).

Forecasting models of particular product markets are often excellent ways of assembling and storing market information. Even when their output bears little resemblance to the eventual outcomes in reality, they enable company managers to assess their current position, to understand complex relationships, to impose coherence and consistency on their thinking, and to evaluate forecast errors in order to learn from their mistakes.

Corporate strategy

The demand for forecasts in business is driven by the need to make forward commitments. Companies investing in new factories need to be sure that their increased output will be in demand; and companies contemplating significant changes in their products' prices need to be able to predict the reactions of their competitors. Forecasts of required inputs of labour and capital are essential elements of all management decisions, from corporate level planning to departmental budgeting. And while a company can assemble a huge volume of information about itself and its environment, it needs to be able to organise it effectively as a basis for planning and the formulation of corporate strategy.

A widely used planning technique, associated with Shell, is that of scenario planning. This approach develops a model of the business environment, as a means of forecasting the future of the business and how it might be influenced by internal and external developments, such as changes in input prices, or in the level of economic growth. Alternative scenarios can be built into the model, allowing the company to assess how it might react to a variety of potential outcomes. Such models might simulate a business unit, the whole company or a whole economy, as with the large macroeconomic models; and relationships between variables may be estimated statistically or econometrically from extended time series of data (see chapter 4).

Sophisticated planning procedures of this kind enable firms to take account of expectations of economic growth, likely developments in their markets, and the effects the implementation of their plans might themselves have on markets and economies. For example, a business might use the best estimates of key variables (inflation, interest rates and demand) from macroeconomic models to construct a scenario in which it appears advisable to go ahead with a new investment. But it must also build in sensitivity analysis, assessing the degree of riskiness, to what extent small shifts away from favourable conditions might make them highly unfavourable.

Corporate planning of this kind is widespread. As William Keegan writes in his book *The Spectre of Capitalism*, 'there is no doubt that the typical capitalist corporation looks many years ahead, and is continually responding to market forces and trying to develop new products and new markets.' This may have a threatening side from the point of view of the customer facing monopoly or oligopoly power (see chapter 1): in *The New Industrial State*, John Kenneth Galbraith writes 'high technology and heavy capital use cannot be subordinate to the ebb and flow of market demand. They require planning; it is the essence of planning that public behaviour be made predictable, that it be subject to control'; and Keegan adds 'It is the natural desire of any primitive capitalist to make a buyer's market into a seller's market'.

INDEX

Africa 40–1, 50, 56–7, 70
  African Development Bank 197
  see also individual countries
aggregates, principle of 63
agriculture 104, 112(and check before not in), 113, 118
aid 49–51, 55–60
  see also developing countries, FDI
Argentina 50, 197
ASEAN (Association of South-East Asian Nations) 50–1
Asia 40–1, 56–7, 59, 60, 70
  see also individual countries
asset valuation
  efficient market hypothesis 160
Australia 208
Austria 55

balance of payments *def* 29, 47, 56, 85, 164, *165*, 166–74, 176, 197
  current account balance *165*, 166, *def 167*, 168, 205
  forecasts 190, 200
  statistics 70, 164, *165*, 166–9, *167*
  visible account *167*, 167–9, *169*, 190
  see also trade balances *under* trade
Bank of England 54
  forecasts 192, 204
  and foreign currency reserves 174–5
  and inflation 38, 136–7, 137, 192
  and interest rates 32, 148, 156
  and money supply 31–3, 144–5, 150
  open market operations *def* 31, 150
  statistics 38, 137, 144–5, 150, 192
Bank of England Quarterly Bulletin 68
banks, central 34, 48, 150, 192–3, 193
  independence of 37–8
  see also Bank of England
banks, commercial 144, *144*
  deposits 6, 19, 31–2, 143, 147–50
  and foreign exchange 47
  interest rates 155
  lending 31, 33, 145, 150
  statistics 67, 145, 147
Baring Securities 60
BCC (British Chamber of Commerce) 69, 107
benefits *see* social security and benefits
Bentsen, Lloyd 183
Black, Fisher 209
black economy 79, 89
'Black Monday' 163
'Black Wednesday' 38, 48, 53–4, 175, 195
Blue Book (CSO) 67, 78
bonds 6, 10, 18, 30, *def* 147, 156, *157*, 158, 180
  and employment 71, 112
  and inflation 71, 152, 156
  and interest rates 20, 147–9, 153–4, 156–8, 162, 202
  'junk bonds' 158
booms 25–7, 30, 79, 153, 195
  indicators 116
borrowing
  consumer 24, 35
  corporate 154, 156, 160
  government 28, 30–1, 53, 96
  indicators 145
  see also interest rates, PSBR
'bottlenecks' *see* supply constraints
brand loyalties 6, 15
Brazil 50, 197
Bretton Woods conference (1944) 197–8
British Bankers Association 145
British Retail Consortium 110
Brittan, Samuel 27, 190, 192
Britten, Andrew 206
'broad money' *def* 143, 147
Brunei 50
budgets 28, 30–4, 69, 92–4, 192
  budget balance 28, *def* 29
  deficits 30–4, 36, 200
  and demand 33–4, 36–7, 92–4

building societies 6, 144, *144*, 145
Bundesbank 131, 151–2
Bush, President 195
business confidence indices 120
business cycles 21, 25–8, *def* 26, 63, 79, 84, 103, 111, 153, 168, 172
  cyclical effects *def* 30, 84–6, 156
  government management of 30, 32–3, 79, 85
  indicators 63, 106, 111–12, 118–20
BZW 208

'call money' 32
Cambridge Econometrics 205
Canada 41, 196, 208
capital goods and investment 8, 10, 27, 77, 87, 96, 97, 105–6, 108, 211
  see also under companies
capital growth 7, 78, 154
capital markets 3, 18–20, 39, 48–50, 49, 58, 164, 198
Cardiff Business School 206
CBI (Confederation of British Industry) 69, 107–11, 204–5, 209
CDs (Certificates of Deposit) *146*, 147
CEF (Centre for Economic Forecasting) 204, 206
CEPG (Cambridge Economic Policy Group) 205–6
Chartered Institute of Purchasing and Supply 119
Chile 197
China 56, 197
City University Business School 205
Clinton, President 195
commodities 39, *122*, 127
  prices 18, 126–9, *127*
Commonwealth 172
companies 3, 7–11, 20, 64–5, 84, 182–3
  capital 8, 21, 23, 28, 75, 117
  forecasts 209–12
  statistics 67
  takeover bids 159–60
  see also multinational corporations
competitiveness, national 70, 137–42, *138*, 200
  determinants and indicators 87, 121, 137–9, *138*, 140–1, 194
Conference Board 209
Congdon, Tim 206
consumer confidence 85, 109, 116, 119
consumer goods 13, 85, 96, 97, 106, 111, 120, 122
consumption 3–7, *def* 4, 22–4, 26, 30, 76, 77, 83, 84–7, 96, 109–10, 115–16, 190
  determinants and indicators 4, 23–4, 24, 121, 145, 148
  see also demand
'contracting' economy *def* 79
costs *see under* employment, production
credit 23, 32, 120, 144, *144*, 145, 150, 153–8, 197–8
  statistics 143, *154*
  see also debt, interest
CSO (Central Statistical Office) 67–8, 78, 96–7, 105, 107, 118–21, 132–4, 166–9, 172
  Family Expenditure Survey 133–4
currency markets 18–19, 39–40, 46–8, 50–5, 147, 158, 180
  exchange rates 45–50, 164–85, *165–6*, *181*, 182–3
  determinants 47–8, 170, 173, 178, 180, 200
  fixed 43, 52, 170, 182
  forecasts 18, 208, 211
  impact 47–8, 111, 129, 156–7, 176, 180–2, 194, 202
  management 29, 31, 52, 193–4, 211
  statistics 67, *138*, 139–40, 140–2, 175–83, **176–7**, *179*, *181*, 182, *183*, 205
  reserves 47–8, 54
Currie, David 206
customs unions 50
Czech Republic 55, 197

debt 29, 40, 57, 175, 194
  national debt *def* 29, 55, 200
  see also credit, interest
demand 4–6, 16, 22, 35, 75, 85–8, 126, 212
  determinants 5, 11–12, 17–18, 95, 100, 116, 156, 193–4
  growth of 19–20, 23–4, 26, 28, 82, 98, 100, 108, 117, 120, 129
  indicators 85, 109, 129
  management of 30, 36–7, 85, 192

statistics 83, 87, 162–3, 189
see also consumption, supply constraints
demography 35, 81, 116
Department of the Environment 98
depressions 25–6, 33, 79
deregulation 17–18
developing countries 40, 44, 55–60, 57, 174, 198
'sustainable development' 58
see also aid, FDI
discounting 16, 20, 111, 160
discount houses 31–2, 148
'dissaving' *def* 24
dividends 7, 78, 84, 87, 149, 154, 159–60, 168
DoE (Department of Employment) 68, 70, 113–15
DRI (Data Resources Inc) 205
DTI (Department of Trade and Industry) 68
Dun and Bradstreet 120

Eastern Europe 40–1, 56, 58, 195, 197
EBRD (European Bank for Reconstruction and Development) 197
EC *see* EMS, EMU, ERM, EU, Maastricht Treaty
econometrics *def* 62
Economic Outlook (OECD) 70, 196
Economic Trends (CSO) 67
economies of scale and scope 9
Economist, The 71, 208
Intelligence Unit 208
'Ecowas' (Economic Community of West African States) 50
ecu *165*, 166, *def* 166, 184–5
education and training 27, 57, 90, 107, 116, 118, 125, 194, 203
emerging markets 48–9, 59, 59–60
employment 3, 16–18, 21–3, 27, 34–5, 54, 67, 70–1, 75, 86, *102*, 103, 112–18, *def* 116, 118, 164, 203, 205
costs 17–18, 59, 126, *138*, 139–40, 140, *141*, 142
determinants 8, 12, 23, 27–8, 32, 34–5, 95–6, 100, 116, 194, 200
forecasts 190, 192, 200, 205, 211
government management of 28, 37, 95–6
indicators 107, 112–16
international 40, 43, 55, 112–13, *113–114*, 117
regional unemployment *115*, 115–16
statistics 40, 70–1, 101, 103, 112–18
see also migration, wages
Employment Gazette (DoE) 68
EMS (European Monetary System) 51–2, 52, 129, 131, 141, 170, *183*, 183–4, *184*, 185
'EMS grid' *183*, 184–5
EMU (European Monetary Union) 50, 54–5, 183, 185
environment 57–8, 203
equity markets 7, 10, 18–20, 30, 59, 60, 153, 158–63, 180–1, 205
'blue chip' shares 163
interest 19–20, 153–8, 156, 162, 202
international 145–9, *146*
prices 65, 67, 120, 154, 158–9, *159*, 202
determinants 162–3, 163, 180–1
statistics 65, 67, *146*, 147–8
see also bonds, dividends, investment
ERM (Exchange Rate Mechanism) 38, 52–4, 185, 194–5, 206, 208
ESRC (Economic and Social Research Council) 204–5
EU (European Union) 41, 51–2, 55, 59, 60, 197, 202
monetary policy 38, 40, 141, 183–4
statistics 66–7, 68
trade 40, 44, 50–4, 51, 170, *171*, 172
see also EMU, EMS, ERM, Maastricht
Eurobonds 18
Eurostat 89
exchange rates *see under* currency markets
expectations 23, 31, 48, 120, 136–7, 160, 202
expenditure 22, 24, 75, 78
see also GDP *and under governments*
exports 41, 56, 68, 84, 119, 170
determinants 98, 111, 140, 172, 176, 180, 182, 185
impact 22, 26, 47, 108, 173
statistics *76*, 77–8, *83*, 87–8, 166–7, 167, *167–8*

'factor incomes' *def* 82
FDI (Foreign Direct Investment) 24–5, *25*, 45–6, 49, 51, 56, 58, 69
see also aid, developing countries
financial markets *see* money markets
Financial Statement and *Budget Report* (Treasury) 68
Financial Statistics (CSO) 67
Financial Times 26, 40, 50–1, 59, 60, 63–5, 69, 79–80, 150–1, *151*, 156, 183, *183*–4, 189, 202, 209–10
Balance of Payments *figures* 166–74, *167*, *169*, *171*, *175*
bonds *157*, *157*
Commodities and Agriculture page 127–9
Currencies and Money page *178*, *179*, 184–5
Economic Diary 66–7
FT-Actuaries world index 147–8

Gross Domestic Product table 82–9, *83*
International Economic Indicators 145–9, *146*, 164, *165*, 166, 176
Prices and Competitiveness table 137–42, *138*
Money and Finance tables 145, *146*, 147–9
National Accounts Table 75–89, 76, 84
Other Currencies table 180
producer prices chart *131*, 131
'PSBR by sector' table *94*, 95
Purchasing Index *119*
share prices 158–9, *159*, *161*, 161–2, 162
UK Economic Indicators table 103–12, *104*, 174–6
Financial section 143–5, *144*
Inflation section 121–4?, *122*, 175–6
Output section 96, 96–100
UK Government Expenditure and Revenue table 90, 91–2
Financial Times Guide to Using the Financial Pages 6, 10, 161
Financial Trade check 68
Finland 55
fiscal policy 28, 30, 36–7, 51, 54–6, 79, 95, 163, 192–4, 200
see also taxation
foreign exchange *see under* currency markets
France 41, 53–4, 75, 101, 147, 159, 164, *165*, 173, 197, 208
statistics 70, 103
unemployment 113, *114*
free trade 50, 58, 113
futures and options markets 18–20, 128

Galbraith, JK 212
GATT (General Agreement on Tariffs and Trade) 50–1
Uruguay Round (1986–93) 45, 51
GDP (Gross Domestic Product) *def* 22, 23–4, 55–6, 67, 75, 75–8, *83*, 97–8, 99, 101, 109
GDP-I 78, 82–90, 97–8
GDP-A 78, 88, 97–8
GDP-E 78, 84, 88–9, 97–8
GDP-O 78, 88, 97–8
growth in 79–80, *80*, 82
indicators 120
models and forecasts 190, *191*, 192, 205, 208–10, *210*
multiplier 22–4
nominal 80, 84, *def* 87, 112, 200
see also GDP-E
real 80–1, *81*, 81–2
statistics 70, *def* 77, 82–9, *83*
world 42
Germany 41, 52–4, 75, 78, *131*, 131, 139, 145, *146*, 147, *152*, 152, 157, 159, 166, 173, 196–7, 208
currency *177*, 178, 180, 182, *183*, 184–5
statistics 70, 101, *102*, 103
G7 (Group of Seven) 41, 196, 202
gilts *see* bonds
Giscard d'Estaing, Valéry 196
GNP (Gross National Product) 78
Godley, Wynne 206
Goldman Sachs 204, 208
'Goodhart's Law' 152
governments 26, 28–33, 49, 84, 96, 125, 163, 194–6, 202, 208
borrowing 10, 30–1, 53, 149–50, 197
consumption 24, 28, 75, 77, *83*, 84–5
debt 90, 92
expenditure 84–5, 90, 91–2
forecasts, models and statistics 67, 190–2, *191*, 200, 206–7
and foreign exchange 47, 49, 52
international co-ordination 39–40, 49, 202–3
involvement levels 32, 34, 36–8
revenue 90, 91–2
social policy 29–30, 34, 67, 118
spending 22, 26, 29–31, 36, 84–5, 90, 91–2, 95, 175, 193
see also political influence *and under business cycles money supply*
Greece 185
growth 6, 25–9, 82, 163
determinants 26–8, 95–6, 190, 200
and environment 58
'export-led growth' 56, 173
international 40, *42*, 200
statistics 77, 192, 200

Henley Centre 205
HMSO (Her Majesty's Stationery Office) 68
Hoare Govett 208
Holland 54, *183*, 184–5
housing 77, 96, 99–100, 103, 118, 120, 145, 155
forecasts 190
human development index 89–90
Hungary 55, 197

IBB (Invest in Britain Bureau) *25*, 69
IEA (International Energy Agency) 196

IFC (International Finance Corporation) 59, 60
ILO (International Labour Office) 114
IMF (International Monetary Fund) 40, 57, 89, 120, 175, 197–8, 199, 200
  forecasts 200
  statistics 69–70
imports 40
  determinants 85, 113, 170, 176, 182, 185
  impact 26, 85, 129, 168, 173
  statistics 22, 78, 80, 83, 88, 166, 167, 167–8
income, national 75, 78, 82–90
  circular flow of 21–5, 84
  see also GDP
India 56
Indonesia 50
industry see production
inflation 21, 43, 89, 93, 132, 134–5, 164, 166, 194–6, 212
  adjustments 25, 77, 81, 105
  determinants 23–4, 26, 31–2, 37, 85, 112, 116, 136–7, 156, 173, 200, 206
  forecasts 190, 192, 200, 205
  and foreign exchange 47, 55
  impacts 34, 53, 119–20, 132, 163
  indicators 11, 71, 108, 112, 121–4, 122, 128–9, 129, 131, 140–1, 145, 148, 150–3, 153, 175–6, 192–3
    see also RPI
  management of 30, 34, 36–8, 38, 56, 85, 195
  statistics 63, 67–8, 175–6
  and unemployment 34–5, 116
infrastructure investment 56, 57, 77, 198
interest rates 7, 18–20, 57, 205, 212
  determinants of 19, 26, 84, 131, 153
  and foreign exchange 47–8, 48, 52–4, 55
  government 29, 32, 149
  impact 19–20, 23–4, 32, 54, 71, 99–100, 108, 112, 120, 134, 154–8, 180, 194–5, 202
  indicators 145, 148, 156–7
  and inflation 37–8, 54, 153
  management of 32, 38, 150, 194
  and shares 19–20, 153–8, 202
  statistics 67, 77–9, 143, 145, 146, 147, 168
International Bank for Reconstruction and Development 49
International Development Association 49
International Finance Corporation 49
International Financial Statistics (IMF) 69
investment 6–7, 10, 22, 24, 30, 84, 86–7, 100, 107, 126, 128
  determinants 10–11, 19–20, 24, 34, 85, 87, 96, 107–8, 120–1, 170, 200
  equity markets 158, 160, 162–3
  forecasts 190, 208–9
  government 28, 49, 84
  'hurdle rate' 10–11
  impact 26, 129
  indicators 86, 99, 148
  international 43, 46, 48–50, 59, 76–8, 77, 170, 181–2, 185, 198, 203, 211
    see also FDI
  'payback technique' 11
  statistics 67, 69, 75, 77, 84, 86–7, 107, 132
investment see also infrastructure investment
Italy 41, 53, 75, 76, 101, 139, 147, 166, 196–7, 208
  currency 185
  statistics 70, 103
Item Club 209–10, 210

James Capel 208
Japan 23, 41, 44, 51, 66–7, 70, 75, 76, 78, 101, 103, 139, 141, 145, 146, 147, 157, 159, 172, 175, 196 7, 200, 202, 208
  currency 177, 178, 180, 182–3
JP Morgan 208

Keegan, William 212
Keynes, JM 32–3, 36
Kredietbank 208

labour see employment
land 21, 23, 77
  see also housing, rents
Latin America 40–1, 50, 56–7, 59, 60
  statistics 70
LBS (London Business School) 204
Lehman Brothers 208
LFS (Labour Force Survey) 114
LIBOR (London Interbank Offer Rate) 147–8
Liverpool University 205–6
Lombard Street Research 206
Long-Term Credit Bank 208

Mo-4 indicators see under money supply

Maastricht Treaty (1991) 52, 54
Malaysia 50
manufacturing industry see production
markets 11–18, 28, 50–5, 82, 113, 174, 200, 206
  see also capital markets, currency markets, emerging markets, equity markets, futures and options markets, money markets, OTC, product markets
'Mercosur' 50
Merrill Lynch 208
Mexico 40–1, 196
Middle East 59, 60
migration 58, 81, 116, 203
Minford, Patrick 206
'misery index' def 35
M4 (money supply, and under FT too) 145
monetarism 34, 36–8
monetary policy 28, 30–1, 32, 37, 51, 54 poss bef, 79, 112, 150, 163, 192–3
money markets 12–13, 18–20, 30–1, 39, 45–50, 65, 70, 88, 104, 112, 143–63, 178, 207–9
  see also capital markets, currency markets, money markets, money supply 35, 37, 79, 103, 143–63, 206
  control of 31–4, 150
  and inflation 37, 136–7, 151–3
  Mo indicator 143, 144, 145, 152–3, 153
  M1 indicator 143, 144, 146, 147
  M2 indicator 143, 144, 146, 147
  M3 indicator 146, 147, 151, 152, 152
  M4 indicator 143, 144, 146, 147
  and 'money multiplier' 31
  statistics 143–5, 146, 147, 149–53, 152
monopolies 14, 16
Monopolies and Mergers Commission 194
monopsonies 14
Monthly Digest of Statistics (CSO) 68
Morgan Stanley 208
mortgages 38, 134, 136, 154, 155
motor trade 14, 15, 111, 120, 190, 205
multinational corporations 39, 59, 89, 115–16, 117, 142
multipliers see under GDP, money supply

NAFTA (North American Free Trade Agreement) 41, 50–1
national debt see under debt
National Insurance 84
  see also social security, taxation
NEDO (National economic Development Office) 207
NICs (Newly-Industrialised Countries) 41, 56
NIESR (National Institute for Economic and Scoial Research) 204–5, 205
NIESR (National Institute for Economic and Social Research) 206
Nigeria 50
NNP (Net National Product) 78
Nomuta 208
Nordbanken 208
Norway 55

ODA (Oversaeas Development Assistance) see aid
OECD (Organisation for Economic Cooperation and Development) 26, 40–1, 72, 75, 89, 103, 117, 120, 145, 164, 176, 202
  economic indicators 66–7
  forecasts 196–7, 200–2, 201
  Jobs Study 203
  statistics 70, 101
OEF (Oxford Economic Forecasting) 204–5
oil sector 43, 105, 162, 167, 168–9, 190
OPEC (Organisation of Petroleum Exporting Countries) 41
'optimism index' 120
OTC (over-the-counter) markets 19
output 9, 24 and bef, 26, 28, 35, 37, 78, 120, 164
  and GDP 21–3, 75
  indicators 145, 148
  and monetary policy 150
  statistics 40, 67, 96, 96-100, 198, 205
    see also GDP

Paraguay 50
Paribas 208
peaks def 26, 63, 80
pensions 7, 78–9
personal disposable income see under wages
Philippines 50
'Phillips curve' 35
Pink Book (CSO) 68
Poland 55, 197
political influence 36–8, 43–4, 70–1, 195–6, 202–3, 205–7
  'political business cycle' 195
population see demography
Portugal 52

price 8, 16, 23, 28, 34–5, 121–42, 170
    determinants 8–9, 11–16, 24, 28, 111, 129
    forecasts 192
    impact 5, 11–12, 94, 121, 131
    statistics 70, 77, 111, 121–3, 122, 126–37, 130, 137–42, 138, 139–40
    see also discounts, inflation and under commodities
privatisation 29, 68
production 4–5, 24, 70, 78, 87, 101–11, 102, 103–8, 104, 118–20, 119,
    119, 190, 198, 205, 211
    costs 8–9, 9 poss bef, 14–15, 46, 122, 131–2, 140
    and employment
        statistics 101, 102, 103–6
    factors of see land, labour, capital
    statistics 69, 101, 102, 103–11, 104, 105
productivity 27–8, 28, 140, 163
    capacity def 23, 26, 85–6, 107–8, 108, def 108
product markets 3, 13–16
profits 8, 13–14, 20, 23–4, 84–5, 87, 128, 159, 168
protectionism 44, 113
PSBR (Public Sector Borrowing Requirement) 29, 36, 67, 94, 95–6, 190,
    193–5, 205
PSDR (Public Service Debt Repayment) 29

quotas 172

recessions 25–6, 26, 30, 53–4, def 79, 85–6, 95, 106, 111, 145, 153, 194–5
recovery 6, 28, 82, 85–6, 95, 99, 103, 106, 120, 132, 145, 152–4
    consumer-led def 84
    determinants 172–3
    indicators 115–16
Red Book (Treasury) see Financial Statement and Budget Report 68
regression analysis 62–3, 211
rents 23, 77–8, 87, 133, 168
reserves 90, 91, 169, 174–5
retail sector 86, 101, 102, 103, 104, 107–11, 109, 120, 124, 129, 131–2,
    145, 155, 190
Royal Bank of Canada 208
RPI (Retail Price Index) 68, 121–2, 128, 132, 133, 134, 136
    forecasts 190
    RPIX 134
    RPIY 136, 152–3
Russia 40–1, 58, 196–7

Salomon Brothers 208
savings, personal 4, 22–4, def 24, 26
    determinants 23, 121, 132
    and investment 6, 10, 24
scenario planning 212
Scholes, Myron 209
Scotiabank 208
SDRs (Special Drawing Rights) 175
seasonality 63–5, 64, 99–100, 110, 117
sectoral analysis 87, 96, 97, 107–8, 110, 110, 111, 170
    see also oil sector, retail sector
securities 18–20, 30
    see also bonds, shares, Treasury bills
Securities and Investments Board 194
service sector 45, 51, 56, 58, 64, 68, 70, 89, 97–8, 104, 107, 109, 112,
    164, 168, 173–4
shares see equity markets
Shell 204, 212
Singapore 50
Slovakia 55, 197
slumps see depressions
social security and benefits 17, 78–9, 113–15, 203
    'claimant count' 113–14
Society of Business Economists 209
Society of Motor Manufacturers and Traders 205
South Korea 197
Spain 52, 208
speculators 46–7, 48, 54, 126, 128–9, 175
SS Warburg 208
'stagflation' 35
statistics 66, 66–72
    see also under individual subjects
sterling 122, 123, 129, 175–6, 176, 208
    value indices 121
'structural deficit' 95
subsidies 88
'substitution effect' 4–5, 15
supply 8, 11–12, 16–18, def 22, 23–4, 26, 35, 47, 75, 82, 162–3
    see also production

supply constraints def 35, 85–6, 108, 120
'supply side' economics def 36, 116, 118
Sweden 55, 208
Switzerland 208
'System of National Accounts' (1994) 89

tariffs 44–5, 172
taxation 28, 79, 88–9, 93–4, 136, 193–5, 211
    and budget revenue 29, 34, 36–7, 79–80, 95
    and consumption 24
    and demand 26, 30, 34–6, 79–80, 85, 93–4, 190
    and GDP 22–4, 190, 191
    'hypothecation' 92
    indirect 35–7, 93, 132, 136
    statistics 90, 91
    and wages 17, 23, 84, 125
    see also fiscal policy, TPI
technology 8–9, 27–8, 44, 174, 203, 212
telecommunications 174, 198
terms of trade 167, 168, 170
Thailand 50
TPI (Tax and Price Index) 136
trade 29, 39–45, 56, 58, 89, 104, 164–85, 205
    balances 78, 167, 167–70, 169, 171, 172–3
    deficits 85, 169, 200
    forecasts 200, 211
    international 41–8, 42, 88–9
    liberalisation 39–40, 43–5, 50–2, 58, 172
    statistics 101, 168–9, 172
    see also balance of payments, exchange rates, exports, imports
trade unions 17, 35
training see education and training
transfer payments 77–9, 87, 168
transport 174, 198
Treasury 68–9, 106–7, 120
    and Bank of England 30–1, 38
    forecasts 190, 191, 192–3, 195–6, 204, 206–7, 209–11
    statistics 174–5
Treasury bills 30–1, 150–1, 151, 156
Treaty on European Union see Maastricht Treaty
trends def 26, 63
troughs def 26, 63

UBS 208
UN Development Programme (1990) 89–90
unemployment benefit see social security and benefits
unemployment see employment
UN (United Nations) 89
Uruguay 50
Uruguay Round 45, 51
USA 23, 35–6, 41, 53, 66–7, 84–5, 123–4, 141, 152, 173, 192, 193,
    195–7, 200, 207–8
    employment 75, 112, 113, 192, 203
    forecasts 192–3, 193, 204, 209
    foreign exchange 43, 178, 180, 183, 202
    GDP 51, 75, 192
    international trade 44, 164, 165, 172
    statistics 70–1, 103, 145, 146, 147
    stocks and bonds 127, 158–9

value data 63, 65, 104–5, 111
VAT 36, 93, 132, 136
'visible account' see under balance of payments
volume data 63, 111

wages 4, 22–3, 82
    determinants 17–18, 35
    earnings 139–40
        distribution 29, 34, 42, 43, 64, 81, 121, 123, 123–6, 125, 203
        'earnings gap' 124–6, 125
    impact 5, 84, 99, 116, 136–7
    personal disposable income 25, def 84, 85, 116
    see also employment, income
Warwick University 204–5
wealth distribution 34
WEFA 205
Wharton School 205
World Bank 49, 56–7, 89, 197–8
'World Development Report' (World Bank) 56
World Economic Outlook (IMF) 69–70, 198, 199
WTO (World Trade Organisation) 45